War and Revolution in Russia, 1914–22

The Collapse of Tsarism and the Establishment of Soviet Power

CHRISTOPHER READ

palgrave
macmillan

First published 2013 by
PALGRAVE MACMILLAN

Palgrave Macmillan in the UK is an imprint of Macmillan Publishers Limited,
registered in England, company number 785998, of Houndmills, Basingstoke,
Hampshire RG21 6XS.

Palgrave Macmillan in the US is a division of St Martin's Press LLC,
175 Fifth Avenue, New York, NY 10010.

Palgrave Macmillan is the global academic imprint of the above companies
and has companies and representatives throughout the world.

Palgrave® and Macmillan® are registered trademarks in the United States,
the United Kingdom, Europe and other countries.

ISBN 978–0–230–23985–2   hardback
ISBN 978–0–230–23986–9   paperback

This book is printed on paper suitable for recycling and made from fully
managed and sustained forest sources. Logging, pulping and manufacturing
processes are expected to conform to the environmental regulations of the
country of origin.

A catalogue record for this book is available from the British Library.

A catalog record for this book is available from the Library of Congress.

10   9   8   7   6   5   4   3   2   1
22 21 20 19 18 17 16 15 14 13

Printed and bound in China

The First World War unleashed a powerful, transforming, destructive storm across the European continent. Its consequences were felt as harshly in Russia as anywhere else in the world. A spiral of chaos and violence erupted, continuing to reign throughout years of revolution and civil war.

Leading expert Christopher Read presents a cutting-edge, highly readable introduction to Russia's crisis years. Read synthesises a wealth of newly available material and treats the period 1914–22 as a whole in order to contextualise and better understand the events of 1917 and their impact. As he examines the multiple revolutions, Read asks how and why the Bolsheviks were able to survive the storm, eventually taking over the world's largest country.

Christopher Read is Professor of Modern European History at the University of Warwick. He has written widely on twentieth-century Russian social, political and cultural history.

European History in Perspective
General Editor: Jeremy Black

Benjamin Arnold *Medieval Germany*
Ronald Asch *The Thirty Years' War*
Nigel Aston *The French Revolution, 1789–1804*
Nicholas Atkin *The Fifth French Republic*
Christopher Bartlett *Peace, War and the European Powers, 1814–1914*
Robert Bireley *The Refashioning of Catholicism, 1450–1700*
Donna Bohanan *Crown and Nobility in Early Modern France*
Arden Bucholz *Moltke and the German Wars, 1864–1871*
Patricia Clavin *The Great Depression, 1929–1939*
John D. Cotts *Europe's Long Twelfth Century*
Paula Sutter Fichtner *The Habsburg Monarchy, 1490–1848*
Mark R. Forster *Catholic Germany from the Reformation to the Enlightenment*
Mark Galeotti *Gorbachev and his Revolution*
David Gates *Warfare in the Nineteenth Century*
Alexander Grab *Napoleon and the Transformation of Europe*
Nicholas Henshall *The Zenith of European Monarchy and its Elites*
Martin P. Johnson *The Dreyfus Affair*
Tim Kirk *Nazi Germany*
Ronald Kowalski *European Communism*
Paul Douglas Lockhart *Sweden in the Seventeenth Century*
Kevin McDermott *Stalin*
Graeme Murdock *Beyond Calvin*
Peter Musgrave *The Early Modern European Economy*
J. L. Price *The Dutch Republic in the Seventeenth Century*
A. W. Purdue *The Second World War (2nd edn)*
Christopher Read *The Making and Breaking of the Soviet System*
Christopher Read *War and Revolution in Russia, 1914–22*
Francisco J. Romero-Salvado *Twentieth-Century Spain*
Matthew S. Seligmann and Roderick R. McLean
Germany from Reich to Republic, 1871–1918
David A. Shafer *The Paris Commune*
Graeme Small *Late Medieval France*
David Sturdy *Louis XIV*
David J. Sturdy *Richelieu and Mazarin*
Hunt Tooley *The Western Front*
Peter Waldron *The End of Imperial Russia, 1855–1917*
Peter Waldron *Governing Tsarist Russia*
Peter G. Wallace *The Long European Reformation (2nd edn)*
James D. White *Lenin*
Patrick Williams *Philip II*
Peter H. Wilson *From Reich to Revolution*

European History in Perspective
Series Standing Order
ISBN 978–0333–71694–6 hardcover
ISBN 978–0333–69336–0 paperback
(*outside North America only*)

You can receive future titles in this series as they are published by placing a
standing order. Please contact your bookseller or, in the case of difficulty, write to
us at the address below with your name and address, the title of the series and the
ISBN quoted above.

Customer Services Department, Palgrave Ltd
Houndmills, Basinstoke, Hampshire RG21 6XS, England

To my lifetime friends – Lucy and Slava in
Moscow, Anne in Lahemaa and
Toomas in Tallinn

Contents

The Soviet Union in 1923 (adapted from map 'The USSR in 1927' © Robert Service, *The Russian Revolution 1900–1927*).

MAP xi

OCEAN

PACIFIC OCEAN

R. Lena

Yakutsk

SOCIALIST REPUBLIC (RSFSR)

Sakhalin Island

Krasnoyarsk

Lake Baikal

Irkutsk

Vladivostok

JAPAN

MONGOLIA

KOREA

CHINA

Preface

I have been privileged to devote a large part of my life to Russia, one of the world's most fascinating countries. Its people have achieved some of the highest levels of human culture. They have also endured, and some of them have inflicted, some of the lowest moments of barbarism and collective depravity. The geographical space dominated by Russians is very challenging. Its winters are legendary, its spaces endless, its ecological balance mostly precarious. It is a space containing great variety – mountains, deserts, tundra, permafrost, steppe, immense rivers, inland seas, a coast opening on to vast oceans. There is great beauty. Some of it is natural, like Lake Baikal or Issyk-kul, the Taimyr Peninsula, the frozen magnificence of the Arctic, the deserts of Central Asia and the vast forests teeming with life. Other examples of beauty are of human origin, in the forefront the intricately decorated monasteries and cathedrals of the Kremlin, Kolomenskoe, Sergiev Posad, Rostov Velikii, Iaroslavl', Novgorod, Pokrov na Nerli and the Solovetsky islands. Joining them as magnificent symbols of human hope and faith, often in the face of suffering, are the great mosques, medressahs and minarets of the Central Asian 'near abroad', as it has been called since the breakup of the USSR.

The greatest of all challenges and achievements, however, belongs to the mass of peasants who, for at least a millennium, reproduced their life and culture over an immense landscape. Their success allowed the secular and clerical elites to emerge, though the peasants themselves rarely shared in the riches they made possible. The tyranny of backbreaking labour in the busy seasons and of oppressive governance at national and local level were more often their lot. When situations became intolerable and opportunities arose, the peasantry would respond with rebellions large and small. The Russian Revolution of 1917 was the biggest and most influential of all. Its consequences not only defined Russia's twentieth century but also the world's. Unarguably, it is one of the most consequential events of the modern, contemporary world. The First World War was the mixer into which the nineteenth-century world was fed. The twentieth-century world emerged. The Russian Revolution was second to none in importance among those processes which arose from the wartime wreckage.

I have been assisted by a host of people in my studies, especially by my teachers, colleagues, students and friends (which are often interchangeable categories). To name those who have influenced the present work is an invidious process which will inevitably leave many out. However, I would like to thank my present and former colleagues in the History Department at Warwick who have all been stimulating fellow-historians. I will risk naming Roger Magraw, Gwynne Lewis, Robin Okey, Christoph Mick, Sarah Richardson, Rainer Horn, Steve Hindle and Bernard Capp, not to mention Mark Harrison and Andrei Markevich from Economics. My prime collective debt with regard to the present book is to the Study Group on the Russian Revolution which, as a founder member, I can hardly believe is approaching its fifth decade. Dare I select some of the names here as well? Of the longer-term members Geoff Swain, David Saunders, Peter Waldron, Jonathan Smele, Howard White, Evan Mawdsley, James White, Paul Dukes, Dan Orlovsky, Steve Williams and the late, unforgettable Brian Pearce. It has been especially gratifying to see the constant supply of new talent in the Study Group including Sarah Badcock, Aaron Retish, Matt Rendle, Katy Turton, Jon Davis, Matthias Neumann, Stefan Karsch (who calmly shared a seriously unnerving experience once when landing at Aberdeen airport!), Alistair Wright, Gayle Lonergan, Jenny Grieve-Laing, James Ryan, Susan Grant, Brendan McGeever and Andrew Willimott. Another collective debt is owed to the Russia's Great War and Revolution Centennial Project which, under the expert guidance of John Steinberg, Tony Heywood and David McDonald has brought me in to welcome contact with many scholars including Adele Lindenmeyr, Liudmilla Novikova, Murray Frame, Steve Marks, Michael Hughes, Boris Kolonitskii, Bruce Menning, Oleg Airapetov, Vladimir Soskin and Alice Pate. Colleagues and friends from the Centre for Russian and East European Studies at Birmingham University, notably Bob Davies, Jeremy Smith, Ron Kowalskii, the late Derek Watson, Melanie Ilic and Arfon Rees have been a constant source of help and inspiration. Conversations and friendships with Steve Kerensky, Chris Ward, Bob Service, Edward Acton, Geoff Roberts, Donald Raleigh, Stuart Finkel and Randall

Poole have been illuminating in a multitude of ways. I owe a special debt to the two anonymous readers of my book proposal and typescript who made many valuable suggestions and saved me from a host of mistakes, and to Alec McAulay for his meticulous editing. Any errors which remain are entirely my own responsibility. Finally, my greatest debt – personal rather than scholarly – is to my family, my mother Joan, and Francoise, Alex and Nat, the foundation of my life. My greatest regret is that my father will not read this book, which he would have enjoyed beyond measure.

Notes

- Dates of events in Russia are mainly given according to the Russian calendar up to 1 February 1918, at which time the western calendar was adopted. Dates of international events, such as the outbreak of the First World War and ensuing battles, are given according to the western (NS) calendar. Where a distinction is being made the letters OS denote the Old Style calendar, NS the New Style.
- A *verst* is almost the same as a kilometre, or 0.66 of a mile.
- 1 *pud* equals 36 lb or just over 16 kg in weight.
- Russian names are transliterated mainly according to the Library of Congress system with some adaptations of familiar names such as ones which end in –y rather than –ii and start Ye- or Ya- rather than E- or Ia-.
- Referencing is a modified Harvard system with author, year, volume, page in brackets in the text and the full reference in the Bibliography. Where appropriate, English editions have been preferred to help English-speaking readers to follow up sources where possible.
- Inserts in square brackets in quotations have been added by the author.

Chapter 1: Into the Storm: Russia Enters the Twentieth Century

As the summer of 1914 became hotter across Europe, so the political temperature also rose. A sense of foreboding lay as heavily as the summer sun. War was in the air, but war was not like a social engagement or a sports fixture: no one knew when, how, or even if, it would come. Nor did they know what it would be like, as it was nearly a century since a continent-wide war had been experienced. There had been plenty of regional wars. Between 1854 and 1871, Russia, France, Prussia, Austria, Piedmont, Turkey, Britain and many smaller states had taken part in wars with and against each other in various combinations. The Crimean War and the wars of German and Italian Unification had changed the map and the balance of power. Increasingly, the Balkans became a cockpit of conflict. The Russo-Turkish War of 1877–8 picked up unfinished business from the Crimean War and brought into existence the independent states of Bulgaria and Romania. In the early twentieth century Balkan struggles broke out again, in 1912, the appetiser for the chaos to come. In the wider world the Scramble for Africa engaged most of Europe's great powers, and the United States continued its long-drawn-out process of challenging Spanish power in the Americas and the Pacific with yet another war in 1898. A modernising, industrialising, expansionist Japan was stepping out in East Asia.

Underlying these conflicts was a dreadful grinding of the tectonic plates of empire. Old, even feudal, empires – Ottoman, Habsburg, Spanish – were being forced under by new, dynamic, capitalist empires driven by science, new technology, an armaments revolution and an

1

insatiable desire for profit, of which Germany, the United States and, in as-yet embryonic form, Japan, were the models. Two previously dominant empires, the French and the British, faced unprecedented challenges from the newcomers and had to re-energise themselves or be ground under as well.

Where did Russia stand in this dog-eat-dog world? As a vast empire it appeared strong, but its weak industrialisation, and ever-increasing protest from its more vociferous minority nationalities, made it more akin to the imploding Ottoman (Turkish) and Habsburg empires than to either the new expansionists or the challenged old guard. In addition to its traditional rival-neighbours, Prussia/Germany, Austria and Turkey, a new, potent threat was emerging to the east – Japan. As Japan's appetite for expansion grew, so it looked on Russia's Far Eastern possessions as a potential target. In 1904 a major war broke out between them in which tsarist Russia's military performance was abject and its humiliation intense.

Political, Economic and Social Stresses in the Russian Empire

Political stresses up to 1905

For more than half a century the political life of Russia had revolved around a paradox. At one level, the state seemed all-powerful and secure. The sovereign autocrat stood at the head of an extensive bureaucracy, a ubiquitous police and informer system, a network of labour camps and, crucially, a vast army dominated by a loyal officer class. At another level, the repression the state engendered was creating greater and greater pressure from below. Pioneer protests against it, from the Decembrists of 1825 to the assassination of Tsar Alexander II (1881), had been easily brushed aside. But there had been a cost. Each round of self-assertion had added to the autocrat's confidence. Traditionalists urged clinging to old ideas as Russia's way forward. Foreign, largely western-European, influences were to be fought off. As the number of adherents of constitutional change and reform grew, so the resistance of the autocracy became more vigorous. On ascending the throne, Nicholas II, also known as Nicholas the Unlucky and, increasingly, Nicholas the Last, extinguished all reformist hopes in a single sentence. They were, he said, 'senseless dreams'.

Not unnaturally, the response to this was a further round of disillusion among the opponents of autocracy and an ever-growing conviction that only revolution would bring about change. By refusing to adapt, successive tsars, especially Alexander III the dates here are reigns not life spans. Is that obvious enough? were stoking up the fires of revolution. In this sense, they were Russia's leading revolutionaries. By closing off all legal avenues of popular representation and imposing censorship and political imprisonment, they left little alternative but revolution. The paradox becomes clear. The more repressive the state, the more revolutionary the nation. Russia thereby seemed to be the most stable and the most potentially revolutionary of the major states of Europe, at least until 1900.

Incredibly, by the skin of its teeth, the autocracy survived a challenge to its authority in 1904–7, conventionally known as the revolution of 1905 even though it was, in the end, neither a revolution nor was it confined to 1905. Only heavy, armed repression enabled the autocracy to ultimately beat back its opponents. But one deep lesson had been learned. The areas of opposition to Nicholas II now extended throughout the country. They reached well beyond revolutionary intellectuals and included not only peasants and workers, who made up the foundation of the social pyramid and provided most of the wealth-creating labour, but also many employers, reformist state officials, the increasing cohort of educated professionals and even landowners worried that if the autocracy were to lose its grip it would bring them down with it. The other side of this lesson was that survival was down to two initiatives. There was a piece of desperate political footwork embodied in the 'October Manifesto', which appeared to promise political reform. True, some of the limited freedoms gained in 1905 survived – notably press freedom, the restricted ability to organise trade unions and political parties, and the emergence of a restricted Duma (Parliament) – but the heart of the autocracy was not in reform. Much more important and much less emphasised in accounts of the period, there was extensive armed repression in late 1905 and 1906, emphasising that the only solid ground on which the regime stood was military strength and loyalty. Nonetheless, the very existence of even a hamstrung Duma from 1906 provided a platform for open criticism of the government. The first two Dumas were very democratic and, consequently, hostile to the regime. In June 1907, the new Prime Minister, Stolypin, disbanded the Second Duma and introduced a system of indirect voting so that the vast majority of delegates were elected by landowners and the propertied elite. There was token representation of the workers and peasants, allowing limited legal status to spokespeople of the left.

Economic and social fracture lines

Politics was only one area of crisis, perhaps best seen as the arena in which Russia's other, multiple, fundamental crises were displayed.

In the forefront of these were Russia's economic difficulties. In terms of wealth, Russia was by no means in the same league as Britain, France, Germany and the United States. What is more, it showed no sustained sign of catching up with the world leaders. But that did not mean Russia was impoverished or even completely stagnant. It had an expanding industrial sector of mines, extractive industries, heavy metalworking, textiles, transport and services. Russia's industrialisation had certain specific features. Among the most important were state involvement, reliance on foreign loans and know-how, and the fact that industrial islands were an archipelago set in a sea of highly traditional peasant and landowner agriculture. The peculiarities arose, not least, from shortage of capital, an endemic Russian problem which also deeply marked the Soviet successor to tsarism. The final set of obstacles sprang from the low national level of education and modern culture (Gregory 1982; Gatrell 1986).

Agriculture itself tended to grow slowly, barely keeping up with a population which grew from around 70 million in the mid-century to 161 million by 1910 (including some territorial expansion into Central Asia). Much of agriculture, especially the peasant sector but also much of the landowner sector as well, remained more or less as it had been for decades, even centuries. There were hot-spots of growth and production for export, Russia being a major grain supplier to western Europe despite intense competition from North America and other new worlds such as Australia and New Zealand. However, the labour of peasants, who comprised some 90 per cent of the population, was geared to subsistence and to limited exchange rather than to surpluses and profit. Peasants lived in their own, largely self-contained, village world, organised round the traditional commune (*obshchina* or *mir*) and its self-governing meeting of elders, the *skhod*. Peasants, as we shall see, had a sharp eye for their own interests but, by and large, since they were scattered across an immense landscape, they found it difficult to organise and exert themselves as a group in proportion to their numbers. Nonetheless, peasant protests were a constant feature of Russian life. They were usually driven by disputes with local landowners over ancient rights, such as pasturing on common land or gathering firewood (a life-or-death issue given Russia's long, harsh winters) or, most sensitive of all, land distribution. As long as they remained localised, the authorities could pick them off one at a time.

However, when a national stimulus came along, as in 1905, and enormous swathes of the peasantry were goaded into action simultaneously, they could become a formidable force. Indeed, one of the key policies of the post-1905 architect of tsarist re-structuring, the prime minister Peter Stolypin, was to attempt to break up the commune, since it appeared to be a basic cell of peasant revolutionary solidarity (Waldron 1998; Ascher 2001).

The commune, in many cases, was the official holder of the land, which, apart from a family garden which was kept permanently, was periodically redistributed by most communes. This complicated the formation of stable divisions within the peasantry since the above-average allocation of a large family would likely be diminished as marriage led to the formation of new families which would themselves receive land taken from the families declining in number (Shanin 1972; Durrenberger 1984; Chaianov 2006). Nonetheless, conventionally there was deemed to be a small (maybe as much as 10 per cent) sub-class of poor peasants with insufficient land to support themselves who lived largely on wages; a thick layer of so-called 'middle' peasants of, about, 60–80 per cent of the whole and a small layer of 'rich' peasants of around 5–10 per cent. The middle peasants were not exactly prosperous but nor did they starve. They lived semi-secure lives and enjoyed a rich culture of traditional clothes, food, festivals, songs, dance, folklore, superstition and religion. They might have been relatively poor, but they were not abject.

The trickiest group to define, however, was the 'rich' peasants. Objective definitions which distinguish the three layers of the peasantry are hard to arrive at. It has often been thought that a key criterion for definition was the employment of labour. In some definitions, rich peasants were employers, middle peasants neither employers nor employees, and poor peasants were labourers. Real villages were not like that. Rich peasants largely worked their own land but, like middle peasants, might employ labour at key times of the year such as harvest or sowing. Poor peasants might have enough land to provide half or more of their subsistence and hire themselves out to make up the rest. Even some middle peasants had to seek employment to make ends meet. The problem of definition is made even more difficult by the intrusion of the term 'kulak'. The word is derived from the term for 'fist', and seems to depict the grasping fist of the moneylender, since peasants largely applied it to such people. However, for Marxists in particular, the term was often equated with rich peasants. This enabled them to construct, in their own analyses, a rural society akin to that of the capitalist city. Kulak equalled bourgeois, middle peasant was considered to be akin to the petty bourgeois, and the poor peasant was the equivalent of the proletarian. While there was some truth in this model it had crucial flaws which led to disastrous policy-making by both Lenin and Stalin. In particular, peasants themselves did not see fundamental antagonisms within the commune and, as they did in 1918 and beyond, tended to join together to protect the village from outsiders. Also, for them, 'kulaks' were outsiders, traders and entrepreneurs rather than communal peasants. Those flaws were derived in part from wishful thinking – the desire to find rural allies for urban radical classes – and in part from ignorance. Most Marxists were urban and even those who knew rural life, like Trotsky and Gorky, often hated what they saw. They incessantly denounced the peasantry as a doomed, disappearing class in the grip of petty localism, superstition, conservatism and an attachment to private property.

Considering peasants in this way leads us into examining other areas of social tension and to defining the contours of Russia's social structure. In an important sense, Russia around 1900 had two, intertwined, social structures. There was the vast majority of the population who lived in the traditional, largely rural and small-town, way – notably, peasants, clergy, landowners and merchants. Alongside them, however, a smaller but vital urban, industrial and proto-capitalist society was evolving, composed of workers, employers, financiers and professionals such as managers, lawyers, doctors and engineers. Caught between the two were important groups such as army officers, state bureaucrats and the creative and critical intelligentsia. To complicate matters, it should also be borne in mind that the traditional sectors were being influenced, if only slowly, by modernisation. Peasant society, in particular, was being affected by industry in many ways. One of the most important was that localism was giving way to industrial recruitment and systematic outmigration to cities, mines and other developing industrial enterprises. Especially after 1900, the extent of outmigration began to undermine some of the traditions of the peasantry. Capitalism, too, was making inroads and increasing areas of production of cash crops for profit – sugar in parts of Ukraine, flax in the west – threatening the subsistence economy of traditional peasants, who were beginning to lose out to larger-scale capitalist estates. In any case, the development of railways had created a national market for grain which, as a key export, had itself become a cash crop, affecting even deeply traditional peasant villages from the 1870s onward.

Industry needed workers. The developing working class was being recruited, by and large from the village. Before 1900, recruiters travelled round to enlist villagers on eleven month contracts. The factories closed for a month or so in the summer and the workers went home to help with the harvest. After 1900 summer closure became rarer as the ever-more intensive capitalist clock ticked relentlessly – not yet 24/7 but increasingly 24/6 with only Sunday off. The working day could extend to 15 or 16 hours.

As with peasants, the complex structure of the working class evoked important arguments and theories, especially among Marxists. While it is beyond our scope to go into them fully, it is important to outline aspects that later affected policies and procedures, not least of the Bolsheviks. For Marxists, workers were the people chosen by history to drag humanity from a once-vibrant but, it was assumed, increasingly stagnant capitalism into the bright end of history, as they thought, in the form of communism, passing through the transitional phase of socialism. While, in Marxist theory, the underlying force for this transition would be fuelled by capitalism itself, Russian Marxists, and Lenin in particular, were not content to let history work itself out. Nor were they prepared to follow Marx's view that the liberation of the workers would be the task of the workers themselves. They thought that since no revolution had challenged capitalism by 1900, perhaps history, and the workers as its leading agents, needed a prod. In order to turn workers into revolutionaries Marx and Lenin believed that they needed to achieve class consciousness, an awareness which would lead them to see that their enemies were not capitalists but capitalism, the system itself not its representatives. However, they diverged increasingly over the way that this was to be achieved. Marx said it would arise from workers struggling to achieve a better life and reflecting on their experiences. For Lenin, they needed an outside agency, the party, to speed this process up. The party would assemble those with 'advanced' class consciousness and help them to spread it to those who had not yet developed it. In actuality, there was a very important core of intellectuals, like Lenin himself, at the heart of this process but, as is often the case with intellectuals, Lenin denied or minimised their role.

However, it was the workers who were the subject of the keenest arguments. It followed from the idea of the advanced worker that there would also be backward workers. The latter were assumed to be unskilled workers who were drawn into the workshops and facto-ries of the city from a rural background. They were deemed to be unsuitable material for the revolutionary overthrow of capitalism on account of their volatility and links to rural customs and cultures such as religion. Advanced workers were thought to be organised, skilled, better-paid, second- or even third-generation workers. However, like the interpretation of rural classes, there was also a large slice of wishful thinking in the Russian Marxist, especially Bolshevik, attitude to workers. In some ways, rural background added to the revolutionary potential of workers in that they brought radical attitudes from the village, notably a belief that those who worked should own the means by which they worked and that hierarchies of ownership were built on injustice and were not recognised by the workers (Read 1984). In fact, some of the most belligerent strikes of 1905 and 1917 were conducted by unskilled workers, often condemned by society in general as *chernyi rabochii* (black workers) and by Marxists as 'lumpen proletarians' prone to racism and violence. At the other extreme, some of the best organised, most established and best educated workers, notably printers, were not so much revolutionary as reformist, or, not quite the same thing, Menshevik rather than Bolshevik (Steinberg 1992). In fact, Lenin developed the concept of a 'labour aristocracy' of well paid, reformist, unionised workers. In practice, no 'objective' sociological tool was sufficiently fine to separate those who were inclined to reform and those who were truly advanced workers. As with kulaks, ideological blinkers were interfering with, rather than enhancing, perceptions of reality.

Russia, to reiterate, was populated by two, intertwining social structures. The traditional society derived largely from the old rural Russia, a Russia of peasants, great landowners, lesser gentry, merchants, church hierarchy, clergy and peasants was decaying. A much smaller, modern, largely urban-based, Russia of industrial employers, managers, engineers, accountants, lawyers, doctors, teachers and skilled workers was coming into existence and becoming the backbone of a new industrial, cultural and economic surge. Like deposits of sedimentary rock, between the large conglomerates were layers which were half and half, in the middle of transforming from one to another. These included unskilled, rural, migrant workers; army officers divided between those born to the post and those of humbler background working their way up, 'patricians' and 'praetorians' in Norman Stone's words (Stone 1975); state officials, some of whom were consumed by traditional lassitude while others were exemplars of modernising energy; and even clergy among whom a modernising element was denouncing the immobility of the majority. The resulting society was highly complex. Many Soviet-era historians described late imperial Russia as 'multi-structured'. It had characteristics of being an empire, but it was also, in certain respects, a colony; its social and economic structure was, in Marxist terms, feudal in part, but also exhibited characteristics of capitalism; it was an autocracy but also had a vestigial modern politics of parties, parliament and elections. If it had simply been the case that Russia had a complex, partially modernised society and related economies then violent revolution might have been avoided or postponed. The new, let us call it in a loose sense, bourgeois society would have continued to replace the declining, loosely, feudal remnants. However, one more absolutely crucial factor needs to be taken into account – the state.

Politics, autocracy, the state under Nicholas II

The Russian state had a number of crucial peculiarities and these peculiarities became increasingly the mould for a peculiar politics. Most obviously, the state was an autocracy. Hard to believe that such an anachronism could still exist in a twentieth-century Great Power, but it did. Up until 1905 the tsar retained the plenitude of power in his own hands. The chief ideological prop of autocracy, Konstantin Pobedonostsev, wrote a coldly brilliant defence of the system in 1890 (Pobedonostsev 1965). Western society, he wrote, was degenerate. Vast industrial cities turned human societies into anthills of depravity and disease. Grim factories dehumanised workers. Everything became tainted by the greyness of vulgar, money-grubbing materialism. Spiritual life was squashed out by the gin bottle. Freedom became licence. Much vaunted values of democracy were shot through with the corruption and self-interest of politicians. By contrast, Pobedonostsev continued, Russian society gravitated towards a family-style hierarchy. Everyone knew and accepted their place and the tsar was a benevolent and impartial arbitrator standing above his subjects. Organised politics was unnecessary, for all a subject had to do was to petition the tsar to right any injustice. As another autocratic sycophant put it, the tsar was 'beneficence personified' (Mossolov 1935: 128).

Needless to say, this fantasy world did not exist. 170 million subjects could hardly expect personal hearings of their problems with a benevolent tsar. But we need to note two things above all from this anachronism. First, it is a sign to us that traditional Russia remained powerful. Autocracy had been built up over centuries as the state system needed to police a serf-based society. Under serfdom, there was no question of equality or shared rights. The serfs had to be intimidated into acceptance, and that was the task of the autocracy. Whenever the serf system was threatened the autocracy reacted with an iron fist. Peasant revolts were ruthlessly smashed from the fifteenth century on, as the autocracy formed itself, all the way through to its response to the great rebellion of 1905, which was drowned in a sea of blood. It is also worth noting here that, in Russia, autocratic dictatorship was building just as its equivalents in western Europe began to decay when powerful barons and, later, increasingly bourgeois classes, laid a claim to a place in the body politic. In Russia, even the landowners were among those oppressed by the state until the eighteenth century. No movements for a rule of law, constitutionalism, or even a free press were permitted before 1900. It was also verging on a theocracy since, from the time of Peter the Great, the church had been incorporated into the state system of administration and the church's leadership institution, the Patriarchate, had been suspended. This dragged the church and religion into politics so that to oppose autocracy was akin to rejecting religion. Many, probably most, of tsarism's educated opponents were atheist. Anything that would be recognised in western Europe as political activity was essentially forbidden, and civil society was heavily constrained. There were no legal political parties, trade unions or political institutions worthy of the name. Backed by its army, police and state bureaucracy, the autocracy looked to have firm foundations.

The second point to note, as well as its apparent strength, is that Nicholas II bought into the myth of autocracy in its entirety. Tutored by Pobedonostsev personally, the tsar earnestly believed he held a commission from God to preserve intact the principles of autocracy. This, not unnaturally, made him inflexible and out of touch with the modernising sectors of Russian society. On the other hand, he had a touching faith in the good will and loyalty of true Russians. Great quasi-medieval theatres of the autocratic ideal preserved his illusions. There were several in Nicholas's reign. The first, the coronation itself, was accompanied by a tragic stampede that killed hundreds. Already a pall was cast among the superstitious over the new reign. In 1903, in the province of Sarov, Nicholas led a pilgrimage on the occasion of the elevation to sainthood of a nineteenth-century elder and ascetic named Serafim. It was an apparently splendid moment of bonding between the tsar and some hundreds of thousands of peasants and others come to participate. For Nicholas this was the reassuring embodiment of the anti-western, slavophile myth of autocracy. The peasants loved the tsar, the tsar loved and protected his peasants. They were children, he was their little father (*batiushka*). Any disturbances were, it followed, obviously the work of Russia's foreign enemies led by the Jews. Xenophobia in general and anti-semitism in particular were instinctive reactions of many (but not all) tsarists to the increasingly extensive movements of mass discontent in the early twentieth century. However, the ominous indifference shown by many to the energetically promoted celebrations of the 300th anniversary of the Romanov dynasty in 1913 told a different story. Anyone with any sensitivity would have realised that time was running out for the dynasty and emergency repairs were urgently needed.

This repressive, antiquated and backward-looking system generated a kind of politics unknown and unnecessary among the developing democracies and quasi-democracies of the capitalist and imperial powers. Because of its intolerance of any opposition, almost all critical activity became revolutionary. The intelligentsia was in the forefront of this process. In Russian terms the intelligentsia was unique. Direct definition of it is almost impossible, but the populist leader and inspiration, Peter Lavrov, called them 'critically thinking individuals' in the 1870s. Most were politically active at least indirectly. Through adoption of disguised stories and practices – so-called Aesopian language, named after the great classical writer of moral fables – even writers and philosophers were political activists. Mid-century discussion circles were subject to official disapproval. Social issues were wrapped up in fictional form to avoid the ubiquitous censor. More directly political acts would often lead to imprisonment or exile.

Around 1900 the three main intellectual-political tendencies began to form into actual political parties. In 1898, at a secret founding congress in Minsk, the Marxist Social-Democratic Party (often known as the Russian Social Democratic Labour Party, RSDP) was founded. Apart from adopting the first party programme, the Minsk Congress was a false dawn. Only in 1903, at the better-known second congress, did the issue of amalgamating the party take centre stage. This is often deemed to be the congress at which Lenin 'split' the party. In truth, there was no party to split. Rather the pre-existing factions failed to come together and for many years, arguably until the 1917 revolution itself, attempts were consistently made to bring the factions – notably Bolsheviks and Mensheviks – together (Read 2005 ch. 3; Mullin 2010).

In 1900, the populist movement coalesced more successfully into the Socialist-Revolutionary Party (the SRs). It was, throughout the period from 1900 to 1918, by far the largest party on the left in terms of members, activities and effect. As we examine the revolution itself more closely later on we have to ask why the SRs did not succeed in coming to power as much as looking at why the Bolsheviks did. From the beginning they were immensely active. Parallel to the political party they set up a terrorist wing, which engaged in numerous armed attacks on government officials from leading ministers down to local police. They are often thought of as a peasant party because their main policy called for the redistribution of land to peasants but they, too, were influenced by Marx and also sought actively for worker members. They appeared to have been in the majority among the workers in St Petersburg's giant Putilov factory throughout the revolutionary period except for the fateful months around October 1917 when the Bolsheviks briefly and with great consequence overshadowed them.

Finally, in 1903 the liberals organised themselves into, first of all, the Liberation (*Osvobozhdenie*) organisation which, in the turmoil of 1905, became the Constitutional Democratic Party (Kadets for short, from the Russian acronym). They looked to western parliamentary models for their inspiration, though, in fact, all three parties put the convening of a Constituent Assembly to draw up a democratic constitution in place of the autocracy as the first item in their programme. Significantly, two of these three groups had to found their movements abroad, the Social Democrats' Second Congress started in Brussels but settled down in London, while the Liberation movement was set up in Schaffhausen in Switzerland.

It was not only political parties that were forced underground. Trade unions, too, were illegal. Strikes were also banned. This had the effect of politicising industrial relations. If every strike brought the police out to repress the strikers it meant every serious dispute between workers and bosses was immediately and unnecessarily turned into a conflict with the state itself. Early in his career Lenin saw how opportune this was for radicals. One only had to get workers to press the button and, like a jack-in-the-box, he argued, a gendarme would emerge with a big stick to threaten those around. In the run up to 1905 the police were increasingly overloaded in beating back hundreds of rural and urban incidents of rebellion. In most cases, despite the traditional tendency to talk about 'economic' and 'political' strikes in Russia, most of these were complaints about working and living conditions in town and country. Almost all strikes with 'political' demands were rooted in the economic. Hardly any were purely 'political'. They really showed how the autocracy itself was ramping up the significance of simple disputes and turning them into political crises. Lacking legal outlets for the expression of work-based grievances turned strikes into political rebellions. For political parties, demanding the right to exist and to discuss issues freely and openly was also equivalent to sedition. Even after 1905, the situation was only partially improved. Trade unions had to register and were frequently either forbidden registration or de-registered if they showed even mild signs of militancy. Political parties remained semi-underground and the main leaders of socialist parties were usually either in exile in Western Europe and occasionally North America, or they were in judicial exile in Siberia. The heartless massacre in 1912 of 200 or more miners and some of their family members by tsarist police, in response to a strike in the British-owned Lena goldfields in Siberia, showed how hollow the concessions forced out of the autocracy in 1905 actually were. After being cowed by massive repression in which thousands died in 1906, the old forces were reasserting themselves, fracture lines were reappearing. On the eve of war, in July 1914, barricades were once again to be seen in the streets of St Petersburg (Haimson 1964, 1965, 2005). The autocracy was still proving itself to be its own worst enemy. Nicholas II continued to be the chief recruiter for the radicals and revolutionaries (Read 2000).

When the autocracy had last faced rising political pressures in 1903 one minister, Vyacheslav Plehve, the Minister of the Interior and former chief of police, supposedly argued that a 'small, victorious war' was needed to drown the revolutionaries in a flood-tide of patriotism. It came too late for Plehve, who was a victim of assassination by SR terrorists on 15 July 1904. The war was no better-favoured. When it came, in the form of a war with Japan, it was not especially short, dragging on for almost a year and a half, and was spectacularly unsuccessful. Far from pacifying the population, the disastrous military performance by land and sea undermined the expected patriotic outburst. In the end, military debacle sparked political crisis. Economic crisis had also been kicking in since 1900 and the two intertwined to fuel the 1905 revolution which the autocracy only survived by the skin of its teeth (Harcave 1965; Mehlinger and Thomson 1972; Trotsky 1972; Ascher 1988 and 1992; Verner 1990).

It is not true that people never learn from history. In 1914, there was also a tendency that urged war as a means of subduing rising internal political tension, though a much more muted one than in 1904. Even more significantly, in February 1914 Pyotr Durnovo, one of Plehve's successors as head of the secret police and as Interior Minister, wrote an extraordinary memorandum to the tsar arguing the opposite of Plehve. In his view, nothing was more likely to further the cause of the revolutionaries than the looming war with Germany. The prophetic power of Durnovo's memorandum is worth dwelling on, not only for its focus on the process of revolution but also for its sometimes shrewd, but always revealing, comments on other aspects of the current crisis. In the most quoted section of the document Durnovo wrote:

> the trouble will start with the blaming of the Government for all disasters. In the legislative institutions a bitter campaign against the Government will begin, followed by revolutionary agitations throughout the country, with Socialist slogans, capable of arousing and rallying the masses, beginning with the division of the land and succeeded by a division of all valuables and property. The defeated army, having lost its most dependable men, and carried away by the tide of primitive peasant desire for land, will find itself too demoralized to serve as a bulwark of law and order. The legislative institutions and the intellectual opposition parties, lacking real authority in the eyes of the people, will be powerless to stem the popular tide, aroused by themselves, and Russia will be flung into hopeless anarchy, the issue of which cannot be foreseen. (Golder 1927: 21–2.)

As the war developed, events bore an uncanny similarity to Durnovo's prophecy. Durnovo blamed the political class for leading Russia astray and it was, indeed, the Duma, which, from August 1915, became a focus of opposition to the autocracy. This was all the more remarkable in that this Duma, which was the fourth, had been elected on a very restrictive franchise which gave most weight to property-owners, especially the landowners, and only token representation to the mass of workers and peasants. By all criteria the Duma was conservative but it, none the less, was in the forefront of challenging the emperor. For Durnovo it was simply that they were the mischievous followers of alien western creeds of democracy. On this issue he was a fully paid-up follower of the slavophile line exemplified by Pobedonostsev.

These beliefs, shared widely among the governing class and the tsar himself, led to two crucial delusions. First, it deprived the opposition of all legitimacy in Durnovo's eyes. It was just a bunch of troublesome westward-looking intellectuals and their Jewish financial allies and mentors who were sounding off. The real reason for opposition from within the elite was never identified. What was stirring these rather conservative figures in the Duma to question their loyalty to the tsar? It was not difficult to work it out. Already, in 1905, they had shown their deep fears. In order to prop up their own elite status, they wanted to reform the autocracy, which they saw was no longer fit for purpose. If the anachronistic autocracy crashed – and here they agreed absolutely with Durnovo – it would bring them down, too. The October Manifesto had been enough to bring them back on board but the history of all four Dumas showed that this was, at best, an uneasy truce. At other times, the Duma was a cockpit of conflict between significant parts of the elite and the government, whose members did not belong to the Duma and were only responsible to the tsar who appointed them, not to the Duma through which their legislation was supposed to go.

The second delusion was that Duma opposition did not matter because they were not really representative of the true Russia. They were part of an alien, largely capitalist, industrial and financial elite, and as such they were seen as the enemy by the masses. Right to the end tsarist officials and the tsar himself dismissed Duma complaints as unimportant. They were, of course, very important. What the Duma and most of those it represented were trying to achieve was to join the old landed super elite in the business of governing Russia. They wanted little more than to help steer the autocracy away from the threatened revolution it was causing, and thereby defend the propertied classes as a whole. Was there a Bismarck in Russia who could bring industrialists and agrarians together in a united front against the socialist left? The leading candidate had appeared to be Stolypin, who was Prime Minister from 1906 to his assassination in 1911. While he did succeed in saving the autocracy in 1906–7 by severely repressing the masses and making minor concessions to the elites, these short-term wins did not add up to a strategic victory. His more fundamental reforms – such as engineering a supposedly conservative Duma; a land reform which redistributed land from one peasant to another without affecting gentry landowning, and the introduction of compulsory elementary education – were either not working or working so slowly they made little difference (Pallot and Shaw 1990; Waldron 1998; Pallot 1999; Ascher 2001). What Durnovo and the autocracy in general were missing here was that the constitutionalists and their allies in the Duma were desperately trying to ally themselves with the autocracy, albeit in a reformed system, not overthrow it. What Durnovo was right about, however, was that the Duma elite did not mean much to the masses. The revolution, when it came, did begin in the Duma but soon swept it aside, as Durnovo had predicted.

It was not just this short paragraph of remarkable foresight which makes Durnovo's memorandum so important. It illuminates a whole host of other questions and gives a deep insight into the autocratic mentality. This mentality was radically different from much of so-called conservative or right-wing thinking in western Europe and

North America. One has to reset the left–right gauge to measure the Russian political spectrum. Liberal conservatives, like the established professionals of the Kadet party, were actually revolutionary in Russia thanks to the stupidity of the autocracy in pushing them into near-illegal opposition. Further right the whole slavophile, anti-western, anti-democratic, xenophobic, especially anti-semitic, package began to assert itself. Russia, in this view, was a unique country with its own indigenous culture. It had its own way of doing things and it would contaminate it to compromise with the decadent and materialist grubbiness of the capitalist west. It was fundamental to this far right that the masses were on their side, acknowledged their place in the happy family that was Russia. Many, usually right-wingers, comfort themselves when assailed by intellectual ridicule of their outlook that, none the less, they retain the confidence of the 'silent majority' of simpler, less-educated people. How much evidence did the Russian right need to demonstrate the emptiness of their claim? A near-revolution, which ranged the entire country, apart from church and army, against the autocracy was, apparently, not enough. Nor was the faltering post-1905 settlement which was bringing anti-semitic trials – notably of Mendel Beilis for ritual murder – massacre of innocent workers and their families in the Lena goldfields and a rising tide of strikes, back into the everyday political scene as war approached (Haimson 2005).

The degree to which even a shrewd observer like Durnovo believed that the masses trusted the government more than the political class and the radical intelligentsia is breathtaking. In his view, the true friends of the workers and peasants were not the Duma politicians but the government factory and land inspectors who, supposedly, prevented the employers from inflicting the worst extremes of exploitation on their employees:

> However insistent the members of our legislative institutions may be that the people confide in them, the peasant would rather believe the landless government official than the Octobrist landlord in the Duma, while the working man treats the wage-earning factory inspector with more confidence than the legislating manufacturer, even though the latter professes every principle of the Kadet party (Golder 1927 20–21)

Here Durnovo is illustrating the gulf which separated the old elites from the nouveau-riche capitalists. The former looked with contempt on the money-oriented materialism of the latter who, it was believed, would abandon all principles and morality to make an extra few roubles. This gulf was endemic in the system. Even though the regime desperately needed the products, especially armaments, produced by the contemptible capitalists, they resented deeply having to deal with them (Gattrell 1994). Durnovo fully shared this dangerous prejudice. Where he made specific criticisms of Russia's unpreparedness for war, such as the state of the railways, shortage of munitions and disorder in the factories, he was quick to exonerate the government ministries and place all the blame on the hated owners and managers. Arguably, this was the most fateful of all the cleavages in Russian society because it split the elite. A divided elite is infinitely more vulnerable to over-throw than a united one (Skocpol 1979).

Paradoxically, despite his apparent belief in the underlying loyalty of the masses, Durnovo also had harsh words for them:

An especially favourable soil for social upheavals is found in Russia, where the masses undoubtedly profess, unconsciously, the principles of Socialism. In spite of the spirit of antagonism to the Government in Russian society, as unconscious as the Socialism of the broad masses of the people, a political revolution is not possible in Russia, and any revolutionary movement inevitably must degenerate into a Socialist movement. The opponents of the Government have no popular support. The people see no difference between a government official and an intellectual. The Russian masses, whether workmen or peasants, are not looking for political rights, which they neither want nor comprehend.

The peasant dreams of obtaining a gratuitous share of somebody else's land; the workman, of getting hold of the entire capital and profits of the manufacturer. Beyond this, they have no aspirations. If these slogans are scattered far and wide among the populace, and the Government permits agitation along these lines, Russia will be flung into anarchy, such as she suffered in the ever-memo-rable period of troubles in 1905–1906. War with Germany would create exceptionally favourable conditions for such agitation. (Golder 1927: 19–20.)

Here Durnovo presents himself as a kind of inverted Marxist, predict-ing an economically based class revolution. The masses are 'uncon-scious' socialists incapable of 'political' revolution and will simply sweep away the educated opposition in a vast land-grab. The extract shows us Durnovo's Nietzschean contempt for the near-animalistic herd who are not capable of lofty, philosophical thoughts, only of vulgar satisfaction of materialist physical instincts. Since they are too stupid and ill-informed to understand 'rights', 'all' they want is land and industrial profits. Is that, indeed, 'all'! To achieve that 'all' would require a complete reshaping of Russian society, which is, of course, exactly what happened in 1917 and after. This extract is, none the less, extraordinarily revealing of elite attitudes and their complete lack of comprehension of the masses. Incidentally, as we shall see, the masses proved themselves adept at pursuing politics, representation and rights in their own way. Durnovo did, however, identify the key issue of peasant land-hunger and its importance for the coming revolution.

The Path to War

Of course, the question arises, if Durnovo had such an accurate view of war being a disaster for Russia, why was he not listened to? Here, there is a straightforward answer. Durnovo's whole argument hinged on an untenable premise. There was, he said, no underlying reason for hostility with Germany. On the contrary, as embodiments of what he called the authoritarian principle in politics, Russia and Germany were natural allies. By comparison, republican France and a Great Britain up to its neck in imperial trickery were poor allies for Russia. Here, once again, Durnovo was showing his credentials as a specialist in internal affairs, a specialisation that was a weakness when he ventured into foreign affairs. There was a crucial set of clashing interests between Germany and Russia. As we saw earlier, the opening of the twentieth century was marked by the grinding together of the tectonic plates of empire. This was the key to international relations. The late emergence, in 1871, of a youthful, dynamic and expansionist German Empire in the midst of a politically overcrowded central Europe, where the Russian, Ottoman, Austrian and French-empires were already in conflict, was a major destabilising element. (For a still stimulating overview see Calleo 1978.) The German tactic of propping up, and thereby infiltrating and taking over, the Habsburg Empire (Austria-Hungary) was a direct threat to two other empires, the Russian and the Ottoman. The flashpoint was the Balkans including the Straits, the narrow sea channels leading from the Black Sea to the Mediterranean and the site of the ancient city of Constantinople (today named Istanbul). Rather than take on both empires, Germany performed the rather impressive trick of allying with both the Habsburg Empire and its enemy the Ottoman Empire.

These two had been in conflict through the nineteenth century as a whole raft of countries, from Egypt in the south, to Greece, Serbia, Romania, Bulgaria and many smaller states and territories, emerged from the wreckage of the declining Ottoman Empire. Religious and ethnic affinities sucked Russia into the mix and it was this, above all else, which led to a de facto rapprochement between the Germanic and Turkic Empires. Both opposed Russia more than each other. For Russia, the greatest geopolitical ambition of all was the recovery of Constantinople from Islam. The city was known as Tsargrad (City of the Tsar) in Russia and in 1878 Russian troops had come within sight of it as they supported Bulgarian independence. It took the Berlin Congress and Treaty of 1878 to force them to back off under the united weight of all the other European Great Powers. Germany, however, had also played the role of honest arbiter at the conference and, to cut a long story short, came closer to Turkey. The prospect of a Berlin–Baghdad railway was raised. Had it been completed it would have been an axis of German imperial expansion, her route not only to what the Kaiser claimed as Germany's 'place in the sun', but also as a route to what was becoming a key commodity, oil. In part, the First World War was the first of the major twentieth-century oil conflicts. But the immediate problem was that the proposed railway lay right across Russia's path of expansion in the Balkans and also threatened to cut off its crucial right to navigation through the Straits. This route was not only of strategic importance to Russia but crucial because its Black Sea ports – Odessa was the largest, with Sebastopol the second largest – were among its only year-round, ice-free outlets to the west. Russia's Baltic ports, including St Petersburg, all froze for part of the year. Only distant Murmansk, connected in 1915 by a fragile railway corridor, also looked west and was largely ice-free.

Clearly, there were crucial conflicts between Russia and Germany which invalidated Durnovo's plea for an alliance between them. Indeed, his whole Memorandum could have been dismissed as special pleading in the German cause. Durnovo was not the only one who believed in the German alliance. Many Russians were ethnic Germans, especially some of the landowners in the Baltic States. Many of them were prominent, like von Rennenkampf in the military and Witte in politics. Witte, in particular, lobbied for avoiding war with Germany, not least because he had substantial investments there, as did many others. But the leading advocate of a German alliance had been none other than the tsar himself. He had, in 1905, even taken advantage of a private meeting with his cousin, Kaiser Wilhelm II, on the royal yacht in a Finnish bay, to draft the Treaty of Björkö, an agreement of non-aggression and co-operation between the two countries. It was a sobering lesson in the limits of even autocratic political power that the Russian foreign office quickly tore it up and disabused their 'sovereign' of any similar transgressions in future since he had threatened to destabilise the whole European alliance system. Nonetheless, Nicholas remained sympathetic to its principles and tried to avoid war with his cousin until the last moment.

However, in one fundamental area, no doubt based on his observation of the bitter war fought against Japan, Durnovo was full of completely justified gloom about the nature of the coming war. It would, he said, be a 'stubborn' war testing not only every aspect of military preparation but also the industrial, economic, financial and infrastructural (notably railways) sinews of the nation:

> Are we prepared for so stubborn a war as the future war of the European nations will undoubtedly become? This question we must answer, without evasion, in the negative. That much has been done for our defence since the Japanese war, I am the last person to deny, but even so, it is quite inadequate considering the unprecedented scale on which a future war will inevitably be fought …
> It should not be forgotten that the impending war will be fought among the most civilized and technically most advanced nations. Every previous war has invariably been followed by something new in the realm of military technique, but the technical backwardness of our industries does not create favourable conditions for our adoption of the new inventions. (Golder 1927: 10 and 11–12.)

Perhaps if the horror that was about to be unleashed had been more widely understood more would have been done to prevent it. But in spring and early summer 1914, no one was sure. Those who were away from their homelands wondered what to do. More and more of them decided to make their way home. An ever-more urgent set of criss-cross journeys threaded along the railway networks. Anxious not to be caught on the wrong side of any military divide that might emerge, thousands of people scurried to their own countries. The crisis deepened by the week. From the assassination of Franz Ferdinand on 28 June it grew into a German-supported ultimatum from Austria delivered to Serbia. As Serbia prevaricated, Russia stepped in to support its distant protégée. As the Central Powers bristled with hostility towards Russia, Britain and France stood firm in support of their eastern ally.

Even so, many believed war was not inevitable. In some respects, the final ignition came from St Petersburg. Nicholas continued to believe that it was impossible for his cousin to declare war on him. However, contrary to that instinct, he opposed advice that it would be provocative to start Russian mobilisation. In a fateful decision, driven by the assumption that its mobilisation time was longer than that of Germany, Nicholas ordered the military to call up its citizens and begin its deployments. Once the process had started, mobilisation could not be stopped halfway without provoking chaos and leaving the country vulnerable until it was sorted out, a process of weeks, maybe months, rather than days. Nicholas still clung to the belief, against all reason, that even now, war did not have to follow. Events were, however, viewed differently in Berlin and Vienna; Germany and Austria-Hungary felt they had no alternative but to respond by ordering the mobilisation of their own armed forces. Inevitably, that triggered France and Britain to join in. The Great Powers were sliding down the slipperiest of all slopes into an unforeseen catastrophe of unimaginable proportions. The initial Russian mobilisation, on 28 July (NS), was aimed only at Austria-Hungary in response to the latter's invasion of Serbia on that day. Last-minute intensive negotiations with Berlin led to the realisation that such a partial mobilisation would only encourage Germany to attack before full mobilisation took effect. On 29 July (NS) Nicholas, under pressure from his generals, ordered full mobilisation. In response Germany declared war. The population regroupment took on a final frenzied surge but almost immediately the trains were emptied of civilians. Thousands of military trains threaded their way to each participant's frontiers. They were crammed with uniformed men, often in unexpectedly high spirits, on the way to their national borders. Not only men were called up. Russia mobilised a million horses (Keegan 1997). By 4 August 1914 the unthinkable had become a reality. A general European war had begun.

Not everyone had managed to get away before the cataclysm began. Unnoticed in the seething anthill of mass movements of civilians and military, two little known Russian revolutionaries relocated. One, living with his German mistress, left the small Bavarian town of Murnau near Munich. Obviously a Russian/German couple would have difficulties finding somewhere where both partners were acceptable. Not surprisingly they headed first for Switzerland. Their sojourn did not last long. Under pressure they split up, one returning to Moscow, the other to Munich. The other revolutionary had moved to Cracow in 1912 in order to be near the Russian border and keep in closer touch with his home country. The outbreak of war, however, put him in peril. An educated Russian near the border of the Austro-Hungarian Empire was an obvious suspect in the spy-mania that accompanied the war just about everywhere. It was imperative to move. Using the good offices of fellow-radicals in Vienna – whose approach to socialism he roundly despised – this revolutionary obtained a passage to Switzerland, just in time. It was another two and a half years before he made it back to Russia. Both of these obscure, unknown figures had no awareness that the events exploding around them would raise them to prominence and make them major figures in revolutionising their particular fields. The former was Wassily Kandinsky who pioneered the transition from figurative art to abstraction, to what he called the spiritual in art. The other was Lenin, leader of a faction of the tiny and uninfluential Russian Social-Democratic Labour Party. Neither could have predicted that they would become leading figures, in totally different ways, in the re-making of their worlds. The nineteenth century was about to commit suicide, the twentieth century was beginning to undergo the most painful of all births. Nothing would ever be the same again.

Chapter 2: An Empire Collapses: August 1914–February 1917

The jauntiness with which so many in all countries approached the outbreak of war is both incredible and poignant. The seductive slogans of nationalism had led many on all sides to believe their country was the best and that victory was a formality. Shrewder observers, like Durnovo, knew this was an illusion, but Russia was wrapped up in it. Patriotic crowds flooded city streets. The authorities had calculated that the call-up would only be answered by some 80 per cent of those eligible. In reality, Russian recruiting posts were submerged by an over-response. The nation and the autocrat were feted everywhere. The number of strikes fell (Golder 1927: 186–7). It seemed as though the sacred cause of national defence was sweeping away all social problems and divisions. The 'small, victorious war', dreamed of by Plehve in 1904, seemed to have arrived.

From Advance to Retreat: The Emergence of Social Unrest

For Russia, the war only went right for a matter of three weeks. From then on it was neither short nor victorious and the deep-rooted fissures in Russian society gradually took on a critical aspect. But those few weeks were almost decisive. The First Russian Army, commanded by General von Rennenkampf, and the Second, commanded by General Samsonov, were able to march forward. The first real encounter, at Gumbinnen, starting 20 August, turned a German attack into a retreat. Fearful of the Russian predominance in numbers – two armies in the field to Germany's one – the German commander, von Prittwitz, felt it prudent to order a defensive withdrawal, effectively abandoning East Prussia. The consequences of such an act might have changed the war completely. German strategy was based on the rather ambitious principles of the Schlieffen plan. The chief war would be between Germany and Russia. To avoid a war on two fronts the plan envisaged the rapid defeat of France in, effectively, a repeat of the Franco-Prussian War of 1870–71. Only a thin holding screen of troops was left in East Prussia with limited reserves in the German heartland ready to move either east or west as need dictated. However, if East Prussia were to be lost, the second part of the plan, the attack on Russia, would have been made much more difficult.

But even before that, the first half of the plan was hitting trouble. France was also obsessed by the memory of 1871 and had taken precautions to avert a repetition. The German advance through Belgium was anticipated (and cemented Britain into the war) and, despite spectacular advances, the main objective, Paris, was not reached and the Battle of the Marne (6–12 September), followed by the so-called Race to the Sea (September to November 1914), stabilised the western front. The conflict metamorphosed into trench warfare and brought about the collapse of the Schlieffen plan. The 'stubborn war' predicted by Durnovo was becoming a reality.

The German High Command responded to von Prittwitz's order to withdraw by replacing him and sending two men who were to symbolise the German war effort more than anyone else: von Hindenburg, who was called out of retirement, and von Ludendorff. They arrived on 23 August. Their impact was immediate. The retreat was halted. In a risky manoeuvre, based in large part on the sadly correct assumption that Rennenkampf and Samsonov hated each other so much that they would never co-ordinate their armies' movements, Ludendorff counter-attacked. For a week the battle raged around the town of Allenstein (today Olsztyn in Poland). Samsonov's army was cut off and eventually destroyed. On 29 August, Samsonov committed suicide. The Second Army was no more: 92,000 Russian troops were captured. 78,000 killed or wounded; only around 10,000 are thought to have escaped. German casualties were much lighter: they suffered some 20,000 casualties and captured sufficient Russian equipment to fill 60 trains (Showalter 2004; Sweetman 2004). Despite it being twenty miles distant, Hindenburg decided to call the battle after the town of Tannenberg, a name that evoked memories of historic victories of the Teutonic Knights.

Ludendorff turned his attention to the Russian First Army which, at the First Battle of the Masurian Lakes (9–14 September), was driven back into Russian territory. The only incursion on to German soil of any army during the First World War had been beaten back. There was, however, one incalculable bonus. Rather than face the loss of East Prussia, von Moltke, the German Army Chief of Staff, ordered troops to withdraw from the battle for Paris and redeployed them to the east. Ludendorff vehemently disagreed with this decision. They would, he said, arrive too late to be of use in East Prussia and crucially weaken the attack on France. Ludendorff was right on both counts. Von Moltke's error may have lost the war for Germany. Be that as it may, the end of the war was still far off. Its main shape was now emerging in the form of trenches of unimagined length, stretching from ocean to mountain, and of unprecedented pressures on entire societies and economies. Total war had begun. Was Russia in any state to be able to endure it?

As autumn gave way to winter, fighting on the eastern front ground to a halt, but not before the German army had made major incursions into Lithuania and had taken Łodz, only some 50 miles from Warsaw. For a few months both sides had time to prepare for the next stage, to form and equip new armies and to think about the new kind of war that was emerging. It was Germany that took most advantage of this. Although the Schlieffen Plan had failed irretrievably and Germany was bereft of a strategy and facing its ultimate nightmare of a war on two fronts, the decision was made to put greater effort into attacking Russia. Once its reinforced armies in the east began to advance they created defeat, disaster and chaos for Russia on an unprecedented scale. 1915 was one of the worst, and arguably, most decisive, years in Russian history. Retreat became rout. Rout became internal chaos. By 1917, internal chaos became, much as Durnovo had predicted, revolution.

The German spring and summer offensive in 1915 was devastating. Warsaw was taken on 5 August. The rest of Poland and large swathes of Bielorussia (now Belarus) were also occupied. The Russian armies were pushed back some 300 miles. In five months from April to the end of August, Russia lost a million men killed and wounded and another million captured (Wildman 1980: 89). In an early advance against Austrian troops in the first weeks of the war, Lvov and much of Galicia had been occupied by Russia. By the end of 1915 nearly all the gains had become losses. The panicky Russian Commander, General N.I. Ivanov, sent waves of indignation through the government by announcing it was necessary to prepare for the evacuation of Kiev. Only in the Caucasus theatre had Russian forces held their own, in this case against the old enemy, Turkey. Altogether, Russia's losses were enormous. By the end of the year, 'Russia's enemies had seized fourteen provinces with a combined population before the war of 35 million' (Gatrell 1999: 31), which constituted about one-third of the population of European Russia.

Even stated in these simple terms the losses were clearly devastating, but they represent only half of the story. Several factors made matters even more complicated and politically damaging. These were first, that frontline areas were under military control. Second, that the areas of fighting contained most of Russia's Jewish population. Third, that in addition to what one might call natural refugees, that is those 'spontaneously' fleeing the fighting of their own free will, the military organised mass deportations, especially of Poles, Lithuanians, ethnic Germans and Jews. These factors added further circles to the primordial chaos of military retreat. The pioneering, magisterial study of these events by Peter Gatrell provides astonishing information. Official figures claimed there were 3.3 million refugees by the end of 1915 and a further 500,000 in 1916. But Gatrell considers these to be underestimates. A total of 6 million by the beginning of 1917, including 367,000 in the Caucasus, was calculated by E.Z. Volkov in 1930 (Volkov 1930: 104). As Gatrell points out, this represented about 5 per cent of the total population and outnumbered the industrial working class which stood at about 3.5 million in October 1917 (Gatrell 1999: 3). The total number of displaced persons, including conscription and repatriation, amounted to 17.5 million people by the end of 1917 (Gatrell 1999: 221 fn. 9).

Social unrest in 1915 often began with refugees but it did not end there. Defeat on such a scale spread nervousness through almost all levels of Russian society. There were many responses, from the foundation of nursing organisations sponsored by female members of the royal family, through voluntary organisations bringing employers and workers together with a view to increasing output of military goods, to rebellions and strikes where pressures became intolerable. Not all the responses helped Russia to deal with the situation. Some were massively counterproductive, none more so than the reaction of some of the military leaders at the front.

For obvious reasons the front was under the complete control of the military authorities but, as with many aspects of Russian administration, it was not that simple. In the first place the notion of the front expanded to include some 100 versts (60 miles) behind the actual front. In addition, Russian armies were notorious for their independence and lack of co-ordination, often arising from rival ambitions of their commanders, so each front area developed its own rules. And, of course, the front line was falling back, sweeping up and through more and more territory further and further away from the original borders. In these envelopes of direct military control administrative chaos grew exponentially as the army was sucked into tasks of civilian government for which it was totally ill-suited. Its incompetence, backed by its taste for strictly enforced martial law, including capital punishment, was a recipe for disaster, especially as panic spread through the army from top to bottom. Even relatively natural and simple requirements, such as requisitioning of food, horses for their haulage power and even some industrial products like tractors, was done with such insensitivity, brutality and frequency that local populations were pushed to the brink of protest and even rebellion. Even more serious, as panic spread, so did the blame game. Army chiefs claimed the failures could only be blamed, Stalin-like, on spies and saboteurs. Who did they accuse? Their chief targets were ethnic Germans, Poles, Lithuanians, Latvians and, especially, Jews. Adding disorder to chaos, certain generals ordered mass deportations of civilians, which catastrophically augmented the 'spontaneous' refugees.

However, it was Jews who bore the most direct wrath of the army. Much of the fighting was, of course, taking place in the western borderlands of the Empire which coincided with the area, known as the Pale of Settlement, where Jews were allowed to live. Only small quotas (which, in practice, were often exceeded) were allowed to live in other parts of European Russia. So the great majority of Russian Jews lived in or near the war zone. This made them a handy scapegoat, enabling the generals to palm off responsibility for their own incompetence. It is no accident that what Norman Cohn called 'the warrant for genocide' – since it played a key role in anti-semitic ideology leading up to the holocaust, and even beyond, since it still crops up from time to time as an authentic document in Iran and elsewhere – had been forged in this very area some fifteen or so years earlier (Cohn 1964). These so-called *Protocols of the Elders of Zion* claimed to reveal a blueprint for Jewish world domination emanating from a fictional meeting of powerful Jewish figures from around the world. Not only were the *Protocols* most probably forged in eastern Poland or western Russia but young army and police officers were the most likely forgers. It was precisely these people and their like-minded successors who were ruling the roost in the chaos of 1915. They were able to direct massive violence on to the peaceful local Jewish population. Whole communities were accused of spying for the Germans. Some were deemed to have sent signals across the front line by use of large mirrors or even windmills. People, property and livestock were savagely attacked and villages looted by rampaging troops egged on by senior officers. Many were killed. Up to 600,000 others either fled or were deported (Klier and Lambroza 2004: 291).

Many non-Jews were also deported for supposedly military reasons, and sometimes subjected to looting and violence. By the end of 1915, 400,000 Ukrainians are thought to have fled from Galicia, through Volhynia towards Kiev. Hundreds of thousands of Poles and Lithuanians also fled or were driven eastwards by the military authorities, whose only thought was to deprive the advancing enemy of potential sources of manpower for their armies. Latvians were also forced along the coast through Estonia towards Reval (Tallinn) and St Petersburg.

It was not only at the front that social order was fracturing under the pressure of continuous, catastrophic defeat. By early 1915 the already volatile situation of pre-war factories was being made worse as trained workers were whisked out of them and into the army to be replaced by newly-recruited workers, many of them women. Pressure to produce in armament and military-related factories increased rapidly. Inflation began to spiral, and wages lagged behind prices. Food shortages began in certain cities. Not surprisingly, worker militancy, driven by desperation and a bemused search for who was to blame, began to take hold. Racist scapegoating was a major component of worker, and even some peasant, protests. Factory masters and landowners with German names were subjected to reprisals. Newly-arrived Jewish refugees were also blamed. Employers in general were accused of being unpatriotic. In the major cities an unseemly demi-monde of crooked arms contractors and nouveau-riche agents mingled with prostitutes, spies – real and imagined – in a free-spending café culture which contrasted starkly with the increasing hardship of the metropolitan working-class. Beautiful women of unknown origin and uncertain loyalty kept a close eye on the goings-on (Farson 1940: 126–50; Read 1996: 40).

Strike figures show the changing situation. According to one source:

in 1915 there were 1,063 strikes, 15 times more than in the second half of 1914 (i.e. the first six months of the war). The number of strikers reached 569,999—more than 15 times more. The strikes affected especially the big factories. The upswing in the strike movement began in April–June 1915. In these three months alone there were 440 strikes and 181,600 strikers, double the figures for the eight previous months of the war. (Woods 1999; figures from Fleer in Golder 1927: 186–7.)

Strikes were often poignant affairs and were signs of real desperation, which was often met with incredible harshness. To take one
example, in June 1915 a group of textile workers in Kostroma, a city
in the Moscow region, felt they had no alternative but to strike as
their living standards and working conditions rapidly worsened. They
were not militant, unionised workers but largely young women and
working mothers. The dispute escalated from a simple demand for a
wage rise on 2 June, which the company flatly refused, to an all-out
strike by 6,000 workers of the Great Kostroma Flax Factory. There
were barricades in the streets by 5 June as other factories joined in.
The response of the governor was harsh and brutal. Police fired on
the crowds and killed ten. The profile of the strikers was reflected
in the casualties. Of the ten, five were girls or young women. The
youngest was ten and three more were under seventeen. Naturally
enough, such barbarism horrified the women peasant-workers and
the whole region joined in out of sympathy. The plaintive plea of
the strikers has been preserved. They called for local soldiers to
defend them, since their own husbands and sons were at the front
so that:

> we, defenceless and unarmed [women], are being shot at by
> healthy and well-fed police guards ... [The employers] say, work
> calmly, but we are hungry and we cannot work. We asked but we
> were not heard: we began to demand and they shot at us. They say
> there is no bread! Where is it then? Or is it only for the Germans
> that the Russian land produces? (Inozemtsev 1934: 5–27; docu-
> ment translated in Daly and Trofimov 2009: 10–11.)

Here, in microcosm, was a revelation of the fracturing of Russian
society. Simple people driven to extreme action by desperate need; a
cruel and unnecessary response by the Governor which made the situation worse; hints of treason in high places; instinctive nationalism
and an appeal for solidarity with other components of the *narod* (the
people), in this case the soldiers. It was also common for soldiers'
wives, known as *soldatki*, and their daughters to be involved in protests
of this kind (Badcock 2004).

This was just one among many ominous signs of things to come.
Perhaps the most portentous were the Moscow riots around the
same time, in which economic and 'patriotic' motives became inex-
tricably entwined. Once again it was women workers and *soldatki*
who took a leading role, protesting that their husbands were being
called up while 'enemy aliens' were exempt. For three days crowds

went on the rampage, targeting businesses with German names and therefore presumed ethnic German owners. Shops, warehouses, workshops, even factories were attacked looted and then often set on fire. According to one estimate, from the most detailed study of the event by Eric Lohr, the damage done amounted to 72 million roubles (Lohr 2003: 31–54). This was, according to the leading specialist on Russia's economy of this period, Peter Gatrell, equivalent to a quarter of all annual investment in industry in 1914 (Gatrell 2004). In September, one of the biggest strikes of the year took place in Petrograd (the name of the imperial capital had been altered from St Petersburg for patriotic reasons). It began in the Putilov armaments factory in response to the arrest of 30 Bolshevik workers, in part on spurious grounds that they were pro-German. According to some estimates, 150,000 workers joined in the protests. Once again, the crude reflexes of autocratic rule had rebounded spectacularly and provoked a greater crisis than it had started off with. This, and the other strikes and protests of the time, were only overcome through a combination of factors. These included the as-yet weak position of the workers, who had no means to sustain a strike and had to go back to work to earn even a meagre living; the unavoidable fact that a war had to be fought and no one envisaged surrender; the repressive instincts of the authorities, which sometimes solved the immediate problem but stoked up hatred and resentment for the future and, finally, limited concessions to the strikers. Not surprisingly, demands began to escalate from the original simple wage rises to issues of national importance, notably the convening of a Constituent Assembly and the transition to a democratic republic; the redistribution of landowners' estates and, in factories, the eight-hour day. The old radical programme of 1905 was beginning to resurface. In the face of this escalating challenge, the propertied elites of Russia began to scurry around more rapidly than ever in search of protection for their privileges.

The Eclipse of the Government and the Formation of the Progressive Bloc: The August Crisis of 1915

The crisis began to concentrate minds. Members of the Council of Ministers were enraged and horrified by the incompetence of the military leadership in dealing with civilians. A summary, by the secretary to the meeting, A.N. Iakhontov, of the ministers' discussion on

30 July 1915 pulls no punches and graphically describes the situation. It is worth quoting the central description at some length:

> Headquarters has completely lost its head. It does not realise what it is doing, into what kind of an abyss it is dragging Russia. One cannot refer to the example of 1812 and transform the territory left to the enemy into a desert. The present conditions ... have nothing in common with 1812 ... To depopulate tens of provinces ... is equivalent to condemning all of Russia to horrible disasters ... but ... civilian reasoning must be silent before 'military necessity' ... The external defeat of Russia is being complemented by an internal one. In the flood of refugees one can distinguish three currents. First of all, the Jews who are being chased out of the frontal zone with whips and accused – all, without discrimination – of espionage, signalling, and other methods of helping the enemy, despite the frequent objections of the Council of Ministers. Of course, this whole Jewish mass is extremely irritated and arrives in the new regions it will inhabit in a revolutionary mood ... the local inhabitants ... receive the hungry and homeless Jews in a by-no-means friendly manner. Secondly there are the service personnel ... with dozens of railway waggons of goods. While tens of thousands of people are trudging alongside the railway lines, they are passed by speeding trains loaded down with couches from officers' clubs and carrying various junk, including the bird-cages of bird-loving quartermasters. Thirdly, there are voluntary refugees, driven in most cases, by rumours of the incredible bestiality of the Germans. Finally, and fourthly there are refugees who are being forcibly driven out on the orders of military authorities, for the purpose of depopulating territories being given up to the enemy. This group is the most numerous and the most irritated. People are torn from their birthplaces, given a few hours to collect their things, and driven towards an unknown goal. Before their very eyes, their remaining supplies, and frequently their houses, are set afire ... And this whole bewildered, irritated, tired-out crowd rolls like a continuous flood along all the roads, getting in the way of military transport and bringing complete chaos into the life of the rear. Along with it come wandering cattle and carts filled with junk. To feed, to water, to warm this multitude is impossible. People die by the hundreds from cold, hunger and disease. Infant mortality has reached horrifying proportions. Unburied corpses lie along the roads. Everywhere there is carrion and an unbearable stench. This human mass is pouring over Russia in a wide wave,

everywhere increasing the burdens of wartime, creating supply
crises, increasing the cost of living and exciting already heightened
tempers in various places. Only very recently … has Headquarters
begun to understand that this cannot be allowed to continue and it
has tried to cooperate with the government's demands that civilian
authorities be involved in the regulation of the refugee movement.
(Cherniavsky 1967: 38–40.)

It is hard to believe that this was a government discussion not a revolutionary manifesto. The government was deeply exercised by the
rapidly deteriorating situation and made great efforts to try to deal
with it, not least by trying to point out to 'Headquarters' (*Stavka* – the
military HQ) that policies of withdrawal and scorched earth were
potentially disastrous for Russia itself.

The ministers' next meeting, on 6 August, began with a discussion of the Jewish question. It highlighted several features. First,
there were deeply anti-semitic sentiments among some of the ministers but they were heavily outweighed by others who defended the
Jewish refugees. A.V. Krivoshein, Minister for Agriculture, thought
the influx of Jews into European Russian towns, but emphatically
not villages, would 'be useful not only politically, but economically'
(Cherniavsky 1967: 65) because their entrepreneurial skills would
stimulate the provinces. Others were horrified on simple humanitarian grounds by the 'violence and damage' inflicted on Jews by
General Ianushkevich, which was 'unthinkable in any civilised state'
(Cherniavsky 1967: 68). But this sentiment was intertwined with
a third, more practical issue, expressed by the Finance Minister,
P.D. Bark: the difficulty of raising money from abroad, including
from Jewish bankers of Paris, London and New York, when such
disgraceful pogroms were being conducted. He was fully supported
by S.D. Sazonov, the Foreign Minister, who welcomed the inevitable
decision taken by the Ministers that day to allow Jews free access to
most provincial towns, saying 'it will make discussions with the allies
much easier for me' (Cherniavsky 1967: 71). Bark agreed. 'Our decision today will have a very favourable effect on our finances, and
make easier the task of feeding the war with money.' (Cherniavsky
1967: 72.) Within a few hours, pressures of this kind had brought an
end to the 150 year-old Pale of Settlement, a clear example of war as
the locomotive of history.

Presumably, the ministers thought they had done a good day's work
at this point and reverted to their constant theme of the inefficiency
of military rule. However, they were about to be hit by a devastating

blow from a completely unexpected direction. As a result of it they were left fighting for their political lives, a battle they quickly lost.

The meeting turned to a routine item, a report on the situation at the front from General Polivanov. Again, Iakhontov's brilliant notes give the substance and atmosphere of the moment. He notes that Polivanov 'had participated little in the exchange of opinions during the meeting ... It was clear something was bothering him. The usual tic of his head and shoulders was particularly pronounced.' (Cherniavsky 1967: 75.) The report itself was bad enough.

> One can expect an irreparable catastrophe at any moment. The army is no longer retreating it is simply running away ... Headquarters has completely lost its head: Contradictory orders, rushing from solution to solution, feverish rotation of commanders, and universal disorder – all this bewilders even the most steadfast people. The psychology of retreat has eaten its way so deeply into the organism of Headquarters that, outside of the notorious scheme of luring the enemy into our great spaces, no solution, no struggle, is being recognized or sought.(Cherniavsky 1967: 76.)

But, terrifying though that was, it was not what was bothering him. He went on: 'But, no matter how terrible things are at the front, there is a far more horrible event which threatens Russia.' The ministers must have been on the edge of their seats when they heard such dreadful words. Polivanov continued:

> I am deliberately violating the secrecy imposed by my post and my word to remain silent for a time. I feel obliged to inform the government that this morning, during my report, His Majesty told me of his decision to remove the Grand Duke [Nicholas] and to personally assume the supreme command of the army. (Cherniavsky 1967: 76.)

Iakhontov described the response: 'These revelations ... evoked the greatest excitement ... Everyone spoke at once ... the majority were shaken by the news they heard – the latest, stunning blow in the midst of the military misfortunes and internal complications which were being suffered.' (Cherniavsky 1967: 76–7.)

The tsar's motives for taking this step are not entirely clear. Mainly he was driven by his fatal sense of duty to God and Russia. To stem the retreat, he thought, required the symbolic sacrifice of his distant cousin and a need to stand foursquare with the army himself. This would, he thought, wrapped up in his illusions of the inner loyalty of the population to the dynasty, provide an example for all of Russia to stand firm and stop panicking. While such a move may have validated Tsar Nicholas's personal courage and sense of duty, it also exemplified his political imbecility.

When he was informed of the decision, Polivanov, aware of Nicholas's 'suspiciousness and stubbornness about all decisions of a personal nature' tried tactfully to dissuade him (Cherniavsky 1967: 79). The elderly Prime Minister, I.L. Goremykin, confirmed Polivanov's bombshell and added that the tsar's 'conviction was formed a long time ago ... According to his own words, the duty of the Tsar, his function, dictates that the Monarch should be with his troops in moments of danger, sharing both their joy and their sorrows.' Goremykin had concluded that any attempt to dissuade him was 'useless' (Cherniavsky 1967: 79). It could also be added that the decision was as unnecessary as it was foolish. Grand Duke Nicholas was not responsible for the situation and he even remained a relatively popular figurehead.

On the face of it, one might wonder why the ministers reacted so deeply. After all, in most people's minds, surely, the person of the tsar was already intimately linked to the war effort? Research carried out by Boris Kolonitskii into arrests for expressions of public disloyalty indicates that the assumption of supreme command made little difference to the number of cases (Kolonitskii 2011). However, many of the minister's comments revolved around this issue. Polivanov had even presented the problem directly to the tsar, informing him 'about the possible consequences for the internal life of the country if the personal leadership of the troops by the Tsar were not to improve the situation at the front'. Since even local successes were unlikely, 'it is horrible to think what impression would be made on the country if His majesty the Emperor were to give the order for the evacuation of Petrograd or, God help us, Moscow in his own name.' Nonetheless, the tsar replied that his 'decision was final' (Cherniavsky 1967: 77). Polivanov was immediately backed up by Prince Shcherbatov who, as Minister of the Interior, had access to reports on the mood of the country. He had also tried to dissuade the tsar, telling him it was 'the most unfavourable moment for such a decision.' It was a time of 'growth of revolutionary feelings.' He even showed the tsar 'letters obtained through military censorship, from people of various social classes, including some closest to the Court' which showed vividly:

the dissatisfaction with the government, with the regulations, with the confusion in the rear, with the military defeats, and so on.

Moreover, the Emperor himself is held responsible for much of this. In such circumstances, His Majesty's taking over direct command of the troops will make a very bad impression and can greatly complicate the internal situation. Besides, Grand Duke Nicholas has not lost his popularity despite everything that is happening at the front.' (Cherniavsky 1967: 77–8.)

Shcherbatov's comments are especially significant, pointing out as they do that as early as mid-1915 the advance of revolutionary sentiments included people close to the Court itself, plus the fact that the tsar was already widely blamed for the situation while the Grand Duke, who was directly in charge of the army, was more popular, as confirmed by Kolonitskii's research (Kolonitskii 2011). This suggested that there was more to the ministers' response than the issue of the tsar's links to military failure, and indeed there was an even more important issue, but one which they spoke about less openly. They were ultimately concerned about their own authority and the risks to the country of a more military-dominated administration. In his summary of the meeting Iakhontov hit on the key point. Given the secrecy of the tsar's decision the main issue was that the whole affair showed that 'there is no confidence in the Council of Ministers.' (Cherniavsky 1967: 84.)

The ministers' authority was being encroached upon from three sides. The tsar himself, the military leaders and the semi-parliamentary Duma were all challenging it. The imminent danger, as most of the ministers were aware, was that if the tsar intervened more in government and gravitated to the military, the nightmare of disastrously incompetent military government would replace the relatively sophisticated pragmatism of the Council of Ministers. As we have seen, the ministers had zero confidence in the competence of the military to govern civilians. In the midst of the crisis two further military decisions aroused their deepest fears. The military was proposing an extension of the area behind the front which they would rule directly. The ministers were distraught. Polivanov alerted the Council to the problem at the meeting of 16 August. The military, he said, wanted to extend the war theatre 'up to the approximate line of Tver'–Tula', that is almost to Moscow. In his view this would mean that 'what was already bad in Germany and Poland, will be a national disaster close to Tula and Tver'.' Shcherbatov, seeing the territory over which he was supposed to preside as Minister of the Interior shrinking so much, said the Council should declare the move to be impossible. He scarcely had to remind his colleagues that 'The picture in the military rear area is one of sickening outrages, anarchy, arbitrariness, and absence of authority. One cannot hand over the central provinces to be abused by the redheaded Danilov [General Yuri Danilov, so-called to distinguish him from another General Danilov] and his horde of rear-echelon heroes.' He concluded emphatically and unequivocally that 'We have accumulated enough sad experiences to be able to say that the abolition of normal authority serves the cause of revolution.' (Cherniavsky 1967: 120.)

The second blatant example of military incompetence and panic came three days later, when a relatively minor minister reported that the military were ordering the evacuation of Kiev. Again the ministers were stunned. Kharitonov asked if there were a real threat or if it was just another Headquarters panic. General Polivanov said there was no immediate threat to Kiev and complained he had heard nothing about it 'as it is considered unnecessary to keep the Minister of War informed of the course of events.' (Cherniavsky 1967: 147.) Kharitonov pointed once again to the Headquarters taking a military decision while ignoring the wider consequences. Abandoning Kiev, 'the Mother of Russian cities' was not like abandoning a Galician village. For all the ministers knew, he went on, 'one fine day we will find out that one brave general has ordered another general to evacuate Petrograd. The devil knows what is going on here!' (Cherniavsky 1967: 147.) They all had the unedifying spectacle of the evacuation of Warsaw fresh in their minds. Indiscriminate mass arrests of Poles and Jews in the last 24 hours before the troops departed had created popular outrage. At the 16 August meeting the situation in Warsaw had been described by Sazonov: 'The men who are in control there are simply mad. Instead of leaving behind a population well-disposed toward us, the gentleman generals do everything possible to have our retreating troops followed by curses.' (Cherniavsky 1967: 123.) To have this replicated in Kiev was too much.

Such considerations had given additional urgency to the government's attempts to avert the catastrophe of the tsar's decision to become supreme commander. Poignantly, a few minutes before the Kiev bombshell exploded, Krivoshein appeared to have found a compromise. He suggested that 'The Tsar assumes Supreme Command and appoints the Grand Duke as his assistant' (Cherniavsky 1967 143). The ministers greeted this suggestion quite warmly. However, it was to no avail. As sceptics had argued, the tsar would not modify or reverse his decision because of personal stubbornness and his mystical understanding of his role. He had made his compact with God, not his government. In despair, a group of key ministers wrote a final appeal to him to change his mind. All the letter did was to establish, in the tsar's eyes, that they were disloyal, and most of them were almost instantly dismissed. Some, like Sazonov, were kept on a little longer, but the outcome of the August crisis was the virtual destruction of Russia's civilian government.

For the last eighteen months of its existence ministers came and went in what has been called ministerial leapfrog. In the course of 1916 there were three Chairmen of the Council, three Ministers of the Interior, three Ministers of Justice and three Foreign Ministers (Waldron 1997: 153). The reputation of autocratic government hit new lows. Unfounded rumours of the influence of Rasputin and of a pro-German party at the court led by the Empress, who was of German birth, grew exponentially. The reputation of the regime was in tatters. The tsar himself spent more and more time at the General Staff Headquarters and insofar as Russia was governed at all in these last pre-revolutionary months it was more military dictatorship than anything else, with the civilian ministers reduced to the role of errand boys for the generals. The ministers had foreseen this disastrous outcome in the midst of the August crisis. In the words of Krivoshein, the internal situation:

> allow[ed] of only two solutions: either a strong military dictator-ship, if one can find a suitable person, or reconciliation with the public ... We must beg [His Majesty] to ... change fundamentally the character of internal policy. ... From all sides one is forced to listen to the grimmest predictions [of what will happen] if no deci-sive steps are taken to calm public anxiety.

Forebodingly he pointed out that 'this is said by people whose loyalty to the Monarch cannot be doubted' (Cherniavsky 1967: 142). The tsar was squandering his best reserves of support.

But what about the alternative mentioned by Krivoshein, 'recon-ciliation with the public'? The crisis had caused all parts of the elite to begin to work out a survival plan. Outside the triangle of tsar–ministers–Stavka wider interests had begun to assert themselves. Local authorities banded together, giving new energy to the Union of Towns and the Union of Zemstva (local government institutions). Employers set up War Industries Committees to try to improve the quality and quantity of military production. They very soon took the unprecedented step of including workers' representatives on many of them. Voluntary societies also tried to make up for the inadequa-cies of government in other areas. Perhaps the most notable were the various nursing associations which were formed to assist with the care and treatment of wounded soldiers and civilians. The main focus of all these groups was, however, the Fourth Duma which had been elected in 1912 on the restricted Stolypin electoral system. This gave a great preponderance of seats to parties of the right. Despite its political complexion, in August 1915 it took fateful steps which, incredibly, eventually turned it into a revolutionary body. The Duma was, in addition to the tsar and the Stavka, the third force challenging the authority of the government. Not surprisingly, government ministers were divided in their attitude to the Duma. Some simply hated it and everyone associated with it. The elderly and old-school prime minister, Goremykin, considered the Duma President, Rodzianko, himself a guards officer so by no means a plebeian, to be a 'madman.' Samarin was softer, agreeing that Rodzianko was 'carried away by his self-imagined role as chief representative of popular representation' but, nonetheless, he was 'a well-mannered man and loyal to the monarch' (Cherniavsky 1967: 117). Schcherbatov and Krivoshein could not resist adding that 'he undoubtedly suffers from delusions of grandeur' 'and withal, in a very dangerous stage of development' (Cherniavsky 1967: 117–18). Beyond personalities, the government tended to mistrust any initiative associated with the Duma. A suggestion to co-ordinate voluntary associations of every kind to help their efficiency was vehemently opposed by Krivoshein, who compared it to the French Revolution, as 'either some kind of a Convention or a Committee of Public Safety.' He continued, 'under the cloak of patriotic anxiety, they want to create some kind of second government' (Cherniavsky 1967: 118).

His comment summed up the attitude of the ministers to the Duma and also showed how deeply divided the elite was. Already, conservative and centrist landowners, factory owners and professionals were being treated as radical revolutionaries. It was a self-fulfilling judgment. Excluding the 'moderate' Duma politicians from real decision-making drove them, gradually and reluctantly, to greater extremes. For the moment, however, they took a first tentative step to develop their power. Alarmed by the appalling internal situation, sharing the government's view of the dreadful incompetence of the military administration and increasingly fearful that the tsar was turning from a bulwark of order into a liability, the majority formed a pressure group, calling themselves the Progressive Bloc. There were even some members of the even more illustrious and largely tsar-appointed upper chamber, the State Council, who signed up. On 25 August they produced their programme. First and foremost they called, deliberately vaguely, for a government 'supported by the confidence of the people'. In one form or another, this phrase became the mantra of the centre-right. What it really meant was not so much a popular democratic government but one in which they, the elite, could participate. They outlined their basic objectives, starting with reorganising the administration to provide a strong government capable of winning the war. Beyond that, the programme called for an end to political imprisonment; equality of all religions; autonomy for Poland; 'a beginning toward abolishing the limitations of the rights of Jews'; greater press freedom, especially in the military zones; restoration of some trade union rights and a legislative programme agreed by the government and the Duma (Vernadsky and Pushkarev 1972: vol. 3, 846). Its limitations are obvious. It was too timid and too divided to call unequivocally for Jewish emancipation, and it recognised a divide between 'the government' and the Duma. It was not attempting to replace the Council of Ministers, still less to attack the tsar, but to agree an emergency programme with them. For all its moderation its pleas fell on deaf ears. The tsar's response, as counter-productive as ever, was to prorogue (suspend) the Duma.

The August crisis was a vivid flash illuminating the developing fissures not only in the social fabric of the empire but also, critically, within the propertied elite itself. It has been argued that a common precursor to revolution is precisely such a split, where elite and state separate from each other (Skocpol 1979). However, revolution did not come about in 1915, not least because there were no significant forces trying to promote it. Left-wingers had little purchase on the situation and were, in any case, hamstrung by the fact that almost all of the leaders were either in prison, internal exile in Siberia and elsewhere or scattered across western Europe and, in some cases, North America. As summer turned to autumn the changing weather brought 'General Winter' to Russia's aid. The pace of fighting slowed down and there was time to regroup. The autocracy survived 1915. Would Russia still have the resources and social energy to recover? There were still significant swings of fortune to be experienced in 1916 before the endgame was complete.

War and the 'Prison House of Nations'

The Russian Empire had been formed over centuries by a process of sprawling expansion across an often inhospitable, sparsely populated set of territories on the south-eastern margins of Europe, that is the area between the Black Sea, the Caspian and the Caucasus Mountains, and the northern margins of Asia, that is from Central Asia to Siberia and Sakhalin Island. Explorers, monks, traders, soldiers and runaway peasants, the main forces behind Russian expansion, had encountered many difficulties, such as barrier rivers cutting across the paths of advance, forests, climatic extremes, tundra and steppe but, until the Arctic and Pacific Oceans and the Caucasus, Hindu Kush and related mountain chains were reached, they encountered very few natural borders. Even so, Russians were the first Europeans to reach the west coast of North America and trading outposts were set up almost as far south as present-day San Francisco. In the eighteenth century, westward expansion secured a Baltic foothold and the fruits of a partition of Poland. By 1914, the world's largest contiguous land empire comprised upwards of 160 nationalities and ethnicities; demographers fought over the exact number (Martin 2001; Hirsch 2005). The tsar's comic-opera list of titles reflected the higgledy-piggledy nature of the process. Just for starters he was 'by the Grace of God, Emperor and Autocrat of All the Russias, of Moscow, Kiev, Vladimir, Novgorod, Tsar of Kazan, Tsar of Astrakhan, Tsar of Poland, Tsar of Siberia, Tsar of Tauric Chersonesos, Tsar of Georgia, Lord of Pskov, and Grand Duke of Smolensk, Lithuania, Volhynia, Podolia, and Finland, Prince of Estonia, Livonia, Courland and Semigalia, Samogitia, Belostok, Karelia, Tver, Yugra, Perm, Vyatka, Bulgaria and other territories; Lord and Grand Duke of Nizhnii-Novgorod, Sovereign of Chernigov, Ryazan, Polotsk, Rostov, Yaroslavl, Beloozero, Udoria, Obdoria, Kondia, Vitebsk, Mstislavl, and all northern territories; Sovereign of Iveria, Kartalinia, and the Kabardinian lands and Armenian territories – hereditary Lord and Ruler of the Circassians and Mountain Princes and others; Lord of Turkestan, Heir of Norway, Duke of Schleswig-Holstein, Stormarn, Dithmarschen, Oldenburg …', and so it went on. Older readers might imagine Peter Ustinov playing this role. In any case, he would have made a much better tsar! Trying to hold such a diverse set of cultures – from desert nomads to igloo-dwellers and including Jews, Protestants, Roman Catholics, Armenian Catholics, Georgian Orthodox, Muslims, Buddhists, animists alongside the majority Russian Orthodox – within a single state structure was an immense challenge. Unlike the British, French and Dutch Empires, which were made up of various parcels around the planet, and which enabled different rules and laws to be developed in each enclave, whether it was large like India or small, like St Pierre and Miquelon, the Russian Empire had to have a more or less uniform legal and political structure for the whole mass. The great late-nineteenth-century Russian historian, Vassili Kliuchevsky, described Russia's history as 'the history of a country in the process of being "colonised". State building and Empire were closely intertwined' (Wirtschafter 2008: 118). As communications slowly improved, through railways, the telegraph, newspapers and so on, the urgency of the need to blend this diversity together increased. The last brainwave of tsarist nationalities policy, developed by the tsar's tutor and mentor, Konstantin Pobedonostsev, had been forced Russification. Between 1881 and 1905, from his official post as secular head of the church, known as the Procurator of the Holy Synod, he launched a series of initiatives prompted by the emergency in 1881 which followed the assassination of Tsar Alexander II. Alongside Emergency Regulations a wave of assaults, some primarily violent, some mainly cultural, were launched across the Empire. Briefly, destructive pogroms against Jews were at least tolerated and often, at local level, encouraged by the authorities. A more sustained policy built the ideological core of the Empire around the Orthodox Church and the Russian language. Local languages were demoted to second place in their own homelands. True, there was a problem here for the state. It needed to build a larger and larger army, but how could it do so effectively if that army spoke dozens of different languages? However, the crude and insensitive imposition of these policies sowed resentment and only a formal, sullen compliance. By the beginning of the twentieth century, significant nationalist groups were forming, from Finland to Georgia. Most revolutionary movements in the Russian Empire had a disproportionate number of members of ethnic minorities, many of them Jewish, among their leading cadres. Not for nothing had Russia, by this time, acquired the description of the 'prison house of nations'. To become involved in a bitter, long-drawn-out and testing war was a sure way to exacerbate those tensions and, during and after the August crisis of 1915, they burst into the open. In particular, two major events illustrated the problems. One was the Armenian genocide, still shamefully disputed and officially denied in Turkey, the other was the Central Asian uprising of 1916.

From the beginning, Russia had not only conducted war on its western borderlands against Germany and Austria-Hungary; it had also fought in the Caucasus on its southern front against its perennial enemy, Turkey. By comparison, the war here was more successful than in the west. At the same time as the battle of the Masurian Lakes in December and January 1914–1915, the Russian Army of the Caucasus inflicted a heavy defeat on the Turkish Army in the mountain battle of Sarikamiş. Enver Pasha's army of over 100,000 troops was reduced by deaths, wounds, illness and capture to only one-third of its original size. From that point on, the Russian army, led by General Nikolai Iudenich, drove the Turkish forces out of the southern Caucasus in 1915 and 1916. Plans were even being made for the Russian army to link up with British forces, moving from Egypt into Palestine, partly under cover of the Arab Revolt incited by Lawrence of Arabia. Baghdad was the planned point of convergence, but nothing came of it.

However, the war provoked catastrophe for the Armenian population, spread beyond its Russian-ruled heartland around the city of Yerevan, into a broad diaspora throughout Ottoman-controlled Asia Minor, with local centres in Van, Trebizond, Adana, Bitlis, Diyarbekir, Erzerum and elsewhere. Ironically, before the war began, the Ottoman leadership sought to enlist its Armenian subjects in its forthcoming war effort. Aware of Armenian hostility to Russia, the leaders of Turkey urged its Armenians to join up with the Armenians living under Russian rule in a joint revolt against the tsar. However, the Ottoman-ruled Armenians had already been subjected to massacres. In 1895 some 100,000 or more had been killed following a protest by them for reform. In 1909, in Adana province, feuding between Turkish groups degenerated into a massacre of some 15,000–30,000 Armenians. While Christian Europe was alerted to the massacres of their co-religionists, divided interests prevented the European powers from taking any serious action to defend the Armenian population. Against such a background, appeals from Ottomans for Armenian loyalty were likely to be met with incredulity. But worse was to come. Like the Jews on Russia's western front, Ottoman Armenians became a scapegoat for Turkey's military disasters. However, persecution of them went much further. Documented instances of forced labour; deportation; death marches; medical massacre through overdoses of morphine especially for children; injection of typhoid-contaminated blood; pogroms; pre-emptive massacre of military-aged males to stop them fighting against Turkey; mass burnings (of 5,000 people in one event); mass drownings at sea of men, women and children; gassing of schoolchildren in a Trebizond school; forced marches into the Syrian desert where people were left to die of thirst and exhaustion, all contributed to an unprecedented disaster, the first genocide. Other Christian groups, such as Greeks and Assyrians, were also targeted. Overall figures mostly suggest there were around 1.5 million deaths in all (Bryce 1916; http://en.wikipedia/Armenian_Genocide; http://www.armenian-genocide.org/index.htm).

Not surprisingly, from the earliest moments of the war Armenians had feared attacks, though no one would have predicted the scale.

Resistance groups joined the advancing Russian forces. In the Armenian stronghold of Van a local uprising held the town against Turkish forces in mid-April 1915 until Iudenich's army arrived in May. Massacre and resistance became a truly vicious downward spiral, each feeding off the other, until the most appalling crime of the century, thus far, unfolded. Russia's role here was, for once, as saviour from, rather than perpetrator of, atrocities against national minorities. Nonetheless, Iudenich did not favour Armenians and proposed to settle a wave of Russian Cossacks on the 'liberated' frontier. The twisted relations of the Caucasus did not, however, end with the war, and the horrors of this particular corner of the battlefield had an important influence in the formation of the USSR in this area.

Further east, equally portentous events were unfolding which had a more direct impact on the demise of the Russian Empire than the relatively successful (from Russia's point of view) advance into the Caucasus. As we have seen, the military crisis of 1915 was forcing a rethink of strategy and a rebuilding of the already-destroyed armies. One aspect of this was the extension of conscription to areas which had been exempt, mainly on grounds of doubt about the reliability of such exempt populations. One of the main exemptions had applied to Muslims of Central Asia, themselves of Turkic stock, though in many cases their practical links with the Ottoman Empire were weak. Even so, it had been initially feared that conscripting them would be more trouble than it was worth. It was especially feared that the indigenous population might sympathise with their Turkish ethnic relatives. However, by 1915 desperation had set in and earlier prudence had been overwhelmed by growing necessity. In the Edict of Mobilisation about half a million formerly exempt males were called up, to work mainly as sappers constructing the defences of the Russian armies in their front areas. A near-simultaneous movement to deprive the local population of what they claimed to be their traditional grazing lands had already inflamed hostility. Not surprisingly, the double whammy was met with armed resistance. Kazakhs, Kyrgyz and Uzbeks rose up. There were fierce clashes in several areas, notably the Fergana Valley in eastern Kirghizia (Kyrgyzstan) and in Kazakhstan. Russian settlers were targeted, and some 2000 were killed. The government sent in an army of 10,000 troops, a larger force than that which had conquered the region fifty years earlier. Disputed figures suggest between 150,000 and 300,000 were killed in the repression and in desperate flight across the mountains via the Boomsk Gorge to the hoped-for safety of the homelands of their ethnic kin living across the border in China (Ali-uulu 2009). For the moment the repression succeeded, but a resistance movement had been set off which evolved into the Basmachi uprising which flared up during the civil war and was not fully put down until the mid-1920s and smouldered even into the 1930s when its last embers ignited a fight against Stalinist collectivisation.

Given what we have already seen of the ethnic conflict and deportations on Russia's western front it is easy to see how the war provoked anti-Russian responses all around the Empire and opened up opportunities for organised nationalities, like Finns, Poles and the Baltic nations to move quickly towards full independence once the tsarist edifice finally crashed down. Central Asia and the peoples of the Caucasus also attempted to escape the prison house of nations but were corralled back in by 1922. However, the stirrings of national groups were an ominous sign, by 1916, that the war effort was creating serious political instability. Ironically, perhaps, the army had some success in 1916 but, in its final eighteen months, the Empire as a whole seemed to be caught in a deadly zero-sum game. Every move to strengthen the military weakened the home front. Redressing the weakness of the home front undermined the prospects of the military. It lacked the administrative ability, strength and resources to sustain both its military effort and its civilian population at the same time. Survival was looking more and more improbable.

The Death Throes of Tsarism

1916 was a terrible year for the Triple Entente: the Somme, Verdun, Jutland. Heavy casualties were suffered, accompanied by failure to make any significant breakthrough in the stalemate. Submarine blockade and encirclement were putting pressure, eventually to the point of famine and mutiny, on both the Entente and the Central Powers. Exceptionally, Russia was the only power to enjoy any notable military success. The winter and spring campaigns on the eastern Front had promised little. Losses in Gorlice-Tarnow had not been recovered and a premature attack at Lake Naroch, intended to divert German forces and thereby to relieve the pressure on Verdun, was another failure in March 1916. The next planned offensive was to be on Russia's Western Front in the area of the Pripet Marshes. Cautious generals told the tsar preparations were not complete when, in May, Italy requested a Russian offensive to counter an Austro-Hungarian offensive against them in the Dolomites. However, General Alexei Brusilov volunteered to attack, and his army launched an assault against Austro-Hungarian positions in the Carpathians on 4 June. For a while they were able to advance. But their success was not consolidated. German reinforcements, made of tougher stuff than their allies, were sent in. In addition, a chronic failing of the tsarist army reasserted itself. Commanders refused to back up the initiatives of other commanders. Brusilov was hung out to dry by his fellow generals and inevitably his armies fell back, losing more ground than they had initially gained. Once again the roads were filled with penniless refugees, shell-shocked deserters and structureless remnants of defeated military units. Potential success had turned into yet another major failure. By the time the battle ended, both sides had lost more than a million men. Austria halted its Italian offensive and Germany had been forced to transfer another 15 divisions from Verdun (see WW1WorldWarOneonline; Dowling 2008).

Nonetheless, it has been convincingly argued (Stone 1975) that Brusilov's initial success showed important features of the Russian war effort. Traditional reasons for failure had included issues like shell shortage, weakness of Russian industry, infrastructural inadequacy especially of supposedly overloaded railways and overconscription, which pulled needed skilled workers out of factories and put them, ill-trained and under-equipped, into often pointless military postings where they were wasted. Stone argues otherwise. For him, generals blamed shell shortage and industrial and railway inadequacy to make up for their own incompetence. Factory owners blamed conscription for their own poor management and weak co-ordination with state procurement of military goods. In Stone's view, what distinguished Brusilov from his fellow commanders was competence, not supplies. Using the same resources as every other front commander, he was able to plan and execute a uniquely successful attack. This indicated to Stone that the real reasons for Russia's failure were to be found elsewhere. The chief villains of the piece were administrative incompetence and inflation. For both of these the state, in the form of parts of the army High Command and parts of the civil service, bore the chief responsibility. Stone's argument was that there were plenty of shells but commanders hoarded them rather than using them. Initial strategic decisions, notably to build up fortresses, had proved to be disastrously misjudged. Fortresses were highly vulnerable to contemporary artillery and the war was fought by spreading resources out in trenches, not concentrating them in small areas like fortresses where they could be targeted, besieged, or simply passed, by advancing armies. Even railways, Stone argued, were not inadequate. Demand on them during war was not substantially greater than in peace time because in war one of the main demands on the railways, to carry export grain, disappeared as no exporting was possible. For Stone, the inadequacy was in failing to reschedule the system rather than in not having the resources. He even shows that, in occupied territories, the German authorities could use the railway resources more efficiently than the Russians despite the broader gauge of the Russian tracks. To add insult to injury, more efficient career officers such as Brusilov and Kornilov were often overridden by officers who held their positions by birthright and failed to understand the modern military world. In 1915, attempts had been made to drag the War Minister, Sukhomlinov, into a dubious spy trial of an officer named Myasoedov who had supposedly passed information to the enemy. Myasoedov had been summarily executed, probably more as a scapegoat for the failures of 1915 than because of real guilt. Senior military figures of the old-fashioned school had long believed Sukhomlinov to be a traitor because he had advocated the dismantling of fortresses. To the old guard this was unthinkable. To the new meritocrats and technocrats it was an elementary necessity.

The ultimate exhaustion and failure of the Brusilov offensive had, once again, knocked all the military cards from the tsar's hand. There was no new perspective and defeat had hastened decline.

The second important corrosive force was inflation. This was also caused by the war, in that a large part of the financing of the war came through simple printing of money. Foreign loans, war gifts and taxation were not enough. The fires of inflation, followed eventually by hyperinflation, ravaged Russian society for some five to six years starting in 1915 (Stone 1975; Gattrell 2005; Markevich and Harrison 2011).

The effects of inflation were increasingly damaging. Prices soared as military demand sucked goods out of the reach of consumers. By the end of 1916 the peasantry, who had not up to that time demonstrated or caused disturbances – with the notable exception of those in areas under military rule near the front – began to exert an important influence on the development of the final crisis. Rising prices encouraged them to hoard their produce. Rather than convert it into money, when few goods were available that they wanted to buy, they simply held on to it. They consumed more themselves and waited for more favourable terms to market the rest. In this way they contributed to supply shortages. The emphasis here is on the word 'supply'. Foodstuffs were available but, as the peasants held on to the surplus, it was in the wrong place. Also, as food shortages developed, particularly in northern Russia, where the climate prevented the region from being self-sufficient in agriculture (a growing season of only about four months a year), it became clear that transport and supply chains were a bigger problem than overall national shortage. There was sufficient grain to feed the country but it was not being supplied to many areas that needed it.

Thus, inflation was having a very damaging effect in several ways: it was causing prices to rise faster than wages; it was distorting peasant marketing of grain and other produce; and, combined with administrative chaos on the railways, it was promoting increasing hardship in the cities. Police reports for 1916 show that the authorities were well aware of the problems. According to their calculations key prices were rising faster than wages. 'While the wages of the masses have risen by 50 per cent, and only in certain categories by 100 to 200 per cent (metal workers, machinists, electricians), the prices on all products have increased 100 per cent to 500 per cent', and shortages that obliged them to queue in the cold and damp had 'made the workers, as a whole, prepared for the wildest excesses of a "hunger riot"'.

The police were also under no illusion that this led to political unrest in many cities. As early as February 1916 the *Okhrana* (Security Police) had detected 'an *anti-dynastic* movement ... of profound resentment against the person of the currently reigning emperor' a movement as strong in Kadet circles as it was on the street. Rumours of German sympathies at court, Rasputin and 'filthy gossip' had 'become the property of the street'. Their picture of the political situation was devastating. Astonishingly, in October 1916 it was reported that, compared to 1905–6, 'the mood of opposition has reached extraordinary dimensions which it never attained among the broad masses during the earlier period'. Clearly, massive efforts to finance and supply the war were wreaking havoc among civilians. A report of the Special Section of the Petrograd Okhrana, also from October, reported that while 'the problem of providing the army with military supplies may be considered solved ... the gradually increasing disorganisation of the rear – in other words the entire country – ...has at this moment achieved such an extreme and monstrous stage that it is, even now, beginning to threaten the results achieved at the front, and promises in the very near future to plunge the country into the destructive chaos of catastrophic and elemental anarchy' (Vernadsky and Pushkarev 1972: vol. 3, 865–6, emphases in the original). The villages were not caught up in the agitated mood, but cities and towns everywhere were on the edge of breakdown.

Thorough research has shown that the economic condition of Russia during the war fell within parameters comparable to those of other combatants.

> According to previous estimates, Russia's economic performance in the Great War up to 1917 was far below that of most other continental countries that entered the war. On our figures, Russia's shortfall disappears ... The average GDP decline for the continental powers was 23 percent, while Russia's GDP was distinctly above the average, falling by only 18 percent. (Markevich and Harrison 2011: 690.)

This also suggests that economic factors alone do not explain the onset of revolution and civil war. Markevich and Harrison concluded on this matter that since:

> economic decline up to 1917 was not more severe in Russia than elsewhere ... we will probably not be able to explain why Russia was the first to descend into revolution and civil war without reference to historical factors that were unique to that country and period (Markevich and Harrison 2011: 691)

We have already examined many such factors. The final twists and turns were to bring out the importance of several more.

The rapidly deteriorating situation sent something akin to panic through large swathes of the politically active elite. The property owners of Russia – both landed and capitalist – were faced with the prospect they had feared since the beginning of the century, that they would be dragged under by the ineptitude of the incompetent tsar. In political circles, especially the Duma, there was great agitation. In December, Pavel Miliukov, head of the Kadet party and also a leading architect and strategist of the Progressive Bloc, made an ill-judged and inflammatory speech detailing the shortcomings of the government. At the end of each paragraph he asked if the cause was 'treason or stupidity'. For such a senior and supposedly responsible politician to promote scurrilous rumours of treason at the top was, to say the least, very unwise. The idea of a 'German party' at court, in the government and even among part of the military had been churned out by the national rumour and gossip mill since the scapegoat searching had begun in the thick of the 1915 crisis. Groundless stories about Rasputin having an affair with the tsarina blended into slightly truer jibes at the influence of the healer and holy man. In the wilder extremes, Tsarina Alexandra herself was deemed to be supporting the German interest. She was German by birth, a fact whose importance was vastly exaggerated in the rumours that discounted completely her conversion to Orthodoxy and faithful support for her husband through thick and thin. However, the rumours are important for two reasons. One is that they point to the decline in the authority of the civilian government, as predicted by Durnovo in 1914 and by the more prescient of the ministers themselves in the August crisis of 1915. Secondly, rumours accusing senior figures, to whom complete loyalty was owed, of being German sympathisers, facilitated the invention of a loyalty higher than that to the tsar in the form of loyalty to Russia. Increasingly, members of the elite, including members of the military leadership and even some members of the royal family, began to assert there was a conflict between their loyalty to the autocracy and their newly-discovered superior loyalty to Russia. Of course, their real, underlying loyalty was to their own wealth and status, but that was unspoken. The new loyalty expressed itself in wild speculation and desperate attempts to prop up the war effort and halt social and economic decline. The voluntary organisations, especially the War Industries Committees, went into overdrive to attempt to make up for the shortcomings of the war effort. At the extreme, cautious, half-baked conspiracies and ill-judged political machinations began to spread in the febrile atmosphere. Indeed, what one might see as the first, violent act of the revolution was actually conducted by young, naïve, self-important and foolish right-wing aristocrats who thought they could save the monarchy and themselves by ridding it of its great disgrace – Rasputin. A small group conspired together to murder him in December 1916. The affair was a sensation and remains one of the most widely known and speculated-upon aspects of the final collapse but, in truth, apart from the sensationalism, it had little effect. Just one more hot flush in the feverish body politic.

By the end of 1916 it is hard to see any outcome other than the collapse of the autocracy. However, even at this extreme moment, the Duma opposition, as it had been since at least the August crisis, was not seeking to replace the tsar but to persuade him to reform. The mantra of appointing (yes, appointing, not electing) a government 'enjoying the confidence of the people' or similar form of words was as strong, even stronger, than in 1915. Every effort was being made to persuade Nicholas to change course. One of the most striking examples is provided by the British Ambassador, Sir George Buchanan. In an audience with the tsar on 30 December 1916, he went far beyond usual diplomatic protocol. He pointed out the failures of the administration which were costing lives through under-equipping soldiers and creating a food crisis. The solution, Buchanan continued, was simply to appoint as President of the Council [of Ministers], a person in whom the tsar and the people could have confidence and allow him to choose his own colleagues. The tsar 'passed over this suggestion'. Incredibly, in some of the most illuminating words spoken by the tsar, Nicholas said 'Do you mean that *I* am to regain the confidence of my people or that they are to regain *my* confidence?' Buchanan increased the pressure. 'You have, sir, come to the parting of the ways ... You now have to choose between two paths. The one will lead you to victory and a glorious peace – the other to revolution and disaster.' (Vernadsky and Pushkarev 1972: vol. 3, 875–6.) By early 1917 the British and French allies had run out of patience and were increasingly open to radical solutions.

The final, fatal, blows to tsarism remain shrouded in speculation and uncertainty about key issues. The main chain of events is clear enough. Among the elites, conspiracies and threats to Nicholas's rule began to multiply. Not surprisingly, one of the most developed conspiracies was being led by one of the major figures in the War Industries Committee, Alexander Guchkov. Other highly placed establishment figures were also being drawn to desperate manoeuvres. Mikhail Rodzianko, Duma President and guards officer, was one of them. He became increasingly worried about the rapidly declining situation. In particular, strikes and unrest were burgeoning in Petrograd as workers fought police in the streets around the Putilov factory and elsewhere. Matters came to a head in the city around International Women's Day (8 March (NS)/23 February (OS)). The women of the city, especially from among the poorer, working-class elements, used it to focus protest about food shortages. These gave a whole new dimension to the unrest from below, and a final element was put in place when the management of the Putilov factory declared a lockout, effectively turning a workforce of around 20,000 into a street-based force with a deep sense of injustice against employers, police and the state. The handful of radical intelligentsia in the city, largely unaware of the massive implications of what was happening, bravely emerged to give some focus to the movements of the street. Above all, they reverted to an important strike-organising body which had emerged in numerous places in 1905, a soviet of workers' deputies. A city-wide Petrograd Soviet was quickly formed and based itself in one wing of the Tauride Palace, another wing of which was occupied by the Duma. When a unit of the Volynsky Life Guards and the Pavlovsky Guards went over to the side of the street demonstrators on 26 February, they were initially kept at arm's length by the rest of the garrison which still feared reprisals. The only place they could go for protection was to the newly-fledged Petrograd Soviet. By joining it they had increased its power and expanded its scope into a Soviet of Workers and Soldiers. The autocracy seemed to be facing the ultimate challenge, maintaining control of its army in the face of mutiny. The final crisis had been generated.

Rodzianko had already embarked on a series of warnings. In February 1917 he circulated a devastating 17-page report highlighting the supply crisis in the main cities. The army, he conceded, was 'better supplied with arms than ever before' but in the rear 'the breakdown is such that it threatens to render useless' all the sacrifices of the war and 'even more, to tip the military scales to the advantage of our enemies.' Moscow was said to require 62 railway wagon-loads of flour per month but received only 42 in January. There were critical shortfalls in heating materials, and the temperature in most homes fell below 10°C/55°F. In some workplaces it was as low as 6°C/44°F. In Petrograd 73 factories were idle, 39 through lack of fuel and 11 through lack of electricity because the power station lacked fuel. According to the report 'The country had everything it needed but cannot make adequate use of it. There is not the slightest doubt that agricultural production is able to satisfy the consumer needs of the Russian population ... Russia has sufficient grain resources.' (Rodzianko 1925: 69–86, quoted in English in Vernadsky and Pushkarev 1972 3: 877–8.) Rodzianko had hammered home the two main features of the crisis. The army was well-supplied but the home front was not, and the failures were not of production but of organisation, especially of distribution.

By late February Rodzianko was beside himself with anxiety at the rapidly deteriorating situation and deep frustration at the tsar's heedless serenity. On 26 and 27 February he sent at least three, increasingly hysterical, telegrams to Nicholas stressing the absolutely critical state of the capital and, remarkably, still calling for a government enjoying public confidence to solve the problems. The first one concluded 'Procrastination is fatal'. The next said 'The final hour has struck' and the third complained that the tsar had, in suspending the Duma, eliminated 'the last bulwark of order' thereby expressing clearly that, for him and the Progressive Bloc, order was what they were looking for, not upheaval, still less revolution. Another appeal for a government enjoying the people's confidence was requested together with restoration of the Duma. 'In the name of all Russia, I beg your majesty to take the above steps ... Tomorrow may be too late!' (Golder 1927: 278; Vernadsky and Pushkarev 1972: vol. 3, 879.)

However, the problem was not getting the information to the tsar and his entourage: after all, his own police reports and Buchanan's personal intervention had done that. The problem was to get the tsar to realise the urgency of the situation. The tsar dismissed Rodzianko's warnings out of hand on 27 February: 'again, this fat Rodzianko has written me lots of nonsense, to which I shall not even deign to reply' (Wade 2005: 37). He also prorogued the Duma. To the very end he lacked all sense of urgency. Incredibly, however, when it was too late, he finally relented and agreed to reforms. The Progressive Bloc and Duma response, channelled through Rodzianko, was that it was too late. Ironically, less than 24 hours earlier, Rodzianko had demanded exactly what the tsar was now conceding. What a difference a day makes! Or does it? The actual final blow was struck from an unexpected quarter. The Chief of the General Staff, General Mikhail Alekseev, had been liaising with Rodzianko and they had become convinced that nothing less than abdication would fix the crisis. Alekseev and Ruzsky (Commander of the Northern Front) tried to get the seven front commanders to accept this interpretation and on 2 March all but one of them, who refused to break his oath of loyalty, called upon Nicholas to abdicate. This block of six telegrams gave Nicholas no choice and, with a surprising sense of apparent relief, almost, Nicholas resigned and consoled himself with a naïve vision of retirement, family life and protection of his haemophiliac son, Alexis, whose rights as heir he also included in the act of abdication. To their great bemusement, when they nervously approached him on 3 March, Aleksei Guchkov and Vassili Shulgin, who had been sent by the Duma to demand his abdication, were informed by Nicholas that he had already done it and signed the papers before they had arrived. The non-confrontation occurred in a railway carriage. The tsar had tried to return from Stavka to his capital but had been forced to abandon his journey when railway workers refused to let his train pass. The 300-year-old dynasty came to an end in a railway siding near Pskov. The tsar did not even have the power to command his own railway train.

However, the final crisis raises more questions than the simple narrative suggests. On the surface the sequence looks fairly straightforward. Food shortages and falling wages cause unrest. Unrest turns into a battle for the streets. Initial police success turns to the danger of defeat when military units side with the demonstrators and fire on the police. The risk of mutiny panics the elite and they force abdication as the only way to pacify what they see as the mob. However, there are many unresolved issues. A similar incident of troops firing on police had occurred in September 1916 at the Renault factory in Petrograd. In that case the mutineers had been arrested. Their equivalents in February were also initially shunned by the rest of the garrison who did not want to face similar reprisals, even the death penalty, to those with which the earlier mutineers were threatened. One of the biggest unanswered questions arises from the fact that the key events were, after all, mainly occurring in one city. The autocracy was under nothing like the pressure it had faced, and conquered, in the worst moments of 1905 and 1906. Why did it succumb with such ease? Why did, almost literally, no one come to its assistance? After all, it still had potential reserves among officers and soldiers at the front who could perhaps be mobilised by persuading them the reservists of the Petrograd garrison were simply refusing to replace them at the front. Clearly, this question focuses attention on the elite, since it was they who controlled the mechanisms by which resistance might have been mounted. Often, even in supposedly 'people's' revolutions in recent times, from the Philippines through Eastern Europe to the Arab revolts of 2011, the street events are usually accompanied by equally, if not more important, manoeuvres by the elites to preserve themselves as much as possible. What exactly was the elite's game in Russia in February? Exactly why did the Putilov management inflame the situation by declaring a lockout at just that delicate moment? In 1905, a handful of industrialists had supported strikes among their own workers as a means of putting pressure on the autocracy, not to fulfil the workers demands, of course, but to use the workers as a battering-ram to get the employers' own agenda carried out by the tsar. Was the same thing happening in February? In particular, was Nicholas's abdication meant to bring the dynasty itself to an end? Plausibly, many of the key actors, such as the generals, later claimed they thought they had been supporting a change of tsar not the end of tsarism itself. Even an apparent democrat like Miliukov was not a republican. However, when he and others tried to rally Petrograd workers by proposing a new tsar they faced insuperable hostility.

Miliukov was one of the last to abandon efforts to get the former tsar's brother Michael to take the throne. In fact, Michael's refusal, on the ostensible grounds that he would only take it on with clear popular support, and his possibly more influential reason that he did not want to end up dangling from a lamp-post should the ploy not work, showed the ineptitude of the plotters. They had not even approached him beforehand to get his consent. To some extent, the dynasty fell by default.

Crucially, where did the allies, Britain and France, fit in? Both had close relations with the Duma and its leaders and both eagerly recognised the new government, not least because the apparent democratisation of Russia removed an important obstacle to the United States joining the war.

None of these questions has been clearly answered, partly because the, from the elite's and the allies' perspective, catastrophic eventual outcome of the revolution in the form of the emergence of Bolshevism led to a great deal of later covering of tracks, obfuscating of the record, playing the blame game and seeking of scapegoats, of whom Kerensky, for various unjust reasons, became the most frequently cited. A rediscovered official Provisional Government enquiry into the February revolution conducted in the summer of 1917 has recently been published. The portrayal of the roles of Kerensky, Rodzianko and an important intermediary named Engelhardt, among others, shows they commanded more respect at the time than has been accorded them in post-October revolution studies and memoirs (Lyandres 2012).

However, the two key features of the February revolution are abundantly clear. First, it was a revolution for the war not against it. The elite and much of the masses were motivated by deep-rooted patriotism. The first charge against Nicholas was ineptitude in running the war. Miliukov expressed this clearly in his memoirs:

> We know that the old government was overthrown because of its inability to carry on the war 'to a victorious end'. It was precisely this inability which assured the co-operation of the military leaders with members of the State Duma in accomplishing the coup. It was thought that the liberation of Russia from the tsarist yoke would, by itself, evoke enthusiasm in the country and would be expressed in an increase in the fighting capabilities of the army. In the first few moments, this hope was even shared by our allies. (Miliukov 1967: 428.)

The February revolution would see a new, more energetic set of initiatives to defend Russia. The handful who tried to turn the demonstrations into anti-war protests had a hard time. They were accused of being pro-German and even threatened with or subjected to beatings by other demonstrators. Even such a convinced supporter of the anti-war movement as Sukhanov was fairly easily persuaded that the slogan 'Down with the War' had to be put aside for the time being because it caused too much dissension within the left (Sukhanov 1962: 11–12). Secondly, the main motivation of the Duma politicians and the property-owners in general was to stem the revolutionary tide, not promote it. The sacrifice of Nicholas was supposed to save them. In reality, of course, it did the reverse. Once the autocracy was gone there was no accepted bulwark and symbol of the old Russia. Durnovo's prediction was holding true. Once aroused, revolution would become an uncontrollable force which risked sweeping away those who had first tried to manipulate it. However, in the nationwide honeymoon which greeted the February revolution, the unanswered questions, the contradictions and the ambiguity of the moment remained out of sight. Very quickly afterwards they began to emerge and to drive forward the history of a tumultuous revolutionary year.

Chapter 3: The Deepening Revolution: February–July 1917

The supreme importance of the February revolution was brought home to the wider nation by the abdication. Distant murmurings of discontent had been followed, in much of the provinces, by the stunning news that Russia no longer had a tsar. The bedrock of political culture had suddenly disintegrated. While discontent had grown steadily all around the empire, few had predicted such a sudden and dramatic turn of events. An autocracy which had fended off almost the entire nation in 1905 and survived had succumbed to a week of protests mainly in one city. It caught most of the country by surprise. Many of those who had been involved in carrying out the February revolution had done so expressly to stop the collapse going too far. Instead, after February, the revolution took on a life of its own and spread – quickly and apparently unstoppably – through all social levels and to all geographical outposts of the Empire.

Honeymoon

In a poetic evocation of the moment, a young writer named Konstantin Paustovsky, who was at that time living in a small provincial town called Yefremov, which consisted of little more than a railway station some 200 miles due south of Moscow, described what happened. It all began, for Yefremov's inhabitants, with a telegram.

> 'Revolution in Petrograd!' he shouted. ... For a moment we were speechless. ... 'When? How? Talk, damn you!' 'Wait... Wait...' Osipenko mumbled, pulling a long string of ticker-tape from his pocket. 'It's all there – read it. I've just been to the telegraph

office.' I took the tape and read out the proclamation of the Provisional Government.

... For months past the whole country had known it was coming, and yet it seemed to have come suddenly, unexpectedly. Out here in this sleepy little town ... nothing had changed for three centuries ... And here it was – the revolution! My mind was in turmoil.

A man came running up to us in the deserted street ... 'Have you heard? ... No Tsar! Now there's only Russia'

The news spread and the small town awoke even though it was one in the morning. 'Suddenly, at this untimely hour, the cathedral bell rang out ... and was soon joined by the bells of all the other churches. Windows lit up. People poured into the streets.' A Provisional Revolutionary Committee soon formed itself and issued a proclamation. The local police were disarmed.

Never in my life have I seen so many tears of joy as on that day ... Noisy muddle-headed, joyful days went by ... Prisons were opened ... Schools were closed ... The town and people were transformed. Russia had burst into speech. Gifted orators sprang up overnight. They were usually railwaymen.' (Paustovsky 1965: 246–50. Paustovsky is unclear on dates but the text implies the news of the revolution reached Yefremov within hours.)

While no two places went through exactly the same experiences many aspects of what happened in Yefremov were repeated elsewhere. In Yefremov, the first instinct had been to select a committee to represent the revolutionary forces. For the present, what form the 'selection' took and who participated remained unclear. But representative bodies emerged and did so at all levels. The best known of them are the soviets but they were not always the most important. In political terms they, and one other set of committees emerging from the local town and city councils, the local dumas, became the main foci. Very quickly, many towns developed both, reflecting at local level the so-called 'dual power' that existed at national level. Certainly the soviets and local dumas shared whatever political authority remained to be shared but, below them, a whole host of representative bodies sprang into political life. These included professional organisations and lobbying groups often descended from the war industries committees and certain of the voluntary organisations that had sprouted since the crisis of 1915. Groups like the Union of Towns attempted to promote the interests of the urban elites (Gleason 1976). The Union of Landowners became increasingly vociferous in the defence of large-scale property rights (Rendle 2006, 2010). Among other things they exploited the new freedoms to form themselves into a political lobby and organised the election of representatives to the new institutions. As the revolution deepened, other groups, of bankers, financiers, capitalists, factory owners and even army and naval officers, began to band together in a defensive circling of the wagons. The threat to them came from the rapidly expanding popular movement of women and men workers, peasants, and rank and file soldiers and sailors. They threw up a whole mass of new and newly-liberated organisations. Trade unions, for example, began to flourish. They emerged from the twilight zone of state control and registration and became what trade unions were elsewhere in Europe: defenders of workers' incomes, conditions of work and rights. They were organised, as the name suggests, by particular trades. Those representing metalworkers and textile workers were among the biggest, as they represented workers in Russia's largest industries. Transport unions were also large, and one of them, the Railway Workers Union (*Vikzhel* in Russian) was the most powerful of all unions, since a railway strike could paralyse a city, a region, a nation or even the entire empire. Not only civil life but the economy and the military would be halted in the event of a major railway strike. Railwaymen have also, along with returning soldiers and sailors, been credited with a key role in spreading revolution to the backward provinces. After all, many of them, train crew and track workers, combined urban and rural life. The rail network linked cities but passed through rural areas, some of them very remote, bringing its operators into contact with both worlds. This explanation was popular with Russian historians of the Soviet era because it apparently revealed a mechanism by which the Leninist and Trotskyist paradigm of worker hegemony over peasant revolution might have come about. However, while not entirely discounting such influences, more recent research has shown that provincial and rural areas needed little coaxing from outside before they stepped in to pursue their own forms of revolution.

A key barometer of the intensity of the revolutionary storm among the masses, of workers, peasants, soldiers and sailors, is the speed with which they organised themselves and set up their own committees as a first step in self-assertion. Within days of the revolution peasants began to form themselves into village and parish (*volost'*) committees. At first sight, such a development might seem surprising. Russian peasants had a long history and could claim to be the foundation of Russia economically, socially and culturally. The fact that they had been repressed and abused throughout their history blinded many observers to the true complexity of the peasant way of life. Their inferior status had helped make them into a strong and self-reliant group. It is, then, not really a cause for surprise that the villages adapted quickly by setting up committees to take advantage of the new conditions.

They were not alone. As a supplement to trade unions, workers began to set up workplace committees which differed from unions. Unions gathered together those who worked in the same trade across a town, region or even the whole country. Workplace committees united all the workers in a single factory or enterprise irrespective of trade. They very quickly became powerful challengers to managerial authority. Not to be outdone, rank and file soldiers and sailors also began to challenge the authority of officers through regimental and battleship committees, uniting all those in a particular military unit. These soldiers' and sailors' committees also spread quite rapidly through the armed services. However, the rank and file also responded to the soviets which were beginning to form.

Soviets are the best known of the plethora of organisations which sprang out of the February revolution. They grew rapidly. By June there were some 400, and by October 900 or so (Anweiler 1974: 113). Soviets shared an important distinction from most of the other organisations in that they were the province of the emerging political class rather than direct representatives of the masses themselves. The people's committees tended to be dominated by actual working peasants, workers and serving soldiers and sailors going about their everyday duties. The lowest level of soviets were very similar but they also began to sprout an institutional hierarchy. Local soviets fed into city soviets, then regional soviets. While no actual permanent national soviet emerged, the Petrograd Soviet effectively took on this role even though it was only formed by people in Petrograd. There was a national assembly, the All-Russian Congress of Soviets, which conferred some legitimacy on the whole structure. The First Congress met from 3 to 24 June and the Second convened on 26 October.

Nonetheless, the soviet structure was somewhat complex, even chaotic. Though we will not encounter the key consequences until later, it is worth elucidating the complexity at this point. Most soviets at all levels operated through mass meetings of representatives, who emerged informally rather than by formal election in the early stages. Their authority was exercised by an executive committee elected by the mass meeting. At times when the larger body did not meet, the executive committee administered in its name. At local level, the executive committees were leaders of the soviet but not substitutes for it. The Petrograd Soviet met regularly as a mass meeting of hundreds of delegates, with the executive dependent on their support from day to day. The most democratic of all soviets was located in Kronstadt, the naval base situated on an island 20 kilometres (12 miles) out from Petrograd in the Finnskii zaliv (Gulf of Finland). It met daily at midday and was open to everyone who came along. Such direct participation was, however, watered down at regional and national level. The pattern here was to send delegates from local soviets to a regional or national conference which, of its nature, would only last a few days, since most delegates had to get back to their jobs or military posts. One of the tasks of the conference was to elect an executive committee to exercise authority once the conference itself had dispersed. Obviously, being a member of such an executive committee was a larger commitment than participating in the localities and, as such, it was the level at which 'professional' politicians began to take over from direct participation. In particular, the All Russian Executive Committee, set up by the first Soviet Congress, was full of leading figures from the leadership of the main left-wing parties, notably the Socialist Revolutionaries and the Mensheviks. They claimed national authority over the Soviet structure but, in practice, had to fight for recognition in the face of competition from powerful local and regional soviets like those in Petrograd, Kronstadt and, eventually, in provincial cities like Moscow, Kiev and Odessa.

While the same political parties held sway at all the various levels the conflicts were limited but, as we shall see, once the different levels of the system were dominated by clashing political groups, the local bodies tended to outgun their supposed superiors. The national and regional Executive Committees could be left dangling in a void, largely because they reflected a political conjuncture which had dominated when they were elected but which had radically altered in the rapidly swirling sequence of events only weeks and months later.

The soviets and the people's committees rapidly chalked up some landmark successes. In Petrograd and Moscow, workers enjoying their newly won right to strike forced employers to accept the establishment of the eight-hour day and the payment of substantial wage increases which partially plugged the gap between rising prices and sluggishly growing incomes. In a matter of days, in the situation of revolution, employers had been forced to agree to concessions they had resisted for years, and even decades in the case of the eight-hour day. Clearly, the balance of power in industry was no longer skewed heavily towards the employers, as it had been from time immemorial.

For the time being, the peasants' gains were significant but much less spectacular. The notion that the February revolution fired the starting pistol for an immediate nationwide land-grab has long been discredited. The first steps in rural revolution were less dramatic and amounted to a cautious testing-out of exactly where the new balance of power lay. By and large, peasants moved slowly but effectively in a series of escalating confrontations, the precise nature of which usually reflected local peculiarities. For instance, if a local landlord had been sympathetic to the peasant community, he and his family would be treated better than if he or she had been harsh towards them, in which case thoughts of revenge began to surface. In particular, memories of those who had been most abusive to their peasants in the years of harsh repression from 1906 into 1908, and even 1909, came to shape peasant tactics. But it was not just peasant–landowner relations that defined the situation. The same was true of relations to the church, to the local intelligentsia of doctors, teachers, local authority engineers and so on. Where they had been 'good' in the peasants' eyes they might be asked for help and advice and some were even invited to participate in the peasants' committees in the early stages. If they were considered hostile, they were excluded.

The evolution of the peasants' actions showed much greater political sense than had traditionally been attributed to them. In terms popularised in the last third of the twentieth century, they exhibited an inbuilt sense of moral economy. They had their conception of what was right and just and they were determined to act accordingly. They also showed greater tactical sense than their 'superiors' had thought possible. From the beginning they chose soft targets and moved only slowly towards their great goal of a mass redistribution of landowners' land. The exact shape and actions were unique to each locality but the methods, tactics and objectives showed remarkable closeness across much of European Russia and Siberia. While there were significant local differences, the Russian and Ukrainian peasantry behaved with far greater uniformity than might have been thought possible. Most striking was the spontaneous emergence of the committees themselves. What the committees then undertook showed great similarities.

In the early stages they aimed at soft targets. This was an escalation of the tactics which had been employed for centuries by peasants – notably, chopping wood the landowners claimed as theirs, illicitly harvesting landowners' crops, gathering firewood in the landowners' forests and many other forms of petty pilfering. All of these were resorted to at appropriate times on an increasing scale. However, new tactics emerged which the landowners found to be more ominous.

Reductions of rent and refusals to pay even the reduced rent began to affect them. The assumption had quickly formed among peasants that the revolution would transfer the land to them, so why pay rent on it in the interim? Instead, some paid it into holding accounts from which they could extract it after transfer. They also began to sow crops in the spring, sowing on land left untended by the landowner. It is hard, at first sight, to understand why there should be unsown land at a time of national emergency and growing food shortages. However, landowners had left land to one side either through lack of labour – as conscription caused peasants to work on their own plots first, to replace sons who had gone to war, and only hire themselves out as a secondary priority – or because the rent was too high in wartime conditions for anyone to take it on. This was something of a scandal and the peasants felt a redoubled sense of moral justification in expanding food production for the war in this way. Fallow land was also sown by the peasants. All these acts began to erode divisions between what belonged to the landowner and what belonged to the villagers. For the time being, actual land transfers were the exception rather than the rule, not because of any doubts the peasants had about their ultimate right to the land, but simply because, as yet, they were afraid they might not get away with it. There were, however, exceptions to this. 'Softer' targets, notably the royal domains, state land and sometimes church land, were attacked as it was assumed, correctly, that there was less likely to be active resistance.

Peasants and agricultural labourers among the minority nationalities faced radically different situations. In the Baltic provinces, where the Russian commune had never been established, the struggles were tinged with ethnic antagonisms. The locals, who were agricultural labourers as much as a peasantry, were, by and large, members of the indigenous groups – Finns, Estonians, Latvians and Lithuanians – while the landowners were from the colonising minorities, mainly Swedes and Germans plus a smattering of Russians and Poles. Here repression had been especially bitter after 1905 and revenge against the harshest landowners was swift and brutal. The proximity of the front also gave a more violent edge to proceedings in this region, in that disgruntled and mutinous soldiers often egged on radical actions. It was also the case that Finland was moving rapidly from semi-detached to fully detached status, and its own revolutionary path was beginning to evolve quite differently from the Russian and Ukrainian heartland. The same was true of Poland, though for the time being it was largely being trampled on by occupying armies and was torn into Russian, German and Austro-Hungarian fragments.

The other great peripheral regions of the Caucasus, Central Asia and the Far East were also going their own way. Landowning and village structures were very different, ranging from mountain shepherd communities in Georgia and Armenia, through camel herding nomads from the Caspian to the Altai mountains, to igloo-dwellers in the Bering Straits. Some of these areas were hardly touched by the February revolution but they were the exception. In addition to class struggles over land and wages, a deep ethnic dimension shaped the actions of Georgians, Armenians, Azeris, Turcomans, Kazakhs, Uzbekhs, Koreans and the multitude of smaller ethnic groups. We should also recall that there were significant minorities within the Russian-Ukrainian lands, such as Jews, Germans, Greeks, the Muslim diaspora and others whose revolutionary path was also distinctive. However, many of them shared a key characteristic. They increasingly began to call for increasing autonomy and even complete independence from Petrograd. The weakness of the centre encouraged the dreams of nationalists in almost all of the larger of these groups, especially Finland, the Baltic provinces, Ukraine, Georgia and Armenia. Later in the year and during the civil war, their moment appeared to have arrived.

The first few weeks after February had catalysed a whole range of radical activities. At first, much of it was contained within the atmosphere of 'honeymoon' in that the initial unifying theme was seen to be national defence and the improvement of the war effort. The extension of the sown lands, to take a notable example, was presented as a national duty to fend off the food supply crisis. Better factory conditions and a better-rewarded workforce were intended to lead to greater productivity and better-quality output from the armaments factories and so on. But in one area in particular, radical activity in the name of greater fighting efficiency became supremely important. That was among the military.

From the very outset, dramatic developments spread like wildfire through the armies and the fleets. While demonstrations by women in the bread queues of Petrograd are often seen as central to the downfall of tsarism, it was actually the activities of soldiers and sailors which turned it into a revolution. In the first place, it was the mutiny of the guards regiments which ratcheted up the threat level posed to the autocracy. Protests by working-class women and men were containable, mutiny much less so. The, from the elite point of view, bad situation became much worse very quickly because they hesitated to confront the unravelling of the garrison. Rather, the elite succumbed to the temptation to use it to obtain their own objective which was, as we have seen, the abdication of Nicholas. However, the pause deepened the crisis in two ways. First, in the absence of determined opposition, the mutiny quickly spread to the rest of the Petrograd garrison and far beyond with stunning speed. Second, at national level, negotiations to set up the Provisional Government led to important concessions to the soldiers' and sailors' movement from the very outset. We will take a look at each of these phenomena.

Immediately after their rebellious act of firing on the police, who were themselves firing on unarmed demonstrators, the mutinous guards felt exposed to reprisal. Their vulnerability did not last long. Within days, soldiers throughout the garrison were refusing to obey officers. In the fleet, where discipline had been savage in order to keep the potential political powder-keg of each battleship under control during long periods of military inactivity, sailors very quickly began to wrest authority away from officers. A revolutionary committee was set up on 1 March which arrested the leading officers. The most hated, including Admiral Viren, the commander and governor of Kronstadt, were summarily executed. Viren was bayoneted to death in the main square of Kronstadt. The most hated admiral in Helsingfors (Helsinki), Nepenin, the commander of the Baltic Fleet, was reported to have been either lynched or shot at the fortress of Sveaborg (Suomenlinnen) on 4 March. Other hated officers were said to have been flung overboard to die under the ice in the freezing waters of the Baltic Sea Nepenin and his associates had stoked up extra resentment by trying to conceal news of the uprising in Petrograd and the subsequent abdication, even though Nepenin had recognised the Provisional Government on 1 March and had also, on 2 March, beseeched Nicholas to abdicate. By 1 March the Moscow garrison was also in open rebellion and its commander-in-chief, Mrozovsky, reported that the local authorities had fled and the city was under the control of the insurgents. By this time, there was no turning back. It was the pressures of the mutiny and the lack of any loyal units in the Petrograd and Moscow regions, plus the fear that it would spread rapidly to the front and thereby endanger the war effort, that led to Alekseev consulting the front commanders and eliciting the demands for abdication. Thus, the soldiers and sailors were, from the very beginning, seen as the most potent of revolutionary forces.

The refusal to obey officers swept rapidly from the reserve garrisons like Petrograd and Moscow to the active ones at the front from Riga to Odessa and on to the Caucasus. Despite local differences, two processes were almost universal. One, as we have seen, was the demand to set up representative committees, something unheard of in any military in the world then or, with few exceptions, since. In itself it was a revolutionary demand. Second, the process of eliminating unpopular officers was present everywhere. Direct violence and execution, like those of the early moments in Kronstadt and Sveaborg, remained exceptions. In the city of Petrograd, while many officers abandoned their posts, at least temporarily, very few were actually killed. In fact, violence on either side was relatively limited, though the February Revolution in the city officially claimed some 1,224 lives. Direct action was quickly replaced by a near-spontaneous movement to elect officers, and throughout the armed services that is what began to happen. Unpopular officers were voted out and often handed over to courts or even sent to Petrograd under arrest to be dealt with. Other officers were elected in their place. There are several important features to note about this process of which three are particularly important. First, the principle of having officers was not questioned. Those removed were not replaced by rank and file but by other senior figures. The second point helps explain the first. The aim of the process was universally acknowledged to be to improve the fighting and defensive qualities of the armed forces. At this stage the revolution was, even among the military, still intended to help pursue the war more effectively, not to unilaterally end it. Thirdly, as with other elements of the mass movement, there was a complete sense of the justness of the activities. While there were some uncontrolled atrocities, the spirit of these acts was one of full justification. It was not mindless mob violence but, once again, the expression of a moral economy. The firm hand of revolutionary justice was being meted out to those who deserved it.

Obviously, such dramatic developments as these could not but be reflected at the national level. However, here we have something of a chicken and egg situation. Did the mutinies wrest concessions from the reluctant Provisional Government as it emerged, or did the concessions encourage the spread of mutinies? A closer look suggests both were true. Key elements of the agreement between the fledgling Petrograd Soviet and Provisional Government, and the famous Order Number One of the Petrograd Soviet, show signs of pressure from the soldiers and sailors. However, the promulgation of the agreement and the order appeared to legitimise further radical action.

The agreement included a key clause forbidding the transfer of troops out of Petrograd. At first sight this seems a very odd and very specific clause to have in an otherwise broad-brush document. The point of it, however, was crystal clear and vital to the defence of the revolution. In these early moments of rebellion no one was sure of the outcome. All those in Petrograd who were involved, whether they were from the Petrograd Soviet or the Duma majority, were afraid that the old regime and/or, above all, its allies in the army might be able to uncover sufficient resources to conduct a counter-revolution. Looking back, we know that no such effort was possible. We also know that, in 1917, the counter-revolution remained weak. It is testimony to the confusion, incompetence and isolation of the opponents of the revolution that they were unable to mobilise enough support to achieve the relatively easy task of resisting the developments in Petrograd. Every day they delayed made their task much harder. By the time the counter-revolution managed to achieve even limited momentum, the opportunity had almost vanished.

At the time the participants, of course, did not know this. On the contrary, they were only too well aware of their own vulnerability. After all, from their perspective it was still largely a revolution focused on one city and a reserve garrison. They could see that there were millions of troops at the front who were, for a brief time, unaware of developments in Petrograd. There were also tens of millions of peasants living passively in their villages. At the time it did not seem inconceivable to the rebels in Petrograd that what had appeared to be the mighty forces of autocracy could muster enough support to engage in at least an attempt to roll back the tide. One obvious tactic, so it seemed, would be to order revolutionary troops out of the city and replace them with less politicised loyal troops from the front, or anywhere else they might be found. The agreement by the Duma to resist any such rotation was partly forced on them by the pressure of the Petrograd Soviet but, at that moment, it was also in their interest: they needed to defend themselves and would have been as much victims of any counter-revolution as the left. Like many aspects of the honeymoon, as time went on the interests of the parties were to diverge, but for the moment the clause was included in the programme of the emerging new government.

Order No.1 (1 March 1917) of the Petrograd Soviet was another unmistakable sign of the leading role of soldiers and sailors in the revolution from the very beginning. According to one of the most reliable eyewitnesses of the revolution, it was drawn up by several leading intelligentsia members of the Soviet, with soldiers commenting over their shoulder as they proposed items for inclusion in the draft. One of those present, Sukhanov, said he was 'extraordinarily interested' by the process and that its contents 'had nothing terrible in them' (Sukhanov 1962: vol. 1, 113). The order had been 'called forth by the general conditions of the revolution. ... This order was in the full sense a popular creation and by no means a malevolent contrivance of individuals or even of a leading group.' (Sukhanov 1962: vol. 1, 114.) Once it was hammered out it became a key influence on developments. It had seven provisions of which the most important were that military units were called upon to set up revolutionary committees; military orders would be carried out only where they did not conflict with Soviet orders and resolutions; soldiers would enjoy basic civil rights; and routine acts of submission, like off-duty saluting and the use of demeaning language (notably the use of the second-person singular *ty*, which, as in French and German for instance, was only used outside intimate circles of friends when addressing children, servants or pet animals) were forbidden. In effect, it ushered in a new set of power relationships in the armed forces. Discipline was to be made less strict, and more humane attitudes were intended to prevail. The acceptance that the war effort must continue, indeed, the hope that the agreement would strengthen it, were visible in the limitations included. In particular, soldiers were urged to observe 'strictest military discipline' when on duty. This aspect was even more obvious in the much less well-known Order No.2 (6 March 1917) by which the Petrograd Soviet denounced the rapidly-spreading process of electing officers. It pointed out that, though it recommended the election of committees, Order No.1 'did not provide that these committees should elect the officers of each unit' (Browder and Kerensky 1961: vol. 2, 851). It was only after a first wave of score-settling and removal of petty tyrants that the soldiers and sailors went along with this ban. Although it theoretically only addressed the Petrograd garrison, Order No.1 became the model for an attempted revolution in relations within the entire armed forces of the country.

It is abundantly clear from the events of the early months of the revolution that the aspiration of the Progressive Bloc, that they should act decisively to *prevent* social collapse, had unleashed something closer to Durnovo's predicted scenario, according to which, once the centre was weak, social revolution would spread rapidly. From the beginning, the new authorities tried to limit the risks and effects of social meltdown. At first, they were aided by the honeymoon moment and the joint fear of all revolutionaries at the time that their revolution was by no means secure. Together, these influences meant that the new government could emerge with the consent of the mass movement and of its Soviet representatives. The two bodies, the Petrograd Soviet and the Provisional Committee of the State Duma, each ensconced in its own wing of the same building, the Tauride

Palace, were able to hammer out an agreed programme for the new Provisional Government which proclaimed its formation on 1 March. Confirming its Progressive Bloc DNA, it claimed to be composed of 'persons enjoying the confidence of the people'. In many ways, this was, and remained, its sole claim to legitimacy.

The head of the new government was an other-wordly elderly Tolstoyan dreamer named George L'vov. His cousin, Vladimir L'vov, had a minor role as Procurator of the Holy Synod from which he later, inadvertently, did as much as anyone to precipitate the collapse of the Provisional Government. The main ministers were Octobrists, a centre-right group of monarchists who had rallied to the October manifesto in 1905, and other conservatives, notably the Minister of War, A.I. Guchkov and Mikhail Tereshenko, the Minister of Finance. The others were barely distinguishable right-wing Kadets (Constitutional Democrats) and their Progressist Party allies such as the leading figure in the whole setup, Pavel Miliukov who became Foreign Minister, Nikolai Nekrasov, Minister of Transport, and Alexander Konovalov, the Minister of Trade. The narrowness of the political spectrum represented is easily explained. Representatives of parties further to the right were not yet prepared to join the revolution. The main left parties in the Petrograd Soviet declared a boycott. The interesting exception to this was the young 36-year-old radical lawyer Alexander Kerensky (1881–1970), who, though close to the soviet as a Labour (*Trudovik*) Party member, declared that he was justified in taking on the mantle of Minister of Justice because it would ensure that there would be no surreptitious deal with, say, the British, to smuggle the tsar and his retinue out of the country. He would ensure that the criminal tsar would face the people's judgment. Thus Kerensky was the only person directly linking the Petrograd Soviet with the Provisional Government. For the moment, there was a clear demarcation between the two new institutions.

The programme projected Russia from being one of the most politically backward countries in Europe, governed by a completely anachronistic, quasi-feudal autocracy, into being, at least on paper, one of the world's most advanced democracies. The programme promised a constituent assembly which would be elected by universal, equal, direct and secret elections the task of which was to establish a constitution. In the meantime, wide-ranging civil rights were enacted. Freedom of speech, assembly, unions and strikes were specifically mentioned. Complete ethnic and religious freedom and equality were proclaimed. All political and religious offenders were amnestied and all pending cases were dropped. The existing police force was to be replaced by a partially elected militia under local authority control. The ambiguous formula of Order No. 1, also published on 1 March, was incorporated insofar as rights were extended to service-men 'within limits permitted by military and technical conditions' while 'strict military discipline' was to be the norm 'during perform-ance of military duty'. The far-sightedness and suspicions of the Petrograd Soviet negotiators were also expressed, in that the conclud-ing sentence of the proclamation stated that the new government 'by no means intends to use the military situation to delay in any way the realization of the above reforms and measures'. This was, of course, precisely what they did. There were several actions which were not strictly mentioned in the programme but were enacted as a result of the negotiations between Provisional Committee and Petrograd Soviet. All senior figures of the old regime, notably the governors of the provinces, were to be replaced.

In addition to the clause preventing the transfer of troops out of Petrograd, the agreement contained several hostages to fortune. Acceptance of the word 'provisional' in its title hardly gave an impres-sion of dynamism and solidity. Granting wide rights encouraged political and social protest, raised expectations and tied the hands of the authorities when it came to dealing with them. An example of the last was the abolition of the police. Such a vast reform needed time and thought but in the short term it encouraged those who were already attacking the police. One notable revolutionary action in Petrograd saw the destruction of one of the city's largest police stations and, more significantly, its vast files on local citizens. Prisoner amnesty, as we have seen in Yefremov, spilled over into the complete opening of jails, releasing not only harshly-treated petty criminals, victims of tsarism's corrupt and class-based system of 'justice', but also many hardened criminals to prey upon the relatively defenceless population now that the police were in disorder. Of course, many of these things were the implications of democracy, but to move rapidly towards them while a war was being conducted was a difficult proc-ess to keep within bounds. Lenin, no admirer of the new system, described Russia as the freest of the belligerent countries upon his return in April. His point was that in wartime other countries had suspended democratic rights, not massively expanded them. The programme also contained two ominous silences. The issues of land reform and policy towards the war remained undefined. No economic policy was visible at this stage.

The members of the new government were inherently conserva-tive. Some of them, notably Miliukov himself, had tried very hard to save the monarchy. The refusal of Grand Duke Michael to accept the throne thwarted any such efforts. The monarchy fell partly by default. Many of those who supported Nicholas's abdication, such as many of the army commanders, were not republicans. They had not expected to end the monarchy itself. But in any case, those who had accepted that the monarchy was too far gone to be salvaged were not, in any other respect, revolutionaries. What they wanted, and what the new government wanted, was a quick settling of social problems, a renewed focus on the war with a view to, hopefully, winning it, along with Russia's allies, and the injection of a new lease of life and the establishment of security for Russia's increasingly diverse property-holders, including financiers and capitalists as well as the traditional landowners.

The instinct of these members of the elite was, first and foremost, to remain members of the elite, and that meant not unleashing any more social change than they had to. They did, however, differ from their tsarist predecessor in realising that they had to give away something in order to preserve the rest, especially when it came to land. They knew concessions had to be made, and that that was the road to their self-preservation. Indeed, their very existence as the new government was down to concession to the popular forces represented by the Petrograd Soviet. In reality, this was a very difficult, perhaps impossible, job description. How would they settle down to try to fulfil it?

Keeping the Marriage Together: The Provisional Government

The omens were not good. The new government was beset by problems on all sides. It had to look over both its right and left shoulders for enemies intent on stabbing it in the back. At first it looked more nervously over its right shoulder. As time went on the left became the more immediate threat. Its mandate to govern was paper-thin. Its self-proclaimed remit was to abolish itself. In the circumstances – that is a strength-sapping war, a disintegrating society and an uncontrollable economy – it is more surprising that it lasted as long as it did than that it finally fell. The same is true of many marriages.

The government's to-do list was formidable. Massive issues of governance, war, land redistribution, economic stabilisation and social cohesion demanded serious action. But at the top, in the short term, was the problem of what to do about the tsar. Plans to short-circuit the problem by smuggling him out of Russia foundered on the twin rocks of British reluctance to shelter the royal family, who could become a future liability, and of Soviet obstruction when they became aware of what was happening. Kerensky proclaimed it his duty to bring Nicholas to trial but, while the case was prepared, the former autocrat and his retinue lived under a loose form of house arrest, or more precisely palace arrest, in Tsarskoe Selo, where he conducted a daily review of his guards. Here he remained until October.

More important problems beckoned. By and large, and this is widely true of all governments, it was driven hither and yon by contingencies. Where a strategy was desperately needed, its day to day perspective barely went beyond immediate survival. A British prime minister, Harold Wilson, coined the phrase that a week was a long time in politics: for the Provisional Government a week was an era. Had it stood back and set up a timetable for the key issue of convening a constituent assembly it might have had a better chance. Other issues could then have fitted in around it. However, it quickly began to put off tough decisions. This then gave out the not totally false impression that it was stalling deliberately, to cling to power in order to preserve itself and the propertied class. More idealistically, it was also trying to maintain national unity in the face of the invaders. However, on most of the big issues it failed to act decisively. It set up committees to deal with land and supply. It began an inquiry into the internal state of the country, supposedly preparatory to calling a constituent assembly. To its opponents on the right such measures seemed to threaten to undermine their property and social superiority. To the left they smacked of manipulation, deceit and possible betrayal. Only the brief 'honeymoon' atmosphere, plus the absence of any immediate alternative, pulled them through the early stages. However, there was one big problem that could not be put off – the war.

Fortunately for the government this was the big issue that, for the moment, united the country behind it. Almost the entire nation supported the war effort. For the right, national defence was a self-evident value. For the middle class, defeat was potentially disastrous and would bring in new, unforeseeable upheavals likely to threaten their newly won freedoms. Before February, some on the left had also supported the war as the only means of fending off a triumph by the Kaiser which would, they argued, have been worse for the prospects of revolution than tsarism. After February, the majority of the left, notably the majority of the Menshevik and Socialist Revolutionary parties, moved to a position of so-called revolutionary defencism. What this meant was that whereas fighting for the tsar had been questionable, fighting for the new post-revolutionary, democratic

Russia was certainly progressive. It followed from this that the war was the vessel containing most of the new government's support and legitimacy. For the moment, potential opposition was spreading, but it was contained by the fear of weakening Russia and opening it up to German invasion. Insofar as the new government had a source of good will, then here was where it lay. It was crucial that it should maintain this good will by coming up with some significant improvement in the war effort. However, in the circumstances it was much easier to identify this crucial point than to be able to do anything about it. The government's first significant crisis showed exactly how fragile this good will was.

One aspect of the war that needed to be dealt with quickly, but did not require vast resources, was to clarify, especially for the sake of the French and British allies, just what the policy of the new government was. Miliukov, who had a reputation as the most European of Russian political figures, had become Foreign Minister rather than Prime Minister not least because he would be a reassuring presence for the allies. For years, he had had close relations with the allied embassies in Petrograd. So close was his relationship that there were persistent rumours that the French and/or the British had supported the overthrow of Nicholas. There has been more smoke than fire on this issue, but it is certainly the case that the new government was quickly recognised by Paris, London and Rome. (15/28 March) It is often overlooked that the demise of the tsar smoothed the way for the United States to join the war. There were many objectors in America to the new, young country getting sucked into the cynical brawls of 'old Europe' but one of their strongest arguments was that there was no way that democratic America should fight alongside an anachronistic dictatorship like the Russian autocracy. Uncle Sam could not befriend the Tsar of All the Russias. February changed all that. The American Ambassador, David R. Francis, welcomed February as 'an extension of the American Revolution.' The United States was thus even quicker to recognise the new democratic Russia (8/21 March) and President Woodrow Wilson's path to joining the war became significantly easier.

It is not, then, surprising that Miliukov thought he was engaging in little more than routine when, on 18 April (1 May), in response to allied pressure, he sent a secret note assuring France and Britain that Russia was still fully committed to the fight on the original terms. It was this last point that created the crisis when the note was, almost inevitably given the fluid situation in Petrograd, leaked to the Petrograd Soviet and the press. Miliukov was forced to resign and this in turn led to a government reshuffle and a significant opening to the centre-left. Why did it have such repercussions? The answer is simple. The terms on which tsarism was fighting the war were geopolitical and imperialist in that, according to secret treaties, victory over the Central Powers, which, of course, included Russia's traditional foe, Turkey, would result in Russia achieving the key goal of taking over the city of Constantinople/Tsargrad, thereby reversing the Islamic conquest of 1453 and giving Russia control over the Straits, and securing its outlet to the Mediterranean. For the left, and for the masses of soldiers and sailors, this was a scandal. It was one thing to defend Russia, which they were still prepared to do, but quite another to waste blood and resources on imperial adventures. On 21 and 22 April there were large, Soviet organised demonstrations in Petrograd and elsewhere. The military right were prepared to do battle but Prime Minister Lvov was not. He chose the path of negotiation. Miliukov resigned, as did the most right-wing member of the government, Alexander Guchkov, who had been War Minister. Henceforth, Miliukov remained outside the Provisional Government but he continued to be a major influence on it to the end. The new power balance resulted, on 5 (18 NS) May, in the formation of a new government. It was the first of three coalition governments. At this time, Kerensky, who took over as War Minister, was joined by six other Soviet leaders, including the senior SR Victor Chernov as Minister of Agriculture, which put him in the front line over land reform, and Irakli Tseretelli, a Menshevik, who became Minister of Posts and Telegraph. Alexander Peshekhonov, an independent socialist, took over another key ministry, that of Food and Supply.

Irreconcilable Differences

The explosion of popular representation and self-government we observed above was looked on with a jaundiced eye by much of the elite. Nowhere was this more true than in the army High Command. Indeed, one of the first measures of resistance had come from General Alekseev, who was retained as Chief of Staff, in part as a reward for his assistance in procuring the abdication of Nicholas. This did not, however, mean that he was favourable to the dilution of military discipline. He had responded to Order No. 1 with strong words, fearing that the apparent dissolution of authority in the army through arrests of commanding officers would 'completely ruin its fighting capacities' and 'result in an unavoidable loss of the war ... since only through disorder can Russia be defeated.' (Browder and Kerensky 1961: vol. 2, 851.) As a result, Order No. 2 had been issued, calling a halt to election of officers. Nonetheless, many military commanders were opposed to the emergence of army and battleship committees, to the extension of civil rights to soldiers, to the ambiguity of lesser discipline when off-duty compared to being in action and, a focal point for all the others, to the abolition of the death penalty in courts-martial. The newly-appointed Military Commander of the Petrograd Military District, General Lavr Kornilov (1870–1918), was one of the most outspoken in his opposition. Alekseev, on the other hand, regarded the existence of the committees as inevitable. The first War Minister, Guchkov, leaned more towards Kornilov's position, not surprisingly since he had appointed him, but his successor, Alexander Kerensky, supported the democratisation of the army, and he and Alekseev worked together to try to transform the committees into agents for implementing the military policies of the government.

But what military policy did it have? Once Miliukov's pledge to the allies had been exposed a new framework was needed to replace the imperialist objectives and to de-emphasise 'war to a victorious conclusion.' Instead, revolutionary defencism became more prominent. In other words, the aim of the war was to prevent the Kaiser and allies from wrecking the new, revolutionary, democratic Russia. However, the new policy shared one vital feature with the old – the war would have to continue until Germany decided to negotiate which, in reality, would not be anytime soon. Indeed, even the emerging ultra-left policy of the Internationalist wing of the Petrograd Soviet (made up of Bolsheviks, Trotsky's independent Interdistrict group and a growing fringe of left dissidents from the Mensheviks and SRs) who advocated 'peace without annexations and indemnities' had the same implication, since there was no way Germany would simply agree to give up its gains and walk home. In all three formulations the war would, in fact, continue. As such, they were political ploys not serious plans for ending the fighting. Still less were they calls for surrender. Before October, hardly anyone supported surrender or, in its more euphemistic formulation, 'peace at any price'. 'Peace' policies as they evolved were certainly complex but the simple truth was that, in the early days of the revolutionary honeymoon, defending Russia, under whatever slogan, united the overwhelming majority of the country.

From the point of view of the Provisional Government and the High Command, military and political imperatives pointed in the same direction, the adoption of an offensive strategy. Militarily it would hasten victory. Politically it would be a response to insistent requests from the hard-pressed allies. They were looking for an eastern initiative to help them out on the western front by dividing Germany's attention and its forces, as in previous crucial moments in the war. But most of all, so the Russian generals thought, a return to action would require a return to discipline. The rot, as they saw it, resulted from inaction. A patriotic offensive would reunite the army and the country.

Not all the leaders were so gung-ho. Alekseev was pessimistic, believing that offensives were not feasible under the current conditions of war. Kerensky, as War Minister, actively supported the soldiers' committees, though he did his best to convert them to patriotism. Nonetheless, the proponents of an offensive, led by Kornilov who was showing his increasing authority, prevailed in the dispute.

The outcome was a major offensive. Preparations were protracted as orders worked slowly through the new structures. Divisional committees claimed the right to scrutinise, modify and even veto all key orders. Nonetheless, the offensive began on 18 June (1 July NS). At first there were some advances, but the reluctance of most soldiers to attack became more marked as casualties mounted. Troops were prepared to die to defend Russia but were considerably more diffident about participating in the political machinations of their commanders or fulfilling promises to distant allies. Initial successes in Galicia, largely against Austro-Hungarian forces, were replaced by a tougher struggle against German units. Just over two weeks into the campaign the advance collapsed. Two days later, on 5 July (18 July NS) a counter-attack by the Central Powers sent the Russian forces into headlong retreat. Only specially formed strike battalions, set up by Kornilov from the strongest troop units, held firm. By 10 July (23 July NS) the Russian Army had been pushed back about 150 miles (240 kilometres). Russian casualties are thought to have amounted to about 60,000.

In a sense, the military aspect of the disaster was the least of the government's worries. Instead of bolstering military morale the offensive had torn it to shreds. Military units of all sizes had refused to obey orders. Defeat undermined the power of the army leaders. Troops were even more determined only to defend, not to attack. Not surprisingly, the crisis spread far beyond the front. In particular, it provoked a near-decisive episode in the capital.

Showing the remarkable political ineptitude that had been characteristic of them throughout the war, the hard-line opponents of the revolution in the General Staff inadvertently poured petrol on the flames. With Kornilov at the forefront, the decision was forced through to supposedly take advantage of the chaos and use it to break the agreement not to move troops out of Petrograd. The hope was that they could be denounced as shirkers who were dodging the front while true patriotic soldiers were dying for the country. Of course, it did not play like that. It was immediately seen for what it was, a cynical power ploy to break the key forces defending the revolution in Petrograd. Even front commanders were unhappy because, if radicalised troops were to be moved, they would have to go somewhere and no commander wanted them on his patch. They would be more likely to spread 'sedition' than to dissolve away in the mass of the army.

But it was not the response of generals that mattered. In the first place, the troops selected for transfer, notably the 1st Machine Gun Regiment, refused to go, picked up their weapons and took to the streets on 3 July. Very soon, they were supported by 500,000 strikers and the city was beyond the authorities' control. It got worse. On 4 July a large detachment of armed sailors, estimated at about 10,000, arrived from Kronstadt ready to overthrow the Provisional Government. In an almost surreal moment they went from place to place in the city trying to urge reluctant politicians of the left to take the decisive step of rebellion. Petrograd Soviet leaders refused. In a moment symbolising their whole endeavour, Miliukov recounts angry sailors detaining Chernov, a leader of the Soviet right. One of them screamed at him 'take power you son-of-a-bitch when it is offered to you!' (Miliukov 1921: vol. 1, 244.) As Sukhanov tells the story, Trotsky had to bravely intervene to save his political opponent from a beating or worse. Trotsky's own description also shows similar characteristics of a movement seeking leadership being fobbed off at every turn (Trotsky 1932: ch. 25).

Failing with the Soviet right of Mensheviks and SRs, the sailors would surely get support from the acknowledged vanguard of the left, the party most hostile to the Provisional Government, the small but growing Bolshevik party? But there, too, they were disappointed. The Bolsheviks, like everyone else, were taken by surprise by the speed with which the demonstrations had sprung up and the fury they exhibited. Although local Bolsheviks in Kronstadt had been warning about the situation, which found them uncharacteristically outmanoeuvred on the left by anarchists who dominated the leadership in Kronstadt, Petrograd had thought they were exaggerating. Lenin had even taken one of his de-pressurising trips to the country as the crisis built. He rushed back and, when the sailors crossed the river Neva to the Petrogradskaia storona near the Peter Paul Fortress, they arrived outside party headquarters in the palace 'requisitioned' from the ballerina Ksheshinskaia and former mistress of the tsar. What would the Bolsheviks do? Lenin had already announced they were ready to take power alone. However, although the government could easily have been overthrown within the hour, Lenin urged caution. He thrust the party orator, Lunacharsky, out onto the balcony. Lunacharsky praised the resolve of the sailors, as you would with ten thousand of them with rifles knocking on your door, and told them to maintain vigilance but said nothing about seizing power. The reason for Bolshevik refusal is still obscure. Lenin later argued that the moment was not ripe. The conditions across Russia had not yet matured and the situation in Europe remained unfavourable. On the other hand, critics argue that Lenin and the Bolsheviks simply did not want to support a movement they did not control. Lenin had a deep distrust of spontaneous movements and his whole career from the early 1900s had been about trying to instil organisation, discipline and consciousness into the revolutionary movement. To gamble everything on a sailors' rebellion dominated by anarchists was not his style. Leaders of the party's Military Organisation, which organised the membership in the armed forces, complained bitterly about being used as 'firemen' to extinguish the revolutionary moment.

While we can never know what might have happened had there been a 'July Revolution' instead of the October Revolution we do know that in the short term the failure of the July Days seemed to be a disaster for the far left and the Bolsheviks in particular. The hesitation of the rebellious forces, when they could not find leadership, enabled the government to rally and fight back. Armed police secured the city, the strikes were broken, the Kronstadters returned to their island base, battered, bruised and politically shaken. Some 700 people are thought to have been killed or wounded. Some, around 15–20, were victims of street attacks by gangs of proto-fascist Black Hundred thugs.

The fiasco had returned the initiative to the centre and the right. In a stroke of political genius the Provisional Government, consisting mainly of Kerensky at this moment, since the government was in crisis even before the July Days, accused the Bolsheviks and the left of being German agents. Turning the demonstrations around from being protests against the ineptitude of the authorities in embarking on a costly, pointless, failed offensive that endangered Russia, they accused the demonstrators of being led by German agents with orders to co-ordinate the protests with the offensive in order to weaken it. In other words, they were blaming the demonstrators for the failure of the offensive! While few on the left were taken in by this barefaced falsehood, those who wanted to believe it did so. Documents which had been in the government's hands for some time, provided by a renegade Bolshevik turned right-wing patriot named Grigorii Aleksinskii, were published. They purported to show that the Bolsheviks were in the pay of the Kaiser. While it is the case that some money from the German special fund for sowing unrest within its enemies' homelands did arrive in Bolshevik coffers, it was and is blatantly absurd to consider any of the radical parties as actual agents of Germany. They took no orders from Berlin. Nonetheless, it did fit in with the fact that many left-wing leaders of most political hues, including Lenin, had returned to Russia in the so-called 'sealed train' which had transported them across the enemy territory of Germany on their way home from Switzerland. It was sufficient 'evidence' for unthinking right-wing gangs to attack leftists. The Bolshevik party was picked out by the government to be banned. Lenin hurriedly left Petrograd and skipped across the border into the autonomous, but not yet independent, Finland, where Russian police had no jurisdiction. He went into hiding, at first in a straw shelter in a field near the border but very soon in a safe house in Helsinki, where he remained until the second week of October. Trotsky, on the other hand, who finally threw in his lot with the Bolsheviks at this point, walked into a police station and offered himself up to be jailed. His aim was to show the fragility of the government's power because, he argued, it would not be able to hold him. He was right. Less than two months later he was released and, like the party itself, gained prestige from the incident in which they had been made to appear as martyrs. The Provisional Government had once again succeeded only in shooting itself in the foot. However, the situation had changed by then. In the two or so intervening months, counter-revolution appeared to raise itself from its unaccountable slumber. However, in the dialectic of the time, its energy only served to rouse up even greater revolutionary resistance. The July Days ushered in a new situation. The contradictions of the February marriage of left and right had emerged with a vengeance. In place of a short and shallow honeymoon, irreconcilable differences had come into the open. Divorce was looming. But who would have custody of the revolutionary child?

Chapter 4: The Counter-revolution Organises: July–August 1917

By the beginning of July the Russian Empire had already undergone a massive transformation. The majesty and pomp of the centuries-old autocracy had vanished like a wisp of smoke. Popular self-government via committees was affecting almost every town, village and even household. Landowners were everywhere on the defensive. The capitalist middle class was struggling to maintain even its minimal hold on events. The war effort was collapsing, society was disintegrating, raging inflation was cancelling out wage concessions to workers almost as quickly as they were made, and Finland, Poland and the Baltic provinces were leading an unseemly charge out of the shadow of empire and into the hoped-for sunny uplands of independence. The fact that over the following six months, and then during the years after October, the pace of transformation became even more frenetic should not lead us to underestimate or misunderstand what had already happened.

Politically, the state, which had appeared so powerful and even unbreakable under the Romanovs, was now but a shadow of its former self, and was weakening all the time. In a sense, it was collapsing into a group of self-governing tribes. The army, the ministries, the judiciary, the civil service continued to run, as the Russian phrase puts it, from inertia, meaning that they just continued doing what they had always done as best they could. The central co-ordination provided by government was becoming more and more marginalised. The government sat in its splendid cabinet room in the Winter Palace but its decisions spread on a hit and miss basis around the country. Even the army, over which the Provisional Government tried to exercise maximum control, responded to its orders selectively. For instance, capital punishment was being used illegally by many commanders who eventually, in the wake of the fiasco of the June offensive, persuaded a reluctant Kerensky to agree, on 12 July, to its re-introduction at the front.

Critics of the Provisional Government on the right and the left adopted the view that there was 'dual power' in operation. The term itself arose before the phenomenon it described. On 2 March, shortly after the formation of the Provisional Government, its representatives agreed to 'take into account the opinions of the Soviet of Workers' Deputies', though they were also determined to prevent 'interference in the actions of the government', which would create 'an unacceptable situation of dual power' (Zhurnal 1917). The notion, in its purest form, was formulated some weeks later by an embittered Guchkov as he was pushed out of his post as Minister of War in April, after objections to his adherence to imperial war aims and a gung-ho attitude to pursue war to a victorious conclusion. In his words 'We (the Provisional Government) do not have authority, but only the appearance of authority; the real power lies with the Soviet'. The concept was also taken up in a big way by Trotsky and, to a lesser degree, Lenin.

In his later reflections in *The History of the Russian Revolution* (published in 1930; English translation 1932) Trotsky devoted a whole chapter to the concept of 'dual power'. He summed up the essence of his idea:

> The historic preparation of a revolution brings about, in the pre-revolutionary period, a situation in which the class which is called to realise the new social system, although not yet master of the country, has actually concentrated in its hands a significant share of the state power, while the official apparatus of the government is still in the hands of the old lords. That is the initial dual power in every revolution ... This double sovereignty does not presuppose – generally speaking, indeed, it excludes – the possibility of a division of the power into two equal halves, or indeed any formal equilibrium of forces whatever ... The splitting of sovereignty foretells nothing less than civil war. But before the competing classes and parties will go to that extreme – especially in case they dread the interference of a third force – they may feel compelled for quite a long time to endure, and even to sanction, a two-power system. This system will nevertheless inevitably explode. (Trotsky 1932: vol. 1, ch. 11.)

Contrary to the comments from the right, Trotsky was arguing that the two forces were not equal. This was also Lenin's view at the time. In his article 'The Dual Power', published shortly after his return to Russia in April, he described the situation thus:

> What is this dual power? Alongside the Provisional Government, the government of the *bourgeoisie, another government* has arisen, so far weak and incipient, but undoubtedly a government that actually exists and is growing—the Soviets of Workers' and Soldiers' Deputies (Lenin 1960–70: vol. 24, 38)

The main feature of Trotsky's and Lenin's definition was that, in Lenin's words, the power of the soviets was 'weak and incipient'. This is a far cry from the right-wing view that the Petrograd Soviet was holding a veto over the Provisional Government in its early stages, but Lenin and Trotsky did imply the relationship was ever-changing and, sooner or later, the Soviet might (neither believed it to be inevitable) gain the upper hand.

With such illustrious sponsorship from both ends of the spectrum 'dual power' became one of the great assumptions of observers of 1917. However, the notion that the Provisional Government was a glove puppet and the hand that manipulated it was the Petrograd Soviet, needs to be modified. First of all, power was being diffused through society way beyond any 'dual' system. 'Multiple' power is a much better description. The massive spread of self-government by committee, to take the most obvious example, diluted both state and Soviet power. The emergence of autonomous and increasingly independent nations with their own rapidly forming governments added to the process. Crucially, at no point before October did the Petrograd Soviet see itself or act as an alternative government. It knew it could not govern alone. In any case, from the forming of the first coalition (5 May), Soviet leaders were becoming part of the Provisional Government. It included six socialists. The Second Coalition, which was formed on 11 (24 NS) July, contained a majority of socialist ministers. Ironically, the Third Coalition (25 September to 26 October), the one overthrown by the Bolsheviks, was dominated by its socialist, soviet-based members. Thus the relationship between the Petrograd Soviet and the Provisional Government was complex but not solely adversarial. The 'moderate' revolutionary defencist leadership of the Petrograd Soviet wanted to keep an alliance with the middle class in order to defend Russia. They were prepared to criticise Provisional Government initiatives before they joined it, but they did so in a spirit of lobbying, not of subversion.

The July events had also acutely demonstrated the emergence of irreconcilable differences over the future of the revolution. Soldiers and sailors would not mindlessly march forward just because officers told them to. They would, they agreed, defend the country but not attack. Workers were getting tired of what they saw as the prevarication and deceit of employers and were being drawn into more and more radical action to maintain their jobs and living standards. In the countryside, the great redistribution of land had hardly begun but peasants were ignoring landowners and establishing their own rules. All of these movements had yet to reach their peak, but for the moment we need to recall that, by July, radical expectations had risen enormously while the delivery of policies by the Provisional Government had been practically non-existent since the initial burst of concessions. Key issues – of the war, the land, the economy and the political system – were being left to fester. Critics argued this was deliberate, since any steps the Provisional Government could take would undermine the class interests of its property-owning wing. Delaying commissions were set up to investigate and supervise issues of land, food supply, war production and preparation for a nationwide election to the Constituent Assembly. But little was actually done to meet popular expectations on any of these core issues. The government was accused of kicking the can down the road in the hope that something, anything, might turn up if they delayed decision-making long enough. In reality, the only thing that could turn up to change the game in their favour would have been victory in the war. Should that happen, they might reap the benefit of a patriotic flush of gratitude. However, victory was about as likely as a trip to the moon at that time.

July had also shown the opponents of radical revolution, from the Kadets rightwards, that their interests were increasingly at risk. The ignominious collapse of the July Days, and the momentum generated by the accusations of collusion with the Germans by Lenin and the Bolsheviks, had stalled what had, until then, been an inexorable radicalisation of the revolution. The right, who deeply deplored the way the revolution was going, began to stir itself. It saw that the conjuncture had, for the first time since February, given them a chance to impose their will on the situation. From July to the end of August, the counter-revolution was on the march.

The Kerensky Moment

In the swirl of events in the first four months of the revolution, no individual had emerged to impose themselves as the national leader.

However, in the wake of the July crisis, it was the War Minister, Alexander Kerensky, who was the first to fill the role. As we have already noted, Kerensky was the only person from the left to join the Provisional Government, having obtained special permission from the Petrograd Soviet to do so. Thus, from the beginning, he was the only person to move freely in both circles. Who was he, and what had put him in this unique position?

Kerensky's historical reputation has been widely vilified. Among Bolsheviks, he was reduced, after October, to a figure of fun and a symbol of bourgeois incompetence. He was portrayed, in Nikolai Evreinov's grand open-air, on-site reconstruction of the supposed 'storming' of the Winter Palace on the anniversary in 1920, dressed in 'capitalist' style morning suit and top hat (Von Geldern 1993: 199–207). In Eisenstein's tenth anniversary film, *October*, he was portrayed as a vain and petty Napoleon, even tucking his arm into his jacket in imitation of his hero. In fact, he did this for a while to conceal the fact his wrist was in a sling as a result of a sprain. He has also been accused of drug addiction. He was said to have fled from Petrograd in October dressed as a woman.

In the usual scheme of things an enemy's enemy becomes a friend, but not in this case. The opponents of Bolshevism were, by and large, no more accurate or more understanding of him. They, too, circulated rumours and falsehoods. In emigration, he was often shunned by fellow émigrés right down to the embarrassing and demeaning, for the church, refusal to allow him an Orthodox burial in New York. In the end, his remains were laid to rest in Putney Vale cemetery in London, a city with which he had relatively few strong associations compared to Paris, New York and Palo Alto in California. It is easy to see why his reputation suffered in this way. For the Bolsheviks, he was one of only a handful of individuals (along with Miliukov and General Kornilov) who had the stature to symbolise the 'bourgeois' phase of the revolution. In itself, this is a kind of backhanded compliment. For the émigrés, the main aspect of their contumely was that he made a very convenient scapegoat. Blame the, from the émigrés' point of view, 'disaster' of October squarely on the shoulders of Kerensky and one had no need to look deeper for an explanation. In particular, by blaming Kerensky, no one had to reproach themselves for fatal mistakes.

The weight of these misleading accusations succeeded in burying Kerensky's real reputation under massive debris from which it is only now emerging (Fontenot 1981; Abraham 1987; Soboleva and Smirnov 1993; Basmanov *et al.* 1996; Badcock 1998; Kolonitskii and Figes 1999; Strongin 2010; Kolonitskii 2011; Lyandres 2012). The three basic foundations of Kerensky's life in 1917 are that he was still very young, only 37, ten years younger than Lenin or Trotsky. Second, he had a serious medical condition resulting from the loss of a kidney. This was at the root of stories of his drug taking, since he took medication for the pain and it also led him to sometimes faint in public at the end of a greatly demanding speech or set of meetings, a characteristic some- times translated by critics into deliberate histrionics or even hysteria. Third, he was a man of the left. He had joined a small leftist party, the *Trudoviki*, literally the Labour Party, a more working-class-oriented group akin to the Socialist Revolutionaries. In other words, he was, in the Russian sense, a populist who believed, as did many radical intel- lectuals, that it was the duty of the privileged to use their talents and standing to better the lot of their underprivileged and impoverished fellow citizens. For Kerensky, a decisive moment had come in 1912 when, as a lawyer, he eloquently defended the victims of the Lena Valley goldfields massacre. His eloquence stood him in good stead in 1917: he stood out as a brilliant speaker and could turn audiences in his favour. He fully earned the nickname of 'Persuader in Chief'. His aim was to maintain national unity as long as possible and thereby defend Russia from the worst of all catastrophes, internal collapse opening the country up to external defeat, dismemberment and occupation by Germany, Turkey and Austria-Hungary. By carefully playing the war card he was, for a while, able to maintain a balance among moderates of left, centre and right who could see the need to stand together as being greater, for the moment, than knocking out enemies within, which risked being mutually destructive. It was, however, a very volatile coalition stretching from Mensheviks and SRs, via Kadets and Octobrists to monarchist generals and landowners. It was a tightrope walk that might succeed for a while under external threat but was bound to end in a fall. The trick was to judge when the moment of the fall had arrived and take decisive action to evade it. It was here that Kerensky was to fail, but that lay nearly four months down the line from when he emerged in July as Prime Minister in place of the elderly figurehead, Georgy Lvov. Appropriately, the government that emerged was expanded to the left so that it, in effect, represented most of the political spectrum of the moment, thereby fulfilling Kerensky's fundamental aim of having a govern- ment of national unity. Its main figures, with party affiliations, were: Nikolai Nekrasov (Finance) and Mikhail Tereshchenko (Foreign Affairs) – both non-party centre-right; Nikolai Avksenteev (Internal affairs – SR); Sergei Prokopovich (Trade and Industry – non-party centre-left); Sergei Ol'denburg (Education – Kadet); Victor Chernov

(Agriculture – SR); Matvei Skobelev (Labour – Menshevik); Alexei Peshekhonov (Food – People's Socialist); Vladimir L'vov (Procurator of the Holy Synod – Progressive). Altogether, there were eight social-ist ministers and seven non-socialist, including four Kadets, who remained very influential.

But even national unity had its limits. The first act of the Kerensky government was to turn on the Bolsheviks who were, incorrectly, accused of being behind the July Days and motivated in organising the mutinies and strikes by German gold. Grigorii Aleksinskii's unreli-able documents (see pp. 77–8) purported to show that large sums of money were being deposited by German agents in Bolshevik accounts (Lyandres 1995). Lenin, among other radical leaders from a variety of parties had, of course, returned to Russia, via Germany and with the approval of the German government. This also weighed heavily against them. Consequently, the idea that they were acting for the national enemy was quickly taken up by the right and the credulous. The Bolshevik party was banned and its press shut down. Neither of these measures was very effective. The party continued to contest elec-tions but under another name. The newspaper also appeared under other titles than simply *Pravda*. The party went partially underground. Significantly, Lenin believed the moment was actually a game-changer. On the advice of his chief lieutenants, Grigorii Zinioviev and Lev Kamenev, he took the cautious line of fleeing the city for autono-mous but not yet fully-independent Finland, beyond the reach of the Russian police. But his writings of the moment, especially his article 'The Political Situation: Four Theses' reflect a really dark pessimism about what had happened to the revolution in those few days.

All hopes for a peaceful development of the Russian revolution have vanished for good. This is the objective situation: either complete victory for the military dictatorship, or victory for the workers' armed uprising; the latter victory is only possible when the insurrection coincides with a deep, mass upheaval against the government and the bourgeoisie caused by economic disruption and the prolongation of the war. (Lenin 1960–70: vol. 25: 179.)

Even worse, it was necessary to envisage a return to the underground. Legal work should be continued but it should not be overrated:

The party of the working class, without abandoning legal activ-ity, but never for a moment overrating it, must *combine* legal with illegal work, as it did in 1912–14. Don't let slip a single hour of

legal work. But don't cherish any constitutional or 'peaceful' illusions. Form illegal organisations or cells everywhere and at once
for the publication of leaflets, etc. Reorganise immediately, consistently, resolutely, all along the line. Act as we did in 1912–14, when
we could speak about overthrowing tsarism by a revolution and an
armed uprising, without at the same time losing our legal base in
the Duma, the insurance societies, the trade unions, etc. (Lenin
1960–70: vol. 25: 180)

Lenin's pessimism was the right wing's optimism. While it would be
going too far to say the right felt things were moving in its direction,
there is no doubt that, as a result of the debacle that the July days
represented for the far left, the right began to organise with a new
spring in its step.

The new government, despite its increasingly left-wing composition, shared many of the anxieties of the right. In particular, it feared
that continued disruption of industry by strikes and the threat of
a massive spontaneous land redistribution would provoke national
disintegration. The right's programme of restoring order was shared,
at least in part, by the authorities. However, repression alone was
not enough and it was, in any case, against the grain of the left-wing
part of the coalition. As compensation for supporting the necessary
establishment of order, the left wanted to see quicker progress on the
fundamental changes to which the original programme had committed the government. This meant not only calling a Constituent
Assembly, which the Menshevik/SR left was confident it would domi-
nate, but also some measures towards land reform and redistribution,
and the ending of the war in an acceptable manner.

From the point of view of the new intelligentsia and middle-class
elite, the most pressing problem was political organisation. For them,
the first priority was to establish a legitimate, democratic system of
government. Only then could the other problems be properly tackled.
Let us note, in passing, that this priority was not shared by the masses.
For most of the peasants and the diverse urban and rural working class,
practical problems of land, wages, work conditions and, increasingly,
unemployment, loomed larger than a new constitution. For soldiers
and sailors the obvious priority was the war, the continuation of which
was a direct threat to their lives. We will examine these concerns in
more detail later but, for now, concentrate on the elites.

In fact, one would have to qualify the comment about a new constitution as a priority even for the elites. True, they wanted an orderly
political process but, as we have already mentioned, it soon became

clear that they would not be able to maintain control over any system which had pretensions to being democratic. This placed them in a major dilemma. Clearly, given the power of soviets, the committees, unions and peasant disorders, any solution had to be democratic. Their initial programme had stipulated a universal, direct, equal, secret ballot. There was no way they could go back on it. But they profoundly mistrusted the masses. For much of the elite, including many on the left, such as the writer Maxim Gorky, the peasants in particular were too uneducated, narrow-minded and traditionalist to be entrusted with the vote and hence the fate of Russia. The educated elite was, on the whole, like Durnovo in 1914, terrified of the so-called 'dark people', the *temnyi liudy*.

The outcome was procrastination. From early on, excuses were presented for not getting on with the business of convening a constituent assembly. Most obviously, such an undertaking was very difficult in the absence of, or unreliability of, updated electoral rolls, and the crudeness of mechanisms for a national election. It became doubly difficult when the war was taken into account. The mobility of soldiers and refugees meant a huge number of citizens, perhaps 15 or even 20 million, were transient and hard to pin down for an election.

In the first place, a commission was set up to enquire into the state of the nation. Its findings are fascinating. Reflecting the fears of the intelligentsia who commissioned and conducted it, it presents an unrelieved picture of mass backwardness and cultural (in the broadest sense) underdevelopment, especially of the peasants. One peasant is quoted as describing the politics of 1917 as a struggle between 'the tsar and the students' (Vulliamy 1929), a depiction that contains more truth than might appear at first sight! The moderate left (that is, largely the right wing of the increasingly split Menshevik and Socialist Revolutionary parties) was prepared to buy the notion that a wartime election was undesirable. The rest of the left, however, believed these were only excuses on the part of the centre and right for putting off the inevitable – an election which would undoubtedly cast them out of power.

Without a doubt the internal situation in Russia was hardly conducive to a crucial election. Ignorance of politics was deemed to be widespread. Passions were already high. Political parties were largely leaderships with no mass members, though they did have followers. However, it should be remembered that national elections had been held for no less than four Dumas in 1906, 1907 and 1912, though the last two were on an indirect franchise. They had shown that peasants had voted rationally in support of their interests and values.

As a man of the centre-left, Kerensky realised that delaying the Constituent Assembly would be as risky as convening it. After all, the 'moderate' socialist part of the political spectrum to which he, and an increasing number of government ministers belonged, was likely to be (and actually was) victorious when the elections were eventually held. So Kerensky turned to more energetic preparations for it. His first step was to convene Russia's first national assembly since the collapse of the Duma. The membership was partly selected from people of influence in the state structure and in civil society, including soviets and trade unions, and partly elected. It had no powers and was purely consultative, set up with a view to preparing the ground for the real thing, but it was undoubtedly the most representative national body to meet in the period between February and the brief meeting of the actual Constituent Assembly in January 1918 and as such deserves attention. It was called a State Conference and it convened in Moscow from 12 to 15 August (25–28 NS), 1917. Some 2,500 persons were in attendance, including 488 deputies from all four state dumas of past years, 129 representatives from soviets of peasants' deputies, 100 from soviets of workers' and soldiers' deputies, 147 from municipal Dumas, 117 from the army and navy, 313 from cooperative organisations, 150 from trade and commercial circles and banks, 176 from trades unions, 118 from *zemstvos* (district assemblies), 83 from the intelligentsia, 58 from national organisations and 24 from the clergy (Gimpel'son 1970–1979). It was deeply mistrusted by the far left, and its proceedings were disrupted by a boycott and strikes in Moscow by transport workers and others, which were largely attributed to the Bolsheviks, who were still, in theory, banned. In left wing mythology, and in the dual power mode, the strikes are portrayed as showing the greater strength of the workers and soviets compared to the Provisional Government and the State Conference itself. Such a view is somewhat exaggerated. The conference did go ahead and was actually the scene of one of Kerensky's greatest triumphs.

The Moscow State Conference very quickly revealed deep divisions between left and right (the following account is based on *Gosudarstvennoe soveshchanie* 1930). The right was dominated by military and pro-military speakers calling for order to be restored by force, and for a form of martial law and a state of emergency to be declared. Russia's newly won freedom would be suspended, soviets and committees disbanded. Many parts of the propertied elite, continuing their programme from before February of protecting their property and privileges at all costs, clustered around the military for protection from the 'anarchy' of social revolution. The main focus of right-wing attention and aspirations was General Kornilov. Kerensky, in a show of his own strength, limited Kornilov's participation in the actual proceedings of the conference. This did not prevent his railway carriage from being the scene for many intriguers, flatterers, anxious property-owners and tunnel vision nationalists to visit him and, in many cases, urge him to take strong action against the left. While Kornilov himself was restricted in what he could say to the conference, one of his associates, the Cossack Ataman (Chieftain) Kaledin, presented the main points of his programme in the form of six proposals: the army should be above politics and meetings and parties should be banned within it; most soldiers' soviets and army and navy committees should be done away with in front and rear, and those which were left should be strictly controlled; the declaration of soldiers' rights should be amended and supplemented by a declaration of their duties; army discipline should be strengthened 'by the most decisive measures' (a thinly veiled reference to the taboo subject of capital punishment); vaguely but menacingly, he said that, since front and rear were united, measures applied to the front should be extended to the rear and, finally, the disciplinary rights (sic) of command personnel should be restored. There were also proposals for the extension of martial law to factories supplying war materials, which could include uniforms and boots as well as weapons and battleships. Kaledin had brought the programme formulated behind the closed doors of the High Command into the public gaze.

Not surprisingly, the representatives of most of the left greeted Kaledin's proposals with complete derision. To suggest militarising factories and suppressing soviets was suicidal. It would be impossible to carry out, not least because it was unlikely that troops or police could be found to implement it. Significantly, a Cossack esaul (lieutenant) denounced Kornilov's mouthpiece for having no standing to represent the Cossacks, let alone the wider society. Although the meeting was boycotted by Bolsheviks, many speakers from soviets and from the trade union rank-and-file spoke up for rejection of the military programme of the right and called for a more rapid transition to democracy and for transfer of land.

The Moscow State Conference also illustrated the growing dilemma of the Menshevik and SR right, especially those in the government. They had to sit passively while those further to the left stood up for the policies, of democratisation, land reform and attempting to end the war which were, in fact, key policies of their own parties. Tsereteli, Chkeidze, even Chernov who was taking a more militant line on land reform than the rest of the right-SR leadership, were forced to

separate themselves from implementation of their own basic principles. This opened up a vacuum in leadership. It enabled Bolsheviks,
Left SRs, Menshevik Internationalist and anarchists – all of whom
stayed resolutely in opposition to the Provisional Government – to
become the main spokespeople for the increasingly restive masses.

The main plank of the Provisional Government's platform was
maintenance of national unity at all costs. This was the essence
of Kerensky's speeches to the conference. Using all his considerable rhetorical skill, he urged the factions to stay united. The only
alternative was national disaster and humiliating defeat. He praised
the army for its defence of the country but, to the exasperation of
the Kornilovites, vigorously defended Russia's new institutions and
continued to declare that, far from threatening the nation, the country could only be saved by using them as channels to improve Russia's
performance in the war. Exhausted by his efforts he came near to
collapse. This was not, as his detractors have said, a piece of hysterical play-acting but a sign of how he had pushed his suffering body
to extremes. Kerensky's speeches to the conference were a tour de
force. He pulled together all his undoubted histrionic and oratorical
ability to emphasise the need for national unity. Each of Kerensky's
perorations was met with enthusiastic applause. Despite this, the
rest of the conference showed that, in the real world, his arguments
seemed to be built on sand.

Kerensky's redoubtable powers of persuasion were at their finest
in confronting the political elite in an assembly like the Moscow
State Conference. Persuading the country to go along with him was
quite another matter. The real political forces were polarising fast.
The strikes and demonstrations in the city had shown that the incipient power of workers was strong. Kornilov's intrigues threatened to
undermine the government among the military and the remnants
of the tsarist order, nostalgically wishing to turn the clock back or, as
dictated by their real interests, attempting to hang on to their fast-
eroding property rights in the only way they knew how – tsarist-style
repression. However, like the February plotters against Nicholas,
Kornilov and his followers precipitated events which were directly the
opposite of what they intended.

The Kornilov affair

Buoyed up by the febrile atmosphere of Moscow during the State
Conference, Kornilov increasingly felt himself to be the man of

destiny, the man of the moment. He would be the 'saviour' of 'Russia', though how he might save it, and which Russia he intended to save are not clear. He proposed to the Provisional Government that he should be allowed to move troops towards Petrograd, ostensibly to establish order in the city but most likely also to disperse the Petrograd Soviet. On 23 August, the government gave its approval, at least for the first part of the plan. However, the intervention of Vladimir L'vov made Kerensky think again and attempt to discover exactly what Kornilov intended. L'vov alarmed Kerensky by warning him, on 26 August, that Kornilov's plan included 'that all military and civil authority shall be placed in the hands of the Generalissimo', that is, Kornilov, and that all ministers should resign until 'the formation of a Cabinet by the Generalissimo' (Browder and Kerensky 1961: vol. 3, 1569). Later on the 26th Kerensky attempted to confirm this, in a curious exchange between the two men over the telegraph-style Hughes apparatus, in the course of which Kerensky imitated L'vov, who had failed to turn up. Kerensky asked Kornilov to confirm what L'vov had told him. Kornilov, oddly, concurred without even asking what it was that L'vov had told Kerensky (Browder and Kerensky 1961: vol. 3, 1571). Not surprisingly, Kerensky then formed the impression that Kornilov intended to overthrow him. He immediately dismissed Kornilov. However, in defiance of Kerensky, on 27 August, Kornilov ordered his subalterns to move towards Petrograd with military units of which the so-called Wild Division (officially the Caucasus Native Mounted Division) was at the core. It was chosen because it was largely composed of Chechens, Ingush and other Muslim mountain-dwellers who, it was believed, would be less likely to be sucked into Russian struggles for which they cared little and from which they would be insulated by their language.

Very quickly, Kornilov's manoeuvres were hit by fatal blows from two sides. His troops moving on the capital were met by delegations of the Petrograd Soviet and other figures from the left. The delegates easily circumvented the language problem by using their own Chechen and Chechen-speaking supporters to communicate with them. It was almost as easy to undermine the supposed insurgents' support for their officers. Using the rhetoric of revolutionary internationalism, they quickly persuaded the troops to disobey their officers and even to threaten to arrest them. Railway workers also blocked military trains. Within days, Kornilov had no troops to carry out his orders and was quickly put under a gentlemanly form of personal arrest and conveyed back to Stavka. The crusade to 'save Russia' had rapidly descended into farce.

Although the basic facts of the affair are known, there remains no end of speculation about who was aiming to do what. Was Kerensky using, or attempting to use, Kornilov to suppress the Petrograd Soviet? If not, why had he ordered Kornilov's detachment to the capital? Did Kornilov believe he was simply obeying orders or did he have an agenda not only to suppress the Petrograd Soviet but to replace Kerensky with himself as military dictator? To what extent were foreign governments, especially the British, involved? The discussions and evidence around these issues is endless. In 1937, in commemoration of its twentieth anniversary, Russian émigrés based in Paris conducted an inquiry into the affair. Its conclusions were weighted in favour of Kornilov's view that he was undermined, even betrayed, by Kerensky. Nonetheless, the enquiry published a great deal of its evidence, some of which supported other interpretations. If the 1937 enquiry supported what James White, in one of the most scrupulous examinations of the topic, has described as the pro-Kornilov explanation, its publications and other sources have fed into alternatives which, again following White, can be described as the 'misunderstanding theory', and finally the pro-Kerensky view (White 1968).

It is still not possible to say with absolute certainty which of the interpretations is correct, though Kerensky's version that he was the one being betrayed and that Kornilov was conducting a 'patriotic' mutiny and a coup attempt, seems very much the most likely. In many respects, Kornilov's political blunderings seem to come from the same source as the hideously counterproductive meddling of generals during the war and February revolution. The same smug, self-satisfied blockheadedness characterises all these disastrous forays of the military into politics. Their simple, politically naive, beliefs were dangerous in a complex and subtle world. The White leaders in the post-October conflict proved fitting successors to their politically incompetent predecessors.

However, when it comes to the key issue of the importance of the affair – its consequences – it is much easier to be certain. The Kornilov affair was a complete game-changer. There were two victims. Obviously, Kornilov and the right had seriously overplayed their hand and caused the national coalition constructed by Kerensky to split disastrously. In a sort of reverse of the July Days, the right had discredited itself and restored the ascendancy of the left. But Kerensky was also a victim. In the eye of the storm he did finally jump to the left. He made an agreement with the Petrograd Soviet, armed it, withdrew the ban on its members, primarily the Bolsheviks, and released Soviet prisoners from jail, notably Trotsky who thereby fulfilled his prophecy that the Provisional Government would be too weak to hold him for long. But it was not enough. Kerensky was seen to have cultivated Kornilov in the first place, not least in appointing him as C-in-C, and was therefore totally distrusted and discredited in the eyes of the militant left. Although it went through one more mutation into a coalition with even more socialist ministers, the Provisional Government in general and Kerensky in particular were living in a political vacuum. The army gave no more than token support to the man who had, in their view, betrayed and arrested 'Russia's best hope' of order and security. The left assumed Kerensky's 'conversion' to alliance with the Soviet was no more than an insincere piece of *realpolitik* necessary to save his neck and position from Kornilov and the military.

If there is no doubt about the victims there is also no doubt about the victors. The left was now moving to a barely-challenged ascendancy. Although Kornilov's escapade was small in scale, in that only a small force was deployed, its impact was off the scale. The attempt was a flash of lighting that illuminated the political scene and galvanised many of the political and social actors into a renewed effort. Kornilov's expedition had sent out an apparent signal to the masses. The gains of the February revolution were under threat. The deeply-held and still unfulfilled objectives – for land redistribution, for democracy, for national independence for minorities, for an honourable end to the war – risked being sent into oblivion by a military reaction. It was a time to either defend the objectives of the revolution or give them up. Naturally the masses opted for the former. The atmosphere of the last pre-October weeks was, in a clumsy but accurate phrase, one of defensive, renewed radicalisation – pushing the revolution forward in order to save it. From his secret outpost in Helsinki, Lenin was one of the first to recognise the importance of the new conjuncture. His extraordinary pessimism of July was replaced by an increasingly unbounded optimism, which amazed and worried his colleagues, who saw far more complications from their various viewpoints in Petrograd, Moscow and the main centres of the eroding empire.

In essence, Lenin's view was correct. Compared to July, the prospects for a revolution looked much better. For the last six or seven weeks of its existence, the Provisional Government was almost without power. In many ways, the basic price of the Kornilov crisis was the dissolution of the last elements of an at best feeble, central power. In late September and October, there was no significant political power governing Russia. The Bolsheviks are said to have seized power but there was none to be seized. Another observer, slightly more accurately, said the Bolsheviks found power lying in the street and picked it up. It was the Kornilov fiasco which had made this possible. In trying to reverse the situation, to stop the revolutionary process, Kornilov had done more than anyone to set it rolling further and faster. In essence, through one group of Russians taking up arms against another in a consistent and organised way for the first time, he had also initiated a civil war. The next six months or so, until Spring 1918, were dominated by the first revolutionary civil war, an intense struggle to re-establish power, conducted between rapidly polarising left and right factions. It is to the essential features of that crucial struggle that we now turn.

Chapter 5:   Bolshevism Triumphant: September–October 1917

The February Revolution had been an odd union of left and right which had started an improbable national honeymoon. The July Days and the Moscow Conference had illustrated the emergence of irreconcilable differences in the unnatural marriage. The Kornilov affair showed there was nothing left but divorce. The fight for custody was on. Unwittingly, Kornilov, who had intended to pre-empt this struggle, had actually fired the starting gun for its most intensive phase so far, a phase which brought an explosion of civil and national unrest to the point of civil war, a Soviet Government and a disastrous treaty with Germany and her allies to end the war. The aim of the next two chapters is to explore the outburst of grassroots revolutionary activity and to analyse its outcome down to March/April 1918 with a special eye on why, of all the parties to the struggle, it was the Bolsheviks who came out on top, for the time being at least.

Defensive Radicalisation: The Popular Movement Accelerates

As we have seen, the first few months of popular revolution had been characterised by radical but restrained steps. The predominant features had been self-organisation, rapidly increased expectations and an escalation of traditional skirmishes. For example, peasants formed committees, encroached on landowners' land, pastures and forests, and went on rent strikes. Workers struggled to improve their living standards through conventional strikes. In the armed forces, the authority of officers was constantly challenged. The restraint – shown by the relatively few land seizures prior to late summer, by the lack of challenge to ownership of factories and by the continuation in authority of much of the old officer class – was attributable to tactics, to patience, to awaiting the right opportunity, not to any lack of commitment to further revolution. In the relatively rosy perspective of the early months the great goals of the revolution – land redistribution, a better deal for workers, a just peace, democracy – were all thought to be inevitable and approaching rapidly. The harsh lessons of July and August were that the old ruling class had at least some powerful elements that would fight to prevent this happy outcome. If success were to be achieved, the masses would also have to fight.

The change of pace can be seen clearly from a few statistics. Government intervention in the countryside was relatively limited before July. After July, it was stepped up, at first as a response to landowner prodding in the light of the renewed opportunity presented by the post-July conjuncture. However, figures for the use of military units against peasants show that, far from being intimidated, increased repression stimulated an angry and aggressive response. Prior to July only 11 military interventions had taken place. In July and August the number rose to 39. In September and October it was 105. In the majority of cases, soldiers opened fire on the peasants (Read 1996: 110). There could be no clearer sign that harsh measures threatened to be counter-productive. The right was continuing on its self-destructive path. The more openly and energetically it pursued its goals, the more it stoked up opposition to itself and undermined its own position. After July the masses were alerted to the newly mobilising power of the counter-revolution. The Kornilov fiasco underlined the message but also showed the right was still disorganised and open to defeat.

Worker militancy

In a pathbreaking study published in 1983, the revisionist historian Steve Smith pointed to new and crucial explanations of why and how the working class of Petrograd was radicalising in late summer and autumn of 1917. The naive assumption about working-class political activity tended to be that it was driven by politicisation through developing values, political ideas, political (and for some, class) consciousness. Both the Soviet and anti-Soviet schools in the cold war emphasised this. For Lenin, rising class consciousness was the key to a successful revolution. However, what Smith showed was that for workers there was also an absolutely crucial element of 'economic' as well as 'political' motivation. In particular, Smith brilliantly deconstructed the drive towards 'workers' control' and factory takeovers that characterised working-class activity in the capital in the post-July and post-Kornilov months. What he showed was that the movement was not so much driven by changing ideas as by changing circumstances. Workers did not joyously encroach on managerial functions but instead were pushed into them. How? Why? By looking at the dynamic of relations between workers and owners in Petrograd factories Smith noted that owners had been trying to regain the initiative by, in effect, threatening their workers with factory closures. Often, such closures were disguised, very plausibly given the growing disruption of the time, as consequences of crucial shortages of fuel and raw materials, rather than presenting themselves as the cynical ploys that they often were. Thus, employers threatened their workforce with unemployment. The precarious nature of working-class life, which was centred on surviving from one weekly pay packet to the next, left little cushioning against such a disaster. Therefore, they tried harder and harder to keep factories going. They formed city-wide committees to seek out wood, coal, oil, raw materials and other essentials of production. As output fell within factories, workers took over more and more managerial functions as the original management seemed to be trying to slow down production, not expand it. The result was the ironic situation whereby owners were trying to cut production and even shut down their own factories and workers were being sucked in to management in order to keep them going and, thereby, preserve their jobs and their livelihoods.

In part, Smith had been building on the insights of a pioneering generation of so-called revisionist historians of the Russian working class such as William Rosenberg, Diane Koenker, David Mandel and others. Many of them were influenced by New Left Marxist ideas translated into historical debate by, as a leading example, E.P. Thompson. Leopold Haimson, a former Menshevik who became a professor at Columbia University, was also very influential. What the new school showed was that the cold war paradigms of Soviet infallibility, preached in the Soviet Union, and of totalitarian terror, preached in the west, failed to account for the facts of the revolution. As far as workers were concerned, their main concerns were 'economic', that is, they revolved round trying to establish a sound and secure living standard. In fact, almost every strike was economic in that it demanded wage increases and/or improvements in working conditions and so on. Many were also political, demanding greater democracy through soviets or the constituent assembly, for example. But the key point is that for workers in a revolutionary situation of that kind, the economic and the political were effectively inseparable.

The great achievement of the revisionist social historians was to show that workers were more complex and better able to pursue their own interests than previously thought. They were not a 'mob' or a 'rabble' as right wing opponents and historians characterised them. Instead, like their counterparts in the French Revolution, they were given the more dignified title of 'the popular movement' or the 'crowd' or the 'masses'. Their way of life was analysed. They were shown to have vestigial organisations in the form of *zemliachestva* (social organisations of migrant workers from the same region) or *artely* (work groups recruited and employed collectively as a group rather than as individuals) (Johnson 1979; Bradley 1985). Simplistic Leninist correlations between established, educated workers deemed to be 'advanced', and therefore Bolshevik-supporting, were shown to be exaggerated. In particular, Smith had shown that even in Petrograd, the main centre of Russia's more advanced industries, the majority of the working class were first-generation migrants. This tendency was reinforced by the effects of the war. Many established workers were conscripted, and a new wave of migrant workers from the provinces was recruited to replace them in the factories. Significantly, many of these new workers were women. Traditionally, women had dominated the workforce in 'light' industries like textiles or cigarette manufacture, while men dominated 'heavy' labour in steel mills, which called for more physical strength. One key implication of the migrant nature of the working class was that it maintained close links with the village. An extraordinary proportion of male workers in Petrograd had wives and children who still lived in their native village. In 1908 a survey showed that between 29 per cent (in a shipyard) and 87 per cent (in textiles) of married male workers in certain Petrograd factories had wives in their home village. They would only meet once a year during the harvest when many workers went home at the end of their contracts. In 1918, 20 per cent of Petrograd workers retained ownership of land in the village (Read 1996: 76).

The new social historians also painted a vivid picture of the difficulties, harshness and precariousness of working-class life but also the growing richness of its culture. Living conditions were often execrable. Families might live in a 'corner' of a room, that is a curtained off section of a large room with several such 'corners' in each one. Single men and women workers might live in sexually segregated dormitories, sometimes sharing a bed with someone on a different shift, enabling the owner to get two rents for it. Incomes were pathetic but, even so, many workers continued to remit funds to the family left behind in the village, which also served as safety net. The precariousness of city life, where unemployment or injury would spell disaster, was partly mitigated by the possibility of returning to the village. The work routine was intense. Despite constant efforts to establish the eight hour day the requirements of war production, rising inflation and the falling value of wages led to workers continuing to work longer hours – ten, twelve per day, sometimes more – six days a week. Not surprisingly, given the harsh climatic conditions as well, vodka blasted a big hole in the health and sobriety of the working class. However, there were also more positive aspects to working class culture. Workers' educational courses were well-supported, zemliachestva preserved regional singing and music-making. On Sunday, the universal day of rest, men and women workers promenaded city streets in their best clothes. Younger men were often devotees of 'dandyism', that is dressing well and showing off, rather than politics (Smith 2008). Obviously, wartime shortages threw a pall over all such activities but they still continued as best they could.

Peasant militancy

One of the weaknesses of revisionist scholarship was that it either ignored or misunderstood peasants. Following the Marxist ideas of Lenin, Trotsky and of other critics like Gorky, peasants were considered to be backward, traditional, petty-bourgeois and even counter-revolutionary. Since the late 1960s there has been a much wider appreciation of the complexity and radical nature of peasant society. Instead of being seen as dumb clods of clay worked on by cunning outsiders such as landowners, priests, loan sharks and traders they were increasingly seen as people with a deep-rooted and rational culture of their own (Moon 1999). To take one simple example, peasant 'conservatism' was the bane of all outsiders who tried to 'modernise' them. However, from the peasants' point of view, conservatism meant survival. By repeating the actions and approaches of previous generations, adapted over centuries to local conditions, peasants were confident they could keep their family, village and society going. Innovations contained a threat, that of the hidden, unintended consequences. Agrarian development programmes all around the world down to the present day have shown the dangers inherent in change (George 1976; Davis 2001). Maybe an irrigation plan looked good, even worked for a while, until extreme conditions created a water-shortage downstream and a disaster. A new type of seed might be more productive but eventually show itself vulnerable to a local pest. For the peasant community the risks were not theoretical, they were the difference between life and death. Best stick to what had worked for centuries. Thus, the reluctance of peasants to take up innovations was not simply cultural stubbornness, it was a rational response to their situation. It was not necessarily the best response but it was one that had helped them for a millennium. Politically and socially, a closer look at peasant societies reveals that other characteristics which infuriated modernisers (including revolutionaries), such as peasants' apparent deference, were often only masks, 'weapons of the weak'. Given they had no power, submission to those who did was only sensible. However, when there was a change in the balance of power, as in Russia in 1905 and 1917, the mask of deference fell away and the peasants became militant and assertive about their desires and rights. In this perspective, peasant action in the revolution should not be seen simply as riot, but as a more rational, if instinctive, approach to getting what they wanted.

Surprisingly, given the need to conform to an anti-peasant version of Marxism, Soviet historians like Danilov were among the first to re-evaluate peasant action (Danilov 1988). Down to the last years of the Soviet system, Soviet historians were ahead of their western counterparts in analysing the peasantry. One example is provided by A.D. Maliavskii (Maliavskii 1981). Influenced by the historiography of the culture of workers' control in the revolution, Maliavskii detected elements of 'peasants' control' in their actions. As we have seen, in the early phases of the revolution peasants did not go for the jugular of the landowners. Instead, they picked away like mosquitoes at vulnerable aspects of the landowners' position. This became increasingly sophisticated and often developed in response to landowners' efforts to extricate themselves from their increasingly difficult situation. Behind the actions of landowners and peasants was one great assumption – in the near future land was going to change hands. The landowners tried to minimise this, whereas, for the peasants, the total takeover of landowner land without compensation was the only solution they could envisage.

On many estates a kind of tit-for-tat game developed. The landowners, fearing expropriation, would try to remove or realise key assets. That is, wherever they could they would remove wealth, from country-house furniture and *objets d'art* to wooden barns. Marketable assets would be sold. To this end the felling of trees would be speeded up, livestock sold off, even tools and equipment would be disposed of.

Obviously, in the prevailing conditions, this would mean bargain base-ment prices, as many landowners would all be doing the same thing and there were few buyers. However, the peasants were not stupid; they immediately saw what was going on and began to veto it. They began to prevent tree-felling and the fire-sale of assets. They were even smart enough to use new institutions of the Provisional Government to put a mantle of legality over their actions. To supervise the issue of land reform the new authorities had set up a Main Land Committee with regional and local branches. As a preparation for the reform, and perhaps as a delaying device, the Land Committee called for the drawing up of a national inventory of property. Obviously, such an enterprise was a mammoth task. A similar inventory had been secretly prepared at the time of emancipation in 1861 and it had taken years. Be that as it may, the peasants realised they could turn the inventory question to their advantage and, as Maliavskii has shown, on many estates the local village committee took on itself the business of draw-ing up such an inventory, on the assumption they would soon be the owners of it all. If landowners tried to downsize that inventory the peasants often insisted on being consulted. 'Normal' transactions, like selling mature animals for meat or regular milk sales, were often approved. However, if anything looked like asset-stripping the peas-ants would not only refuse to allow it, they would often physically prevent it. Incidentally, the Land Committee was not the only body 'taken over' at village level by the peasant committees. The issue of finding food and raw materials for the war had spawned a Supply Committee entrusted with the task of maximising food production for the war effort. Early peasant ventures such as encroaching on landowners' land and sowing their own crops on it were increasingly carried out under the supposed cover of the Supply Committee (Maliavskii 1981; Read 1996: 101–5).

The success of these early strategies emboldened the peasants, and it was only with the beginnings of a more hard-line response, reflected in the figures we saw for increasing armed intervention after the July Days, that they began to meet significant resistance. By this time the peasants had realised it was now or never. If they wanted the land they believed they had the right to they were going to have to fight for it. The Kornilov affair, though had little direct impact on the rural situation, clearly raised the ghost of counter-revolution. Far from buckling under to repression and threat, the peasants responded by increasing the intensity of their attack. They had assumed the land would come to them gradually and naturally. That assumption was looking shaky. Direct action was necessary.

A new wave of militancy, driven by the new conjuncture, set in once the harvest was gathered in and agricultural tasks were less pressing. Nothing shows more clearly how smart the peasants were than the figures for land seizures. In the ambiguous conditions up to October they had held back. Once the green light was shown they hit hard. Up to September land seizures had been rare but in October 3 per cent of manors were confiscated. In November the figure rose to 20 per cent while December and January it was about 30 per cent in each month (Pershin 1966: 200). The momentum had become unstoppable; within months private landowners had been swept away in a vast tidal wave from below.

Although slower to get going than Soviet studies, western studies of the peasant movement escalated apace. Books and articles by early pioneers like Graeme Gill, John Channon, John Bradley, Robert Edelmann and Maureen Perrie were joined by an ever-increasing number of fine, detailed studies. Donald Raleigh and Orlando Figes produced fascinating accounts of the peasantry in the Volga region, centred on Saratov province. They led the way to an increasing number of local studies, made more feasible by the collapse of the Soviet Union and the opening up of many archives. A new generation of historians, including Sarah Badcock, Aaron Retish, Liudmila Novikova, Michael Hickey, Stephan Karsch and others studied important regions like Nizhnii-Novgorod, Voronezh, Archangel, Viatka, Kazan' and Smolensk. In the phrase of a leading group of these historians, they have shown the existence of 'a kaleidoscope of revolutions'.

Such studies have confirmed many aspects of the revolution. In the first place, each of these local revolutions was complex and self-generating. The issues over which people fought were those which impinged directly on their daily lives and their material well-being. Secondly, there was an extraordinary degree of self-organisation. The local movements tended to produce their own leaders. True, the standard political labels came to apply, with most leaders affiliating themselves to the Kadets, for the middle classes, and the Socialist Revolutionaries, Mensheviks and Bolsheviks for the workers, peasants and soldiers. But these affiliations were very weak, in that the localities did not always follow the centre. Thirdly, despite the multitude of differences, there was, by and large, a high degree of solidarity and shared values across the range of popular revolutions. This did not, of course, cross the great divide between the masses and the middle- and upper-class elites. The two camps became defined by the widespread use of the term '*burzhui*', a sort of dialect version of the term 'bourgeois', by the masses to describe the elite. Mass solidarity was expressed in self-identification as '*narod*', the people. This testified to an extraordinary degree of self-generating, if simplified, class consciousness (Kolonitskii and Figes 1999). This is a stark reminder of the polarisation of Russian society, attributable to the late survival of serfdom. Because emancipation only came about in 1861, the formation of intermediate and middle classes had been stifled. There were serfowners and serfs. It was a division that was hard to break down, not least because the serf state had been very slow to reform itself after 1861 and was increasingly anachronistic, as we have seen, in hanging on to autocratic privilege and fighting every vestige of devolved power and democracy.

Critics of simple class division have often pointed to the great diversity within supposed classes, and it is no different in the case of Russia. Not all peasants were the same. Workers also differentiated themselves through many gradations of skill, income, length of urban experience, locality, trade, age, gender and so on. Victoria Bonnell identified over 100 skill divisions in St Petersburg factories before the revolution (Bonnell 1983b). Soldiers and sailors were also distinguished by length of service, military unit, military specialisation (such as infantry, veterinarian, artillery) and many others. Sometimes rivalry within the class and between the subgroups was intense. Overlying all the differences was the question of nationality. The great diversity has led many observers to question the existence of such a thing as class at all. However, the Russian case is a superb example of E.P. Thompson's assertion that class is something that 'happens'. In Russia, at crucial moments, the divergences were set aside and a united front of the narod was presented. Workers and peasants often acted together. In the February Revolution, July Days, October Revolution and on many other occasions right down to the Kronstadt rebellion of 1921, soldiers and sailors responded instinctively to support workers' strikes and protests. Women's rights were acknowledged by all groups in the cities, though rural patriarchy only weakened slowly. Mass actions often incorporated cross-national participants. Attempts to utilise the supposed divisions rarely worked. For example, right-wing officers tried to turn frontline soldiers against workers by describing the latter as loafers and traitors who preferred to strike rather than work to produce the weapons needed at the front. Such ploys were easily counteracted by organising solidarity visits of worker representatives to the front and of soldiers and sailors to the cities. It was army leaders who, in a desperate effort to keep the front going, attempted to reorganise the army on national grounds, in particular to separate Ukrainian from Russian units in late 1917.

The rationale was that, since much of the frontline was in Ukraine, while Russia proper had not been invaded, Ukrainian units would fight harder to defend Ukraine than Russian units whose homeland was less threatened. This ploy did little to stop the post-October disintegration of the armed forces, once again showing revolutionary and class principles overrode national differences, for the time being at least (Frenkin 1978, 1982).

The rich detail being uncovered by the new historiography, and the consequent emergence of a picture of a volcanic explosion of self-generating local revolutions, has brought one danger with it. The great array of diverse components laid out by this new approach has led some to question whether or not they are part of a larger entity which can still be called 'the revolution'. For such observers the degree of diversity is so great that they question the notion of an overriding, general 'revolutionary movement'. In certain respects the debate is another example of the tendency of historians, as J.H. Hexter pointed out in the 1960s, to be either 'lumpers', who clumped things together, or 'splitters' who divided everything into small, separate entities. In particular, Hexter was attacking Marxist historiography in general and Christopher Hill, like Hexter an historian of the English civil war, in particular. Applied to the French Revolution, determined 'splitters' like Alfred Cobban and François Furet have questioned whether there even was such a thing as the French Revolution. However, such an approach can only be sustained, in the Russian case at least, by overlooking the fact that, in addition to local battles, there were central battles which were, in the end, decisive. Obviously, the central conflicts were deeply intertwined with local ones, but it was the outcome of events at the centre which determined the final outcome at local level. Without February, the local revolutions would not have been put into motion in 1917. Without October, the civil war and Red victory, there would not have been a Soviet state with ever-expanding control over the provinces. Without the land redistribution, the class structure of Russia would not have been transformed. Therefore, in order to understand the outcome of the revolutionary explosion we have to examine how the issues were played out at a national level.

Political Conflict at the National Level (September and October 1917)

There was once an odd consensus among Soviet and anti-Soviet historians about the outcome of the events of late 1917. A highly-organised

Bolshevik party and its charismatic leader Lenin, had captivated the revolutionary movement in the soviets, undermined all political rivals, seized power in a party-led coup which then spread out into a national campaign of subversion abhorred by the anti-Soviet historians as a manipulative Bolshevik takeover and praised by Soviet historians as 'the triumphal march of Soviet power'. Obviously, for anti-Soviet historians these developments were 'bad', malicious, deceptive, and for Soviet historians they were 'good', a mark of democracy, popularity and Lenin's genius. Nonetheless, they shared the view that the driving force was a centrally-organised, determined and disciplined revolutionary party with a strong and popular leader who stood at the head of a mass movement. Revisionist historians have convincingly demolished or massively revised, each of these characteristics. The Bolshevik party has been shown to be divided and indecisive. Lenin was a barely recognised figure. The mass movement developed independently of the Bolsheviks. In fact, it has been argued that the relationship between the party and the October revolution was the reverse of the traditional view – 'the October revolution was not the Bolsheviks' gift to the popular movement, it was the popular movement's gift to the Bolsheviks' (Read 1996: 174). In view of these debates what light can we throw on these tumultuous and decisive months?

Preliminary observations

One or two preliminary observations need to be made before we plunge into the maelstrom of national politics at this time. First of all, it is necessary to keep in mind that, although we use a conventional vocabulary of 'political party', 'party leader', 'conservatism', 'liberalism', 'populism', socialism' and even 'civil war', the precise meaning behind these terms is not exactly the same in Russia as in Britain, France or the United States. Political parties in the western sense did not exist in Russia in 1917. This is hardly surprising, since they had only been legal for just over a decade. Most of them were in the process of formation rather than finished products. There were no real party organisations with a stable, dues-paying membership. By and large they were much looser, fluctuating entities. The leaderships were well-defined, the members and followers less so. This was somewhat ironic given the traditional prominence given to issues of membership in the split between Bolsheviks and Mensheviks. Despite the argument, in practice, both parties had very similar structure, or rather lack of structure. In their case, and that of other groups, 'membership' was defined by working for the party, and the central task of party members before 1917 was to distribute the party newspaper. Terms relating to party ideologies were also different. The political spectrum in Russia went much further to the right than in most of western Europe and North America. Proto-fascist, anti-semitic and stridently nationalist, anti-modern, anti-democratic and anti-leftist Black Hundreds and their elite backers (including the tsar and, with reservations, his mentor Pobedonostsev) had a bigger role in Russian politics after 1900 than in any other part of Europe or America. As a result, 'conservatives' were often positioned closer to the centre than their counterparts in, say, Germany. Liberals espoused similar principles to those of British liberals but were much more open to the left. Before 1905 and even, in part up to February 1917, they were partly revolutionary. They stood for a political revolution to end autocracy and a constituent assembly, but on social policy, especially land redistribution, they were to the right of centre. 'Populist' groups like the Socialist Revolutionaries were not rabble-rousers, as the American equivalent tended to be, but were defenders of the narod, the people, which included workers as well as peasants. Socialists, like those elsewhere, stood for some form of sharing of ownership of land and capital but beyond that had very divergent views. Terms have to be used with due respect for such nuances.

The second area of definitional difference, which follows from the first, is that politics itself was more fluid, more volatile, more fluctuating than in more established political systems and more mature democratic political cultures. Once again it is imperative to keep in mind that a new politics was still in the earliest moments of formation. As Lenin himself put it, in 1917 millions of people were awakening to national political life for the first time. They could not be expected to be sophisticated. The movements were immature. It is conventional to describe groups as 'Bolshevik', 'Menshevik', 'Populist' and so on but at grass-roots level today's Menshevik supporter could be tomorrow's Bolshevik voter and vice versa. This was, as we shall see, very well illustrated in 1917 and early 1918. Rather than supporting parties and being loyal to their leaders and the party programme, workers, soldiers and peasants remained loyal to their own programme – land redistribution, material security, peace – and supported parties only in so far as they were instruments for the realisation of their own instinctive aims. This is especially displayed in the soviets in general and in the Petrograd Soviet in particular. These bodies had small groups of party leaders at the head, but the majority of members of soviets were uncommitted. They voted for the leadership group whose stated aims most closely resembled their principles and desires. But it should also be remembered that political parties were also immature and loosely structured. They were themselves in the process of being formed. Russian politics in general and Soviet politics in particular in this period was not an orderly march of disciplined armies conflicting with one another. As has already been pointed out, the leaders were more like surfers in a turbulent sea trying to ride a massive, uncontrollable wave. The one who rode the wave most successfully was the winner, at least until the next wave came along.

It was a wave like this which deposited Lenin on the beach of the October revolution. As we have seen, the forces propelling the wave were rising anger and fear as a response to the Kornilov affair. Soldiers were angry with Kornilov-supporting officers. Peasants feared the return of landowners and the disappearance of their dream of obtaining the land. Workers were threatened by Kornilov's plans to proclaim martial law in defence factories throughout the empire and in key cities and regions near the front. National minorities heard the renewed beat of the imperial drum in Kornilov's rhetoric. But why was it that it was Lenin and his companions who were the most successful surfers? To change the metaphor radically: this question resembles a coin. It has two sides: the question on the reverse is, Why did Lenin's rivals fail?

The rise of the Bolsheviks and Lenin's campaign for an insurrection

It is difficult to say how well-known the Bolsheviks as a party and Lenin as an individual were in 1917. Traditional historiography is peppered with phrases from rivals about how Lenin was the one who would really stir things up. Unsurprisingly, Lenin himself shared this belief and even expressed it for a moment at the First All-Russian Congress of Soviets in June. As described by Sukhanov, Lenin said 'Chkheidze had declared that there is no political party in Russia that would agree to take the entire power on itself. I answer: There is! No party can refuse to do this, all parties are contending and must contend for power, and our party will not refuse it. *It is ready at any moment to take over the Government.*' (Sukhanov 1962: 380, Sukhanov's emphasis.) Quite understandably his boast was treated as a joke, though Sukhanov pointed out that it revealed Lenin was aiming for his party to take the entire power. In that Congress, the Bolsheviks comprised only 105 of the 777 delegates who declared a party affiliation. There were 285 SRs and 248 Mensheviks. By and large, while Lenin and his party were well known to the political elite, they had little support among the masses. In July, as we have seen, they appeared to have undergone a great setback. From then until the Kornilov affair, Lenin was in exile in Finland (where he stayed until about 8/9 October) and Trotsky was in jail. The party was hampered by its illegal status. Nonetheless, there are, as we will see, indications that, even then, their support was growing.

One of Lenin's greatest strengths was his ability to see the underlying pattern of forces in important political conjunctures. He was not always correct, as his overreaction to the July 'suppression' shows, but his instincts were usually correct. From the early moments of the Kornilov affair in late August, Lenin became as passionately optimistic about what he saw as the rising revolutionary opportunity, as he had been pessimistic in early July. From his hiding place in Helsinki he began to write a series of letters and articles calling for an insurrection.

Lenin's campaign of September is quite extraordinary. His first salvo came in the form of a Letter to the Central Committee of 30 August. He did not call for a Bolshevik takeover but, surprisingly, for support for Kerensky to arrest Miliukov and Rodzianko, arm the people and support workers' control. This was no momentary response. In his next article, 'On Compromises', in itself an un-Lenin-like title, he said a Menshevik–SR coalition should take power without any Bolshevik participation. However, political events were moving fast and Lenin was one of the most flexible and penetrating analysts of the moment. Responding, in particular, to the growing support for the Bolsheviks in the soviets, he began to suggest something very different. While arguing that peaceful development of the revolution was possible, he also secretly tried to persuade his colleagues in the party leadership that, since the party now had the support of the majority in both the Moscow and Petrograd Soviets, 'The Bolsheviks ... can and must take state power into their own hands.' Lenin's colleagues, however, were not persuaded. Their slowness to respond unleashed a more characteristic torrent of invective from him. To say that an insurrection such as the one he was calling for was unMarxist was, he fulminated, a 'vicious distortion' and 'an opportunist lie'. His anger mounted further as he, confined impotently to his safe house in Helsinki, watched what he believed was a once-in-a-lifetime revolutionary opportunity slip away. On 29 September he denounced any delay in seizing power. Even to wait for the Congress of Soviets to assemble was '*utter idiocy, or sheer treachery*', a curious echo of Miliukov's dichotomy of treason or folly of the previous December. Lenin was so incensed by the inactivity of the Central Committee that he even tendered his resignation, an act that remained purely symbolic. Two days later, his stridency hit a new peak: 'procrastination is becoming positively *criminal*'. But even then, more than a month after his campaign had begun, nothing at all had been done. It was then that he made a fateful, if strangely delayed, decision. He would have to return to Petrograd. On 10 October, at long last, he confronted his colleagues directly. In an intense debate, conducted from early evening and through the night into the early hours of 11 October, the discussion raged. Inevitably, Lenin prevailed, but it was not a total victory. The decision arrived at was that armed insurrection should be put on the party's agenda. It was hardly the most ringing of endorsements but even so his opponents, led by the next two most senior members of the party after Lenin himself, Grigorii Zinoviev and Lev Kamenev, continued to oppose the Lenin steamroller. On their initiative, a new Central Committee meeting was called for 16 October, giving time for members outside Petrograd to join in, unlike the hastily convened meeting of the 10th. The meeting is notable for several key features, notably the continuation of deep opposition; Lenin obtaining a sizeable majority but not unanimity and the fact that, only nine days before the actual October revolution on 25 October, the party was squabbling rather than planning. No sign of military discipline or revolutionary blueprints can be found in the detailed documents we have of these tumultuous meetings. In many ways we have the reverse, because much of the meeting of 16 October was taken up with reports from key points in and around Petrograd and some from further afield. Asked to comment on the revolutionary readiness of their areas the delegates' reports gave a very mixed picture. Some areas were ready for action, some were not. A few were reported to be ready to respond to a Bolshevik call for action but others were only prepared to respond if the soviets made the call. There is no sign that the masses were straining at the leash (Bone 1974: 97–8. Account of Lenin's campaign adapted from Read 1996: 169–73).

Perhaps the lack of unequivocal evidence from the delegates emboldened Kamenev and Zinoviev to take their opposition to Lenin to unprecedented levels by openly publishing their objections in Gorky's newspaper *Novaia zhizn'*. The furious row in the party had, inevitably, been partially leaked to the Petrograd political class and, hence, to the press and to the authorities. But even so, Kamenev and Zinoviev's transgression was quite extraordinary. Their objections, reflecting the opinion of others within the party, was that the party was risking a repeat of the debacle of July. They were afraid that premature action would be catastrophic and provide a pretext for damaging action to be taken against them, once more. As it was, they argued, the situation was promising for the party. The Second All-Russian Congress of Soviets was about to convene and its members, who had already been elected around the country, seemed very favourable to the Bolsheviks' policies. The government was too weak to further delay the Constituent Assembly, elections to which were only three or so weeks away. The Bolsheviks, the two dissidents argued, were set fair to be the second largest group with some 25 per cent of the vote. Why risk all this on a political adventure of uncertain outcome? (Bone 1974: 122.)

Needless to say, Lenin reacted with fury to this betrayal by his senior lieutenants. They were summarily expelled from the party, an expulsion which, interestingly, remained as symbolic as Lenin's own resignation from the Central Committee less than three weeks earlier. However, the opening of the wound for all to see reminds us that we need to look beyond Lenin and his colleagues to explain why, by 25 October, the Provisional Government finally succumbed and, perhaps more surprisingly, the Bolsheviks were able to stand almost alone as the supposed embodiment of soviet power.

The decline of the Mensheviks and the SRs

Unwittingly, it was Kornilov who had provoked the moment of truth. His ill-planned and overconfident manoeuvre had brought all the underlying political tensions to the surface. Combined with the ever-deepening economic and social crises, he had precipitated the perfect storm and the perfect wave. The underlying, rapidly deepening polarisation of the country was brought into the open. It was no longer possible to balance between the two forces. Kornilov had torn compromise to shreds. Lenin had realised this at once. Many of his rivals failed to do so and doomed themselves to irrelevance.

This was especially obvious in the Moscow and Petrograd Soviets. In the early months of the revolution the Mensheviks had outdistanced the Bolsheviks by a comfortable margin. By the middle of the summer, however, the situation was changing fast. In the August elections to the Moscow City Duma, the previously dominant Mensheviks were reduced to a rump of only 4 per cent, while the hitherto marginalised and technically suppressed Bolsheviks attained 33 per cent of the vote, a rise of 14 per cent. The fundamental changes in Russian politics were not related to overall swings of opinion from left to right or vice versa. Rather they were regroupings on the left and right. The beneficiaries were, on the left, the Bolsheviks, who mopped up the disaffected Menshevik voters and, on the right, the Kadets who became the prime focus of the old elites, largely because they were the most organised and professional party outside the left. Even so, Kadet dominance only corresponded to some 10 per cent of the vote. The SRs started the year as the largest party and continued to hold that position throughout, though they did lose some support. Their situation was complicated by a serious split, resulting in the Left SRs leaving the party and joining the Bolsheviks in a post-October coalition.

The processes bringing about this reconfiguration on the left are not hard to recognise. The overwhelming problem for the Menshevik and SR leaders was that their position in the Provisional Government was causing them to lose support. While they were committed by their programmes and traditions to radical policies of land redistribution, improving workers' rights and standard of living and to the rapid convening of a constituent assembly, once in power they were forced to put off decisive action in these areas. By autumn, when land seizures began to peak, so did armed intervention by the authorities, usually on the initiative of the provincial governor. Many of these new governors were SRs so the peasants were puzzled by having troops sent against them by their own party. Workers, too, began to find that Menshevik leaders were only bringing bad news. In a major example, the government decided to cut the bloated workforce of the Putilov factory by about a third, aiming to reduce it from about 30,000 employees to about 20,000. This time it was workers who were puzzled by having Menshevik commissars telling 10,000 women and men they would lose their jobs.

The Left SRs and the Bolsheviks reaped the benefit. From the beginning, in his momentous *April Theses*, Lenin had, immediately upon his return to Petrograd some five weeks after the February Revolution, declared no support for the Provisional Government. This gave the Bolsheviks in general and Lenin in particular, what the diarist N.N. Sukhanov called a 'wild card' position – that is they could represent anything. They did not have the responsibility of carrying any of their policies out. In fact, once the Bolsheviks came to power and lost this status, their popularity followed the same declining trajectory as the Mensheviks who, after they were expelled from power, saw a rise in their popularity in the first year of Soviet rule. The Bolsheviks, however, were prepared to intervene ruthlessly to maintain themselves in power. In summer 1917, the Mensheviks were not. Instead, the Menshevik and SR caucus showed weakness and ineptitude, though they would say that they kept their honour. Their loss of power in the Petrograd Soviet is a microcosm of their national decline and, in the Menshevik case, eclipse. Bolshevik influence in the Soviet had begun to grow, ironically after the July failure. By identifying them as the most active supporters of revolution in July, the Provisional Government attack on the Bolsheviks made them appear to be martyrs and started their dramatic rise. The Kornilov affair lit the booster rockets.

On behalf of the Bolsheviks, Kamenev proposed a resolution which emerged in the Petrograd Soviet on 31 August in the midst of the Kornilov crisis. The resolution called for an immediate break with the property owners and the right; the proclamation by the Soviet of a democratic republic and transfer of landowner land to peasant committees. The Menshevik and SR leadership caucus refused, even at this extreme moment, to renounce their alliance with the right. Failing to see that this was a decisive moment of change, spokesmen like Tsereteli were forced to argue in public for support for landowners and the old elite just as these supposed allies appeared to be plotting to disband the left and the soviets. It was a crazy situation to get themselves into. Rather than change their line in the face of the inevitable, the caucus chose to sulk, and on 9 September, in a fit of pique, they resigned en masse after a moderate Bolshevik resolution, calling for the executive committee to be composed according to proportional representation, passed by a narrow margin. Fatefully, they left the field open to the Bolsheviks who delightedly took over. Trotsky resumed the post of Chair that he had briefly occupied in 1905. The Menshevik-SR caucus had lost a key power base with barely a whimper.

The end of the Kerensky moment and the implosion of the state

To his credit, Kerensky seemed more aware of the significance of the moment. Once he had ordered Kornilov's arrest Kerensky opened up the armouries to the Petrograd Soviet in order to defend the city. However, he did not gain much political credibility with the left, which considered it a forced and insincere conversion by someone who had, until that moment, been a close ally of Kornilov. However, Kerensky's problem was compounded by the fact that his swing to the left also lost him support on the right. As we have already seen, Kerensky was a lame duck premier. The government had lost almost all authority and for the last six weeks or so of its existence there was a growing power vacuum. Even the army and the navy were rapidly losing cohesion at the national level. Lenin's perfect wave was peaking.

Ironically, it was action by Kerensky and various scattered forces loyal to the Provisional Government which undermined themselves and probably set the final crisis in motion (Daniels 1968; Mel'gunov 1972).

In the weeks after the halting of Kornilov's troops, Kerensky appears not to have realised just how isolated he was. The government continued to meet as usual, and was still supported by the Menshevik–SR caucus which, despite the reverses in key soviets, still represented the largest number of voters in the country as a whole. It has also been plausibly suggested that Kerenky's military adjutants, some of whom now secretly hated him for undermining their hero Kornilov, were falsely underreporting his isolation. In fact, they seem to have been giving him false reassurances that the army was still loyal and, with obvious exceptions like the Petrograd garrison, still responsive to his command (Mel'gunov 1972). In the light of this woefully inaccurate information, Kerensky believed he could try to revive his centrist and defencist policies. Had he realised the true situation and responded to it by abandoning the right, the outcome of 1917 might have been different. However, every day Kerensky continued in this wrong direction was a day nearer to the disorderly collapse of his government.

Despite having turned to the Petrograd Soviet in order to save his bacon in early September, the alliance remained fitful, not least because the leftward swing of the Petrograd Soviet itself weakened his Menshevik–SR allies and strengthened his Bolshevik enemies. Control of the Soviet, even its dispersal, and a renewed ban on the Bolsheviks rose to the forefront of his agenda. Ironically, rebellion by his right wing was leading to him taking action against the left. For him, as for the Bolsheviks themselves, the timing of political action revolved around the convening of the Second All-Russian Congress of Soviets.

As the name suggests, it was the national convention of representatives and delegates of soviets all around the country. That made it the most widely elected body in Russia at the time and, though participation was only open to those affiliated to soviets, that was, in theory, some 80 per cent to 90 per cent of the population. In a world of fragile political mandates, there was a danger that the Congress could claim a greater political legitimacy than the unelected Provisional Government itself, whose right to rule emerged from a highly tenuous connection with the undemocratic Fourth Duma. Though evidence remains unclear, it seems that Kerensky eventually decided to prevent the Congress from meeting. In any case, although voting for it had been running for several weeks and delegates had been elected, the date of its opening was put back several times until, eventually, it was due to convene on 26 October. The date focused minds on left and right. Lenin was determined to act either to pre-empt it, according to some interpretations, or to coincide his actions with it, according to others. For his part, Kerensky wanted to take control of the city, and thereby the situation, before it convened. The increasingly open secret of a Bolshevik attempt at insurrection seemed, or so Kerensky thought, to play right into his hands. It would give him a pretext to arrest the Bolshevik leaders, disperse the party and prevent the Congress from convening. How would he do this? With the phantom loyal troops his adjutants assured him were available? Were they setting a trap for Kerensky or simply being sycophantic, as adjutants often are? No one knows for certain but, given the track record of political interventions by the military in these years, it seems more likely to assume incompetence rather than subtle plotting (Mel'gunov 1972).

In any case, the first moves in the October Revolution were made, not by the insurrectionists, but by the Provisional Government. On 24 October, troops loyal to the Provisional Government were ordered to occupy the Bolshevik printing press and to take up strategic positions in the city, notably the main railway stations, the telegraph and the vital bridges. It is a continuing peculiarity of Petrograd/St Petersburg that, in order to allow commercial barge traffic along the main branches of the River Neva, all the key bridges are drawbridges. This meant that, if they were raised, the city would be divided into subdivisions. Vasilevsky Island would be cut off; the Vyborg and Petrograd Sides (*Storona*) would be separated from the city centre, at least until the river fully froze over, which was usually in late November or December. This would break the unity of different militant areas of the city and hamper mass radical activity.

There was, however, a fatal flaw in Kerensky's actions: his manoeuvres depended on having reliable soldiers to carry them out. But the troops were not loyal. Faced with this government advance, the left began to organise to ensure the opposite of what the government intended. They responded in order to enable the Congress to meet. However, it was not the shambolic and ever-argumentative Bolshevik Central Committee that took the lead. Nor was it Lenin. Incredibly, his attendances at the Central Committee were his only public appearances. Although he was in Petrograd he remained in hiding in a safe house and took no direct part in events. Nor was he exercising much control from his hideout. Instead, it was the Petrograd Soviet that took the lead, and the instrument by which it acted was its Military Revolutionary Committee (MRC).

The MRC had several noteworthy features but two are particularly important for us to take in to account. First, it had been set up to defend the city, but not against its own government. Since the fall of Riga on 21 August, rumours had been circulating that the Provisional Government was planning to abandon Petrograd. This seemed, indeed was, rather far-fetched, but in theory it might have made sense to a desperate government. In particular, if it left the revolutionary city it would no longer be a hostage to the most radical of the soviets. If it moved to Moscow it would find a local political situation that was much more balanced, with the centre and the right retaining considerable influence. However, a government cannot simply catch the next train out. Its papers, its entourage, its communications and so on would all have to be prepared. That could not be done secretly, so as soon as word spread that such preparations were under way, the left could take countermeasures, ordering groups of workers and soldiers to pre-empt such actions. Their trump card was the railwaymen who, as they had with the tsar and Kornilov, could hamper all travel in and out of the city. All this was obvious to the government and, though it might see the wisdom of escape, there was no way it could reasonably be pulled off. In any case, abandoning the city and possibly allowing the Germans to take it, was a massive risk. However, the rumour persisted and helped the left take counter-measures, of which setting up the MRC was the most important. Its role was to defend the city in the event of desertion by the government. To that end, it began to co-ordinate the activity of radical military units and civilian activists like the disparate bands of Red Guards that had sprung up as an armed workers militia. Their regular tasks had comprised defending factories from thieves and, ironically, from employers bent on asset-stripping, and protecting residential areas from vagrants, burglars, armed deserters and other components of the criminal underclass who were taking full personal advantage of the power vacuum.

The MRC was headed by a rotating body of leading figures in the Soviet. This is its second characteristic – it was very much a Soviet institution, not an instrument of any one party. Its history has been somewhat veiled by exaggerations in Trotsky's account. He placed himself at its head and, after 25 October, claimed its main aim had always been to lead an insurrection. Like most effective propaganda, Trotsky's assertions are half-truths. He was head, but one among several and not the permanent chief. Its purpose may have been wider than simply defence against the remote possibility of a German attack, but it clearly was not pursuing a proactive insurrectionist strategy before 24 October.

Nonetheless, on the night of 22 October, the MRC sent a delega-
tion to the headquarters of the Petrograd Military District, situated
near the Winter Palace. It demanded that all orders be submitted
to the MRC for countersignature. Not surprisingly, the commander,
Colonel Polkovnikov, refused. In retaliation, the Petrograd Soviet sent
telegrams to all units stating that 'any orders to the garrison which
are not signed by the Military Revolutionary Committee are invalid'
(Browder and Kerensky 3: 1770). In fact, this was a near-repetition of
point 4 of Army Order No. 1, which had stipulated, in March, that only
orders that did not conflict with Soviet resolutions should be obeyed.
The real essence of the moment was, as usual, caught by Sukhanov.
The MRC's bold step was, he said, definitely an insurrectionary act
but an oddly isolated one whose significance was not fully recognised
by either side. 'War had been declared in unmistakeable terms, but
combat activities were not begun.' (Sukhanov 1962: vol. 2, 592.)

The October Revolution

However, once the Provisional Government had moved into action
the MRC was quick to react. Wherever the Provisional Government
sent its soldiers the Soviet and MRC sent its people out to oppose
them. The confrontations were more often verbal than armed. By
and large, it was not difficult for the Soviet forces to persuade the
government men and, sometimes women, not to risk their lives for
the decaying remnants of the government. Over the next few days,
reactivity was spurred on by the feebleness of the resistance it encountered and turned into proactivity. From initially defending the city, by
24 October the aim was to control it in order to allow the Congress
to convene, which it did.

Only on the night of 24/5 October did Lenin emerge, in a disguise,
consisting of a false beard which, once he had revealed himself at
his destination, was thoughtfully taken from him by his companion
Bonch-Bruevich who, mindful of the fragility of the moment, put
it away saying 'it may come in handy again one day, who knows?'
(Read 1996: 146). Lenin's arrival in the Smolny Institute, where the
Soviet was gathered, coincided with the turn to the most dramatic
piece of proactivity – the overthrow of the Provisional Government.
There is no evidence to definitively link Lenin personally with this
decisive step but there can be no doubt that in the discussions which
occurred, about which we have little hard information, Lenin's voice
would have been one of the loudest in favour of the bold move.

At 10:00 a.m. on the morning of 25 October a revolutionary proclamation was issued by the MRC: 'The Provisional Government has been deposed. State power has passed into the hands of the organ of the Petrograd Soviet of Workers' and Soldiers' Deputies, the Military Revolutionary Committee which heads the Petrograd proletariat and garrison.' It was, unequivocally, a Soviet revolution, not a party one. The Bolsheviks were a powerful component, but they were not the only one.

In itself, 25 October was rather undramatic. Events at the Smolny and elsewhere left much of the city untouched and unaware of the crucial nature of what had happened. There was little fighting. Even likely centres of resistance fell without an exchange of bullets. The most prominent example was the General Staff headquarters which was taken by simply swamping it with Soviet supporters. The much-vaunted 'storming of the Winter Palace' was almost an afterthought. Only after the proclamation of Soviet power had been made did anyone suggest arresting the members of the Provisional Government. The oversight meant that Kerensky was able to make his way out of the city in search of loyal troops. It was only on the evening of the 25th/26th that the Winter Palace was entered by Red Guards and revolutionary soldiers and the government ministers were arrested. They were marched over the river to the Peter Paul fortress but their detention was brief and they were soon released after promising to desist from further political activity. In Sukhanov's words:

> Two or three hours later the capital awoke – without realising who were now its rulers. From outside, the events had not been at all impressive. Except for the Palace Square, there had been order and calm everywhere. The *coup* had begun rather modestly and ended rather swiftly (Sukhanov 1962: 648)

By 27 October, Kerensky had returned with a detachment of troops, mainly Cossacks, who were able to take the tsar's summer residence at Tsarskoe selo on 28 October though the tsar and his family had been moved for protection to Tobolsk in western Siberia in August. However, another skirmish in the expanding civil war was conducted at Pulkovo, just outside the city. Although the Red Guards were ill-organised, they were able to defend the city alongside regular troops from the 1st Division of the Latvian Riflemen, led by I.I. Vacietis. Kerensky's troops were beaten back. Petrograd was secure, but it was only one city. What would happen at the front, in the national peripheries and in the rest of Russia and Siberia? No one knew.

Chapter 6: The First Civil War: October 1917–March/April 1918

The 'Triumphal March' of Soviet Power and Early Consolidation

It had been easy enough to proclaim Soviet power: there had been next to no resistance. The emerging problem was to spread control beyond Petrograd and to hang on to it, in other words, to extend Soviet power in time and space. The first steps had not resembled the mass march of the united proletariat depicted in later Soviet propaganda, but nor was it simply a coup, as portrayed by certain cold warriors. It had been somewhere between the two. There was, indeed, a swiftly exercised political coup but it was only possible given the massive and growing national support for Soviet power, a heightening movement of land seizures, growing weariness with the war and extensive economic desperation. Maintaining power would also require considerable mass support. A coup d'état, is, in its purest form, a change of personnel at the top of a political system, a state, which is seized by the coup plotters and taken over by them. By October, there was precious little state to seize. The first step was to find power lying in the street and to pick it up. Beyond that, however, multiple bitter struggles had to be conducted. The 'wild card' privileges of opposition had played a major role in bringing the Bolsheviks to power. Their supporters and allies favoured them in the first place because they were not part of the Menshevik–SR governing caucus. In the second place, the Bolsheviks had fully identified themselves with the popular programme of peace, bread, land and Soviet power. However, one should not make the mistake of thinking that the masses as a whole were marching to the Bolshevik tune. Only

118

minorities were actively involved. The Bolsheviks themselves were still relatively weak and unknown.

Bolshevism, the masses and October

An examination of Bolshevik strength, even in its heartland areas of the Baltic fleet, Petrograd garrison and northern and western fronts indicates that formal Bolshevik representation was not as strong as one might expect. Even impeccably Bolshevik sources of the period, such as the memoirs of F. Raskolnikov, a leading representative of the party among the soldiers and sailors of the Petrograd region, provide evidence to support this view. Ten days before the October revolution he found, on visits to Novgorod, Staraia Rus' and Luga, that the situation of the Bolshevik party was not uniformly favourable. There was much support for the Bolsheviks, he says, but little in the way of formal organisation. In Luga there were military units which supported the Bolsheviks, but insufficient party members for groups to have been formed (Raskolnikov 1982: 281). In Staraia Rus' the local soviet of 36 members had so few Bolsheviks there was not even an organised party fraction, though it had selected four Bolsheviks to represent it at the local Congress of Soviets which Raskolnikov had been sent to attend (Raskolnikov 1982: 271). In Novgorod there were only 176 party members, up from 102 ten days before his visit. Interestingly, of these, 150 were soldiers and only 26 were workers (Raskolnikov 1982: 272). Other pieces of information fit the same pattern. In mid-October, even after a 'rapid rise', the Bolshevik party organisation on the whole northern front only numbered 13,000 members, concentrated in the Fifth and Twelfth Armies and the 42nd Army Corps. 2000 of these party members were in the Fifth Army (Gaponenko 1968: 595). These numbers were not large considering there were over a million men serving on the northern front at this time. According to Frenkin, the Bolshevik military organisation in Petrograd numbered 500 members in March–April 1917, 1,800 in August and 5,800 in October, at which time there were 271,000 troops in the city and 467,000 in the area as a whole (Frenkin 1982: 203). In the Moscow region, there were 850,000 garrison troops. The Moscow Region Congress of Soviets, held in late-September and early October, comprised 390 delegates of whom 130 were Bolsheviks. A Bolshevik resolution urging the seizure of power by the Soviets received 45 per cent of the votes. The Bolsheviks were at their strongest in the soldiers' section, where the executive committee, based as was normal on proportional representation, was made

up of six SRs, six Bolsheviks and three Mensheviks. They were at their
weakest in the peasants' section, where the executive committee was
made up of 11 SRs and one Bolshevik (Raskolnikov 1982: 310). It is
worth noting that the disparity between Bolshevik support among
soldiers and among peasants is striking evidence that soldiers were
not just 'peasants in uniform' whose politics was limited to the land
issue, but had a distinct agenda of their own (Adapted from Read
1996: 159–60). Finally, an excellent recent study of Karelia has shown
that the important railway town of Petrozavodsk, a strong-point for
defending Petrograd from the north, was in Left SR hands until July
1918. The first town Bolshevik committee was only set up in February
1918 with 100 party members (Wright 2012: 35). Such stories could
be repeated across the entire country.

All this suggests that the undoubted movement towards Bolshevism
among the troops as well as among the wider population was transient. Clearly, Bolshevik numbers were far from overwhelming,
though we must not fall into the trap of underestimating them.
While the impression promulgated by John Reed and Eisenstein of
a united nation striding into the future behind its Bolshevik leaders
has to be confined to the realm of fairy tales, it is, nonetheless, the
case that in a situation of disorganisation the strongest is the one
who is least weak, and at crucial points up to 1921/2 the Bolsheviks
showed that they were the least weak. That said, we must also take
into account another crucial observation by Sukhanov. A second
feature of Bolshevism, he said, kept him from joining their ranks. As
a left-wing member of the executive of the Petrograd Soviet from Day
One he was a supporter of the same policies as those proclaimed by
the Bolsheviks, but, he said, the meaning of those slogans was different for the Bolsheviks. 'We were divided not so much by slogans as
by a profoundly different conception of their inner meaning. The
Bolsheviks reserved that meaning for the use of the leadership and
didn't carry it to the masses' (Sukhanov 1962: 524). They proclaimed
peace but knew the implication of their action was to promote civil
war. They stood for redistributing land to the peasants when their
own aim was to nationalise and collectivise it. For the moment they
supported workers' control but replaced it as soon as they could.
They knew that their action would further disrupt the economy but
proclaimed they would save the workers from economic disaster.
They proclaimed Soviet power and even support for the Constituent
Assembly but what they wanted was something different – Bolshevik
power. One could go further. Bolshevik aims were not just about the
popular movement's programme of peace, bread, land and soviet

power, they were about world revolution, the abolition of classes and the transformation of humanity. This second, but very real agenda, was almost unknown outside a small group of Bolshevik and associated leaders. These wider dreams began to emerge quite quickly after October, but first there were formidable practical obstacles to be negotiated. The first was the Second Congress of Soviets, and it was here that the ambiguity of Bolshevism, to the point of duplicity, began to become apparent.

A survey of delegates to the Second Congress produced cut and dried figures which have been accepted by historians of all persuasions. The composition of the congress, it is confidently asserted, was that 670 delegates representing 400 soviets turned up. 390 declared themselves to be Bolshevik supporters, 160 SRs (of whom 100 were Left SRs), 72 Mensheviks and 14 Menshevik Internationalists. However, we have to clarify what these convenient labels actually meant. Obviously, there had been a 'swing to Bolshevism' in the final weeks before October. Why? As we have seen, disillusion was driving people away from the Menshevik-SR 'right'; Sukhanov called it 'the crisis of Menshevism' (Sukhanov 1962: 524). There was nowhere much else to go but to the Bolsheviks, who were ardently proclaiming the popular programme of peace, bread, land and all power to the soviets. It is perfectly justifiable to infer that the Bolsheviks were seen by their new followers as an instrument to realise the popular programme. The newly minted Bolsheviks knew little and cared less about world revolution and the transformation of humanity. What mattered to them was Soviet power and the popular programme, and here we enter a definitional loop. The Bolsheviks identified with Soviet power so most of those who identified with Soviet power considered themselves Bolsheviks. However, 505 delegates, of many party affiliations, had arrived at the congress already mandated to support 'all power to the soviets'; a further 107 wanted a popular government without participation of the bourgeoisie; only 55 supported the Provisional Government line of cross-class alliance (Rabinowitch 1976: 292).

This interpretation is strengthened when one of the fundamental developments of Russian left-wing politics is taken into account. By October, divisions within the Soviet camp were not about divisions between parties but within them. The relatively clear divisions of February and March had been replaced. Very quickly, the issue of 'defencism' (that is, fighting the war in order to 'defend' the February revolution) versus 'internationalism' (that is attempting to rally radical anti-war groups around Europe to force an end to war and, perhaps, convert it into revolution) began to spill over party boundaries.

As the year progressed other issues adhered to this original distinction, mainly the revolutionary agenda of the masses. At the same time, the balance of power shifted from 'defencists' towards 'internationalists'. The tensions created clear splits in the Menshevik and SR parties. A small group of Menshevik Internationalists, led by Lenin's pre-1903 friend and ally, Iulii Martov, and N.N. Sukhanov, stood up for the radical programme. A larger split in the SR party produced an increasingly separate Left SR party which supported the traditional party policy of redistributing land to the peasants without compensation. In the interests of national unity in wartime and their continued participation in the Provisional Government, the SR right put this vital question on hold and watched their support haemorrhage away. Thus, in October, divisions were more about policies than parties. On one hand, there was the Provisional Government bundle of policies – defend Russia; conduct a measured land reform at some future date; postpone the Constituent Assembly. On the other, the Soviet bundle – peace, bread, land, all power to the soviets.

This was the main fracture line of Russian national politics in October. It was one of the most fundamental and characteristic features of the Russian Revolution. The masses had a programme which included all power to the soviets as one of its main elements, and the programme took precedence over parties. Parties only received support insofar as they adhered to the popular programme. The popular movement had not been converted to Bolshevism. They mainly supported the Bolsheviks because the Bolsheviks claimed they would implement the popular programme, and in many respects they did. A soviet-based government was set up, peasants were encouraged to seize land, and workers increasingly took over factories.

The problem arose, however, because the masses took such steps to be the core of the actual revolution. For the Bolsheviks, they were only a first step. They had a deeper agenda which, they believed, was in the longer-term interests of the workers and poorer peasants. However, at some point they would have to move from the common ground on which October was based, to the more ideological objectives of Lenin and the party leaders. They would have to embark on their aim of constructing socialism as they saw it. At this point they would begin to diverge from the popular programme. Lenin was confident he could persuade the masses to follow, but was he correct? In a sense, the whole history of Soviet Russia and the Soviet Union was a working out of this central belief. All the leadership, repression, experiments, failures, successes were part of the task of building the socialist project and selling it to the masses (Read 2001). While Lenin had made the surprising but crucial statement in his *April Theses* that 'it is not our *immediate* task to *introduce* socialism' it was, nonetheless, his belief that preliminary steps should be made.

The moves began early on, and every one of them took the party away from the popular programme of 1917. Sukhanov was exactly right: the Bolshevik 'inner' meaning of the mass slogans they adopted would soon become apparent. At first, the Bolsheviks were unable to do anything but watch the peasants take the land, but in other key areas the differences soon began to emerge into the light. The first fully-fledged Soviet Government was a coalition between the Bolsheviks and the Left SRs but was not the all-party coalition hoped for by the masses and the majority of delegates to the Second Congress. By spring 1918, workers' control was in retreat and former managers were being encouraged to return to industry with offers of high pay and strong disciplinary powers. Independent militias like the Red Guards were being either disbanded or absorbed into conventionally-structured, centrally-controlled institutions such as the Red Army and the Cheka, the first Soviet secret police force. The channels of democratic activity in 1917 – factory, army and navy committees, trade unions, even soviets and political parties – were being closed down by force or transformed into regime-supporting shadows of their original, vibrant selves. In the countryside peasants were, for a while, beyond the reach of the new authorities, and early efforts to assert control failed. It was only 12 years after October that the full force of the Bolshevik revolution reached the villages and replaced the last vestiges of the popular programme by taking the land back from the direct control of the peasantry. There were many factors behind these processes and many possible forms they could have taken. The 'Stalinist' version was not inevitable. However, much of the rest of the present analysis is geared to examining how these processes evolved.

The first signs of difference between Bolshevik objectives and those of the masses became apparent very early on. In the Second Congress Lenin began by apparently playing to the scenario of support for the popular programme. He presented two major decrees, a Decree on Peace and a Decree on Land. The former called upon the working masses of all warring nations to join together across national boundaries and attack their murderous, imperialist governments instead of fighting each other on behalf of their rulers. It was powerful local propaganda and a clear statement of intent, but it had no international significance. The Land Decree supported immediate handover of land to peasant committees, an unstoppable process which was already well under way. Not surprisingly, hecklers shouted that it was SR policy. In his riposte, Lenin said 'What does it matter who drafted them! As a democratic government we cannot ignore the resolutions of the lower strata of the people, even though we may not be in sympathy with them. Life is the best teacher; it will show us who is right.' (Bunyan and Fisher 1934: 132.) However, the real objection, that this was directly contradictory to Bolshevik policy, went by almost unnoticed as did Lenin's admission, in those few words, that implementation of real Bolshevik policies lay in the future, once 'life' had persuaded the peasants that Bolshevik policies were correct. It was only in 1929, when Stalin undertook the collectivisation of agriculture, that this 'anomaly' was rectified. Lenin also supported the convening of the Constituent Assembly, as did the rest of the left. It is difficult to reconcile this with the proclamation of Soviet power except to judge, as many did at the time, that Soviet power was only a temporary expedient until the Constituent Assembly could come up with a permanent form of democratic government.

Having set out his stall in this enticing and deceptive fashion, it is not surprising that allies came over to mask the nakedness of Bolshevik power. Martov and the Menshevik Internationalists expressed disbelief at Lenin's apparent conversions and denounced his acts as being insincere. Fatefully, Martov and company walked out of the Congress in protest, thereby provoking Trotsky's remark that they were removing themselves to the 'dustbin of history'. However, the Left SRs were less fastidious. They joined the Bolsheviks and, when the congress came to vote for the bodies to exercise its authority after its dispersal, 29 Left SRs were elected to the Soviet Executive Committee alongside 61 Bolsheviks and 20 from a variety of smaller groups. For the moment they stayed out of the first Soviet government, known as Sovnarkom, the Russian acronym for Council of People's Commissars, that was formed at the Second Congress. Lenin chaired both Sovnarkom and the Soviet Executive Committee. Trotsky became Commissar for Foreign Affairs; Stalin was appointed Commissar for Nationalities. Ironically, it initially called itself the Provisional Workers' and Peasants' Government, echoing the less than dynamic name of its predecessor.

The formation of the Soviet government – birth pangs

The new authorities had plenty of problems confronting them. In the first place, power had to be spread beyond the city and be consolidated against counter-revolution. The war was continuing. What could be done about that? Would the rural disruption threaten next year's food supply? Could the downward economic spiral be controlled? Could the Bolsheviks' broader agenda of world revolution and human transformation be realised?

The priority, of course, was to stay in power, because without that nothing else could be done. The first difficulty in Petrograd was that the first Sovnarkom was completely Bolshevik and this caused a reaction. The popular forces behind October had wanted Soviet power, not Bolshevik power. Many were disappointed, even shocked, at the emergence of a purely Bolshevik government when a Soviet all-party coalition was what seems to have been widely expected. This provoked the Bolsheviks' first crisis. Their chief opponents were not the political remnants of the former ruling group – now a completely ineffective 'Committee for the Regeneration of Russia', whose figurehead was the veteran revolutionary, 'father of Russian Marxism' and one-time idol of Lenin, Georgii Plekhanov – but the Menshevik-led railway union, Vikzhel. The response to the crisis spoke volumes about the Soviet future. The Bolshevik leaders fought back in two ways that were to become a common feature of communist politics in and beyond Russia. They circumvented Vikzhel by claiming it was out of date and had lost its mandate, forcibly dissolving its legitimately elected leadership and creating a new, Bolshevik-dominated union called Vikzheldor. The political side was dealt with equally ruthlessly. Because of Bolshevik weakness, Lenin was prepared to negotiate with others about forming a coalition government. He appears to have only been interested in buying time, but others in the Central Committee and its associates took the issue seriously. They believed a coalition would be more stable and more healthy for Russian democracy. When the negotiations broke down Lenin turned on dissident Bolsheviks with fury, accusing them of undermining the revolution and siding with the counter-revolution.

On November 4th – ten days after the October revolution and, therefore, the tenth of the days that shook the world – the following protest against the Bolsheviks was published:

> It is our view that a socialist government must be formed from all parties in the soviet ... We believe that, apart from this, there is only one other path: the retention of a purely Bolshevik government by means of political terror.

The leadership would become cut off from the masses and the outcome would be 'the establishment of an unaccountable regime and the destruction of the revolution and the country.' The signatories to these prophetic words were not Mensheviks or SRs. Astonishingly they included Kamenev, Zinoviev, Rykov and Larin, four of the most senior figures in the Bolshevik party after Lenin himself.

Ominous signs had already begun to appear. Within days of coming to power the Bolsheviks decreed the closure of newspapers of the centre and right. Within weeks, those of the left were also being shut down. Far from his mock magnanimity of September, Trotsky fully confirmed Sukhanov's fears of the concealed message within Bolshevik slogans. On 4 November, he explained that they had demanded freedom of the press at a time when 'we could demand only a minimum programme, but now we ask for a maximum' which, in this case, meant controlling the press. What other U-turns were in store in the transition from minimum to maximum?

The Central Committee's response to the dissidents within its ranks was itself unpromising. They were accused of 'totally disregarding all the fundamental tenets of Bolshevism', 'repeating deeply unMarxist phrases about a socialist revolution being impossible in Russia' and of having 'a state of mind which reflects the exhausted (not the revolutionary) section of the population'. The minority was accused of hampering revolutionary work, 'criminal vacillations', 'disruptive activity' and 'sabotage'. While the word 'wrecking' had not yet been invented, the full panoply of 'Stalinist' accusations was thrown at them. Some of the protestors resigned from the party in disgust. (Bone 1974: 136–40; adapted from Read 1996: 199–200.)

Meanwhile, the explosion in Petrograd was producing echoes throughout the empire. Soviet power began to spread. It had, of course, been established in a few places, notably Kronstadt, before Petrograd but it was events in the capital which caused what one might call a domino effect, maybe one of the few times in history where such a process has actually taken place. In the first phase, rather like Yefremov in February, it only took a message to kick off a local revolution. In innumerable places around the country, local and regional soviets proclaimed their power. In many places the proclamation was more or less unopposed; in many other cases it was purely formal as there were fierce struggles to implement it. In Moscow, for example, where army officers and centre and right wing politicians were prepared to resist the Moscow Soviet, there was six days of bitter fighting and heavy casualties. Reports suggested there were 700 dead. In a third group of places the old authorities were not challenged. There, soviets were too weak or non-existent to act, and the local council, the Duma, took power, often backed by local military leaders. Associated with this last group were numerous areas on the periphery where nationalists proclaimed independence. Within weeks, the Russian Empire had imploded. Finnish independence was quickly recognised by the new Soviet government. Over the next few months Poland, Estonia, Latvia, Lithuania, Ukraine, Georgia, Armenia, the Transcaucasus, Turkmenia, Kazakhstan, Tadzhikistan, Uzbekistan and numerous autonomous regions in Siberia and the Far East had loosened or even shaken off central control. The result was that a political patchwork quilt had been formed which was never completely replaced. Over the next four years or so the colours on the quilt changed but never reverted to a single colour. At the peak of the conflict in 1919 at least 23 groups claimed to be governments of all or part of the former Russian Empire and the central Soviet Government controlled only some 10 per cent of the territory of the pre-war Empire. Even with the formation of the Soviet Union on 31 December 1922, major territories, Poland, Finland and the Baltic States, remained independent, and parts, like Kars in the Caucasus, were under foreign rule, in this case Turkish. Politically, the next four years were marked by confusion and conflict between and within these areas. The chaos was only slightly mitigated by the fact that the core population in European Russia comprised some 50 per cent of the total of the former Empire and was largely under Soviet authority throughout.

In effect, most of these territories quickly escaped the jurisdiction of Petrograd. But even within the Soviet-controlled area the process of spreading the revolution was fitful and uneven. It did not progress smoothly from point to point: pro- or anti- revolutionary forces sprang up in each locality. In November (NS dates) Minsk, in Belarus, Novgorod, near Petrograd, and Ivanovo-Voznesensk declared Soviet power on the same day as Petrograd (7 November). The following day (8 November) there were declarations in widely scattered cities: Ufa in western Siberia, Kazan on the middle Volga, Reval (today Tallinn) on the Baltic Coast of Estonia and Ekaterinburg in the Urals. Moscow did not become Soviet until 15 November, a week after Petrograd. Only on 1 December did Mogilev, headquarters of the army, declare itself Soviet. So it went on. Petrozavodsk had Soviet power on 17 January 1918, but it didn't have Bolshevik power until July. Helsinki was Soviet on 28 January 1918, Odessa, on the Black Sea, on 31 January. Among the last places where Bolshevik–Soviet power was installed in this first wave, were Kiev, capital of Ukraine, and Vologda, in the Russian north, both on 8 February and, finally, Archangel in the far north, on the White Sea, on 17 February and Novocherkassk, in the far south, on 25 February. The list covers a period of four months. The combinations are complex and the 'triumphal march' random and fitful in that each locality responded in its own way to the events at the centre. Each one had its own story to tell. In some cases the proclamation remained of limited significance for some time. Soviet power was declared in the city of Viatka on 8 December but only in spring 1918 did it spread to the remainder of the province. Not all of them remained Soviet for long. Helsinki and Kiev, to name but two, soon fell to right-wing nationalists. Of course, many cities that eventually ended up in the USSR were absent from this list – Irkutsk, Vladivostok, Erevan, Tbilisi, to name but a few – because they were not brought within the Soviet orbit for several years. The fall of Novocherkassk to Soviet forces on 25 February, was considered especially significant because it meant the collapse of a White stronghold and what contemporaries thought was the nominal end of the 'civil war'. In fact, the full scale civil war had not begun but the period from Kornilov to the fall of Novocherkassk marked a smaller but still important first civil war.

The First Transition Strategy

Clearly, throughout at least the first six months, Soviet power was balanced on a knife-edge. No one at the time was confident that it would last. In addition to its internal enemies it also had its external enemies – Germany, Austria-Hungary and Turkey – eager to rip it apart. A first point of celebration came after two months when the new government surpassed the life-span of the Paris Commune. The example of the Paris Commune was very much in the minds of Bolshevik leaders, and it was under that early influence that the first Bolshevik 'state' was called the *Severnaia kommuna*, the Northern Commune. On 8 March 1918 the party changed its name to the Communist Party, in honour of their predecessors as well as of Marx and Engels' *Communist Manifesto*, which they claimed to be putting into practice.

Lenin was well aware of the precariousness of his position. In part, at least, he argued that what they were engaged in was a holding operation to maintain Soviet power until the explosion of revolution in Germany. In particular, it led him to engage in a policy of peace at any price with Germany. Immediately after October the German and allied armies had been delighted to sit back and watch as their enemy imploded. By December, a truce had been agreed and negotiations begun. Germany wanted a quick resolution to enable it to plunder the food resources of Ukraine and South Russia, thereby breaking the increasingly painful allied blockade, and have sufficient security to move the bulk of its troops, who were desperately needed on the western front as the impact of the United States' entry into the war began to be felt. However, as the draconian terms the Germans wished to impose became known, Trotsky, the leading Soviet nego-tiator in his role as foreign minister, was rightly fearful of a terrible backlash against the Soviet Government if it agreed. He attempted to stall negotiations as much as possible, to kick the leaves around until they disappeared in the hoped-for wind of the world revolution. The Germans quickly saw through his 'neither war nor peace' stance and presented an ultimatum – sign or we attack. They did advance and showed that Russia was completely indefensible, not least because Lenin had urged the soldiers to go home after October and take their weapons with them. He had done this to ensure the old officer core could not regain control over the rank and file and to have an armed revolutionary force scattered throughout the country. The crucial side effect, of course, was that it meant there was no chance of defending Russia in the face of its external enemies. Trotsky contin-ued to refuse to sign the proposed treaty but Lenin was in favour. He had two arguments one powerful and one speculative. The former was that there was no choice; the latter that the agreement would be temporary because the other party, the German Imperial State, would soon collapse. It did. Lenin was vindicated, but he was also lucky. He had not known the German Empire was doomed but he was prepared to pay any price to hold out as long as possible.

His writings of these crucial weeks and months show this clearly. In a riposte to a group of his critics within the party, he said frankly: 'we lack strength we must retreat (before Western and Eastern imperial-ism) even as far as the Urals, for in this lies the *only* chance of playing for time while the revolution in the West matures' (Lenin 1960–70: vol. 27, 326). It was considerations of this kind which led him to agree to the Treaty of Brest-Litovsk, one of the most devastating treaties of the modern era and one which, in itself, should be sufficient to show that, far from being badly treated at Versailles, Germany was handled less harshly than it had treated its defeated opponent. According to the terms of the treaty Russia lost 32 per cent of its arable land; 26 per cent of its railways; 33 per cent of its factories; 75 per cent of its iron and coal mines and 62 million citizens. To add insult to injury it also had to pay a gold indemnity.

Not surprisingly, the publication of the terms caused widespread dismay. The paradox of the desire for peace had shown itself again.

While no one was keen to fight, no one wanted national humiliation and defeat. The Soviet Government had to face a serious backlash from the right and the left. One of the most eloquent denunciations came from armaments and metal workers in Petrograd, initially the hard-core supporters of Bolshevism. While they had a vested interest, in that peace meant unemployment for many of them, their resolution still made key points:

> Four months have now passed and we have seen our faith cruelly shattered and our hopes rudely trampled. ... The new regime calls itself Soviet ... however, the most important matters ... are decided without the participation of the Soviets ... They promised us peace ... in fact they have given us a shameful capitulation to German imperialists ... They promised us bread. In fact they have given us a famine of unparalleled dimensions ... They promised us freedoms ... All have been trampled by the heel of police boots and crushed by force of arms.

The meeting demanded the dismissal of Sovnarkom and re-convening of the Constituent Assembly (Bernshtam 1981: 87–90).

Indeed, a turn away from the Bolsheviks was visible in many areas. One historian has posited a Menshevik 'comeback' (Brovkin 1987). In early 1918, those who had moved from the SRs and Mensheviks to support Bolshevism and Soviet power were moving back, for the same reason they had moved to the Bolsheviks in the first place – to defend Soviet power but this time against the Bolsheviks. Of course, the political constraints were changing. At one level, internal dissent only aided the common enemy, consisting of the old ruling class, so many opponents of the Bolsheviks were reluctant to push their disagreement too far. If they did, the newly-formed secret police, the Cheka, were waiting. Set up in December 1917 as the Special Commission to Combat Sabotage and Counter-revolution, it embodied the twin edges of growing Soviet/Bolshevik power. At one level it was a necessary instrument to defend the revolution from ruthless and determined enemies, a swift and just arm of retribution. At another, it risked becoming simply a hit squad for the political leadership, crushing all opposition, illegitimate or otherwise.

But it was not only counter-revolutionaries who objected to the treaty. Lenin had to face the emergence of the first post-October oppositional faction within the party, the referred to as Left Communists. They did not object to the treaty on grounds of national humiliation: as internationalists they cared nothing for that. Their objection was that it was a surrender in the struggle for world revolution. They believed party policy was clear. The task of the party was to struggle for revolution at all costs. That did not mean sitting back but pushing on into revolutionary war, carrying the fight by political as well as armed means to Germany itself, proclaiming insurrection and setting up the class war, the Europe-wide civil war that Lenin himself had called for as early as September 1914.

This was not their only source of complaint. They also accused Lenin of easing up on revolutionary transformation in many other areas. The party, they objected, was abandoning socialism and constructing what they called 'state capitalism'. To understand the significance of this aspect of the crisis, we need to examine what policies of economic, social and political transformation the leadership had been pursuing in these early months.

For a socialist, or, for that matter, almost every kind of mobilising politician, power is not an end in itself but a necessary means so that some kind of transition can be effected. For a socialist, transition is crucial, but complex and fraught with difficulties and contradictions, so much so that, critics would argue, it is impossible to implement. The problem of transition is that, while one might have a very profound critique of the current situation and a more or less clear idea of the goal ahead, how do the two relate? How does one get from one to the other? What is the first step, the second step and so on? Lenin and other party leaders had not spent much time on issues of transition. Given the unlikelihood, until only weeks before it happened, of the Bolsheviks coming to power, issues of transition were not a priority. Nonetheless, any socialist needed a plan of some kind. Lenin's revolutionary strategy was not very systematic in this period. We have to look through a wide range of his writings and pick out significant nuggets of information and analysis to ascertain his views on this question. There are four major elements. These are brief comments from the early stages of the First World War; the *April Theses*, proclaimed on his return to Russia in 1917; the unfinished and unpublished pamphlet *State and Revolution* which he wrote while in his safe house in Helsinki and, finally, aspects of his campaign for insurrection of September and October 1917. For our purposes, the second and last of these are the most important.

Lenin, like any true Marxist, was an internationalist in the sense that nations were bourgeois fictions to hide true social divisions which arose from class. In conditions of modern capitalism, workers shared the same interests no matter what country they resided in. Such a belief had been an axiom of the labour movement of the late nineteenth century and the principle behind the founding of the

First and Second Socialist Internationals. That is why it was such a rude shock that, when put to the test as war approached, internationalism evaporated and the leaders of the largest socialist parties opted to support the war efforts of their national governments. Lenin was one of a small minority who remained faithful to the old principles. It was this that led him into an extraordinary argument which he put forward in September 1914. The imperialist war was, indeed, going to be a humanitarian disaster but it should also be seen as a revolutionary opportunity. Why? Because it would cause the masses to realise they were risking their lives in an alien cause, that of the capitalists. The correct policy for a socialist, Lenin argued, was to encourage 'the transformation of the present imperialist war into a civil war' (Lenin 1967: vol. 1, 663; Read 2005: 114). In other words, the struggle between nations would and should evolve into a war of classes. This remained fundamental to Lenin's outlook right up to spring 1918 and beyond.

In the second of the crucial writings we have identified, the brief but endlessly stimulating and extraordinary *April Theses*, the implications of which are vast and often unexpected, Lenin set out the principles which guided him in 1917. His assumption of the 'wild card' position which was so important in bringing him to power, was made explicit in his injunction that there should be 'no support for the Provisional Government.' Other clauses show that, for the moment, there should not be outright opposition to it either. But as well as political instructions large and small (the latter exemplified by his recommendation that the party should change its name) there was an implicit plan of transition. It was not, Lenin told his astounded listeners, possible to introduce socialism immediately. To start with, one should content oneself with Soviet supervision of production and distribution. One can only conclude that this meant a form of supervised capitalism under the old owners and within the framework of the market as the first step forward. Indeed, Lenin only called for limited expropriation of capitalists in the form of nationalisation of the banks. Later, in the year he extended this to include certain key industries, but the fundamental point remained. Socialism could not be '*introduced*', by which Lenin meant it had to grow organically out of the existing soil (Read 2005: 146–50).

Although it was unknown at this time (it was published in January 1918) and unfinished, *State and Revolution* contains reflections on these themes. The assumption behind Lenin's notion of transition was spelled out. Modern economies were run by routine, bureaucratic processes within the compass of any competently educated individual. In other words, managers ran the world. Lenin believed that the emergence of 'organised capitalism', which controlled the wild forces of markets and competition through monopolies and cartels, meant the beast could be beheaded relatively simply and its surviving body, the bureaucratic mechanisms, be set to work in a new and eventually socialist direction. In an amazing phrase, Lenin argued that running a modern economy was as routine an operation as running the German Post Office (Lenin 1967: vol. 2, 304; Read 2005: 166–172). He was also impressed by state leadership, as he saw it, of the German war economy in a form of state capitalism.

It is only with considerations such as this in mind that one can make any sense of some of Lenin's comments in his campaign for insurrection. He claimed that, contrary to critics who argued that a new round of revolutionary upheaval would add to the chaos, only a seizure of power by the soviets would save the country from crisis and ensure a transition that would be 'gradual, peaceful and smooth' (Lenin 1960–70: vol. 25, 73; Read 2005: 177). There were, he said, 'ample resources, material and spiritual' to conduct the war, they only needed to be properly organised. This would be accomplished by workers and peasants themselves who 'would soon learn' to produce and distribute goods. (ibid) Lenin was either being very ingenuous or very deceptive.

In any event, the first months of the Soviet Government smashed such simple and optimistic expectations. At every level the assumptions came unstuck. The capitalists and their associates refused to play their allotted roles. A whole range of opponents, including owners, managers, civil servants, office workers and clerks, either actively resisted the construction of the new order or refused to recognise the legitimacy of the new commissars. Senior staff at important institutions like ministries and banks resisted the Soviet Government. So desperate was the situation that Lenin eventually began to accept the need to pay higher salaries, many times greater than that of workers, to any managers, engineers, accountants and the like, re-christened 'specialists' (*spetsy*, from the Russian abbreviation) who would stay in post.

The net result was simply that the economy and the banking system, representing the lifeblood of the economy and of government spending, descended into an ever-deeper downward spiral. The new government was pushed into ever-greater acceleration in printing money to pay its way. Its predecessors had done the same but the Bolsheviks eventually raised it to a whole new level, leading, inevitably, to the hyperinflation which began in 1918. Naturally this had massively corrosive economic effects, eventually pushing Russia back into an age of barter. If finance and money circulation was one crucial network on which civilised urban life depended, the railway system was the other. That, too, was imploding. Economic disruption and civil collapse made a mockery of schedules and train fares and so on. Technical problems including flight of managers and engineers plus the impossibility of getting spare parts from abroad or from barely surviving factories in Russia, pushed the railways into a downward spiral as well. By the year's end, far from presiding over an orderly supervised form of capitalism resembling the German war economy, the Soviet Government was living from hand to mouth in a situation of unprecedented chaos. Not surprisingly, the country became vulnerable to epidemic. In the first place, the devastating post-war influenza epidemic that hit the whole of Europe began to ravage Russia in the winter of 1917/18. The country had fallen down several levels of a Dantesque inferno. Though no one knew it, or could even envisage it at the time, it was only a prelude. Russia was entering a holocaust in which some 10 million people would die of illness, hunger, war.

While the priority of the new government was, as we have seen, survival, it also had to take measures to deal with other aspects of the crisis and to try to institute its vision of transition to socialism. They went alongside each other in a curious relationship, and the government also proceeded up a very steep learning curve. Economic policy and political survival soon became very close. There were few 'economic' policies as such, for instance interest rates; spending targets; inflation control and so on. Indeed, for Lenin, economic policy was inseparable from institutional and coercive measures. On the institutional front, the key focus was the setting up, in December 1917, of a Supreme Council of the National Economy (*Vesenkha*, from its Russian acronym) to oversee the economy. In April 1918 a commission of scientists and other experts was also set up, under the aegis of the Academy of Sciences, to review Russia's productive resources and advise on how best to use them. Banks were nationalised but in such an alienating way that they were merely pushed closer to collapse. Relying on exhortation to call upon workers and managers to fulfil their responsibilities became more frequent, more shrill and more empty. As that happened, the void was filled by coercion.

The Cheka, with its task of dealing with 'sabotage' was an instrument of economic policy because sabotage came to mean, first and foremost, disrupting the economy. Peddlers, petty speculators, reluctant managers and even prostitutes quickly came within the remit of the new institution. The destructive relationship of declining consent to Bolshevik measures leading to increased coercion was already beginning to show itself in the first months of the Cheka's existence (Leggett 1981; Pipes 1998).

Needless to say, the same was increasingly true of the political sphere. The coalition crisis of the first days of Soviet power had been resolved by forcibly breaking up the railwaymen's union leadership and replacing it. Other measures shocked even Bolshevik supporters. The new government moved quickly to close opposition newspapers. At first, the target was right-wing papers, which were outlawed on only the second day of the new government's existence, 27 October 1917. However, other obstacles like a ban on advertising which cut off a major source of income and, in 1918, a state monopoly on paper and a near-monopoly on printing presses, gradually squeezed the life out of most other newspapers, including those of the non-Bolshevik left, even before censorship was institutionalised in 1918.

Non-Bolshevik parties also entered a twilight world of arbitrary suppression. In the chaos, prominent figures of the opposition managed to stay in Russia in secret for some time. Kerensky, for example, did not finally leave until May 1918. However, another downward spiral had begun. Opposition led to repression which led to loss of support and therefore more repression. In the first six months such processes were restrained compared to what was to come.

In addition to the stick, Lenin knew it was necessary to have a few carrots. Certain aspects of policy were implemented in order to show what the revolution represented in the long term. Some of the priorities seem curious. A war against the church was conducted. Unsurprisingly, separation of church and state was decreed on 20 January 1918 and the church was excluded from the education system. But legislation went further, nationalising church property including buildings which were loaned back to the clergy on licence. However, the Bolsheviks did not prevent the re-institution of the Moscow patriarchate, that is, the independent leadership of the Russian Orthodox Church, its Archbishopric of Canterbury, so to speak, which had been suspended since 1721. In November, Tikhon was named the first Patriarch of the new era. He protested against the Bolshevik measures against the church and, perhaps unwisely, pronounced an anathema against the Bolsheviks on 19 January 1918. The campaign against the church was largely driven by ideology as, for the time being at least, there was no mass hostility to religion though there was a good deal of anticlericalism. However, from the pragmatic point of view, the assault on the church, when there were more pressing issues, seemed to risk creating unnecessary enemies, not least in the rural areas.

The reform of marriage laws in mid-December, permitted civil marriage and no-fault divorce, also indicated the direction of Bolshevik thinking, though making divorce too easy soon rebounded against the interests of wives and mothers whom it had, naively, been expected to protect. A whole host of other indicative legislation, what Lenin called 'propaganda by decree', democratised army ranks, established elected courts and revolutionary tribunals and abolished the Table of Ranks set up by Peter the Great.

One of the most significant features of the period was the Bolsheviks' inability to prevent the elections to the Constituent Assembly. In the heat of October they had presented themselves as its defenders but this was largely decorative. They had no interest in seeing it meet. The elections went ahead and, importantly, revealed a good deal about the political affiliations of Russia at that particular moment. The most careful study of the elections, conducted in 1950 by Oliver Radkey, showed that the SR group had the largest number of votes, some 40–50 per cent depending on how one defines national subgroups like the Ukrainian SRs. The Bolsheviks also did very well, polling around 25 per cent. The Kadets barely scraped 10 per cent and the Mensheviks were virtually eclipsed. Beyond the overall party figures, the elections reveal a great deal more. First of all, parties of the left gained some 80 per cent of the vote. There was no sign of any mass affiliation to counter-revolutionary groups. Predictions about the innate political 'conservatism' of the peasants and their attachment to the tsar had not proven themselves to be true. The election figures also illustrate important features of the Bolshevik vote. Bolsheviks were massively outvoted by the SRs in the deepest provinces and across Siberia, but the Bolsheviks had power bases where they mattered. They were the largest party in Petrograd and Moscow and were either the majority party or the largest party among the military voters in the Petrograd and Moscow garrisons and the northern front. They were also the majority in the politically important Baltic Fleet, although in the Black Sea Fleet they were heavily outvoted by SRs (Radkey 1989). They were strong enough to disperse the actual Constituent Assembly at the end of its first day of existence on 5–6 January when it refused to ratify the new Soviet system. There were some demonstrations in Petrograd and a significant total of dead and wounded who had attempted to defend it, but, in essence, the long-awaited assembly was abolished without serious practical repercussions, though its dispersal has been a focus of anti-Bolshevik propaganda ever since. Dispersal also meant the Bolsheviks were unable to immediately present a constitution. As a taster of what was to come, they had issued, on 2 January, a Declaration of Rights of Working and Exploited People. It was consciously modelled on the Declaration of the Rights of Man and the Citizen of the French revolution. However, where the French declaration had been universal, the Bolshevik one was based on class principles. Non-working people were deprived of many rights. An obligation to work was incorporated within it, intended to outlaw the possibility of living on unearned income from rents or investments.

The Revolution at Six Months

The first six months, then, were very tumultuous. They had been characterised by multiple processes of securing power, securing peace, facing rapid economic decline, promoting social revolution, restraining spontaneous revolution from below, watching over the dissolution of rural large-scale landowning and transfer of land to peasants, and the first steps in 'reversion' to non-Bolshevik principles of unequal pay and one-person management. In the chaos, two things were clear. On the plus side from the Bolshevik viewpoint, they had survived and they were in control. Their brief alliance with the Left SRs, from late November until the Treaty of Brest-Litovsk, had helped them through, but by March and April of 1918 they governed alone. The death of Kornilov in battle outside Ekaterinodar deprived their enemies of their most respected leader. Indeed, the defeat of the White offensive had even created the notion, which we will examine in the next chapter, that the civil war was all but over. On the minus side, the 'gradual, peaceful and smooth' transition to be conducted by the masses 'who would soon learn' to produce and distribute goods, had proven to be completely illusory. The transition predicted by Lenin in his works of 1917 and earlier was in ruins. The combination of factors – relative political security (again remembering that the least weak is the strongest) and a complete collapse of strategy, meant there was both the possibility and the need for a new set of guidelines. Lenin, who, as ever, was very adept at analysing political conjunctures, realised this fully. In April and May 1918 a change of direction was emerging, where coercion, not consent, would be the driving force. In place of the 'gradual, peaceful and smooth' transition, Lenin began to talk about iron proletarian discipline. A darker day was dawning.

Chapter 7:   Experiencing Civil War: April 1918–March 1921

From the First Civil War to the Second: The Crises of Spring and Summer 1918

From early April 1918 to late May the assumption in Moscow, the new capital since 12 March, was that political conflict in Russia was winding down and that, for the time being, Soviet power had been secured, at least in the Russian heartland. True, large areas of the old empire were beyond central control and independence struggles were taking place. By and large, these were in relatively small, peripheral and non-Russian, non-Slavic regions. The most significant losses were Poland, Finland and the Baltic provinces. The Treaty of Brest-Litovsk, however, made matters much more serious. Most of Ukraine was lost and it became a political vacuum for the next three years during which a variety of movements, from right-wing nationalists to anarchists, played out a bitter struggle for power that, once the German and Austrian occupation collapsed in December 1918, merged almost seamlessly into the Russian conflicts. However, Moscow's tenuous control over Russia itself was exposed in a dramatic and, perhaps, unnecessary incident.

Revolt of the Czechoslovak Legion

Some 30,000 Czechoslovak troops, who had been fighting with Russia on the Eastern Front as a part of their nation's struggle for independence from the Austro-Hungarian Empire, were attempting to return to the fight after Brest-Litovsk dissolved the Eastern Front. Their only recourse was to attempt to reach the Western Front by travelling east, either to Central Asia and India and thence back to Europe or, more practically, via the Trans-Siberian Railway and then across the Pacific to the United States and across the Atlantic to France. Wisely, the Soviet Government was simply letting them leave. However, as they moved east, rumours began to circulate that they were helping the SR opposition to the Bolsheviks. Nerves were taut at this point because the Bolshevik–Left SR coalition had collapsed after Brest-Litovsk. In order to prevent the supposed assistance Trotsky, as Commissar for War since March, ordered the departing Czechoslovaks to disarm. This was one command they could not obey as it would leave them at the mercy of the Soviet Government and any other armed groups, of which there were many still roaming around. In making the order Trotsky was provoking their intervention in Russian internal affairs as much as responding to it. The order was a disastrous error. The Czechoslovak Legion resisted and was, whether it wanted to or not, encouraged to fight alongside others who opposed the Soviet Government. That was not all. Because they were strung out along the Trans-Siberian Railway, they controlled that vast province. In one rash order, Trotsky had lost an immense territory. To get some of idea of just how big it was, one historian compared it to the United States. In those terms, the Czechoslovaks on the Volga would have been at a point 300 miles *east* of New York out in the Atlantic Ocean while the Vladivostok group would have been 1000 miles *west* of San Francisco, out in the Pacific Ocean, well on the way to Hawaii! (Mawdsley 1987: 275.)

The Second Civil War emerges: Territories and participants

Like most civil wars, Russia's was very different from conventional warfare. The main distinction is that it was not fought between easily definable and territorially contiguous entities. Even more than regular warfare, civil war is politics with guns. A major effect of this is that the war was not so much along a frontline but was more like a patchwork quilt, red patches here, white patches there, green patches (that is, freelance, usually peasant rebels who tried to avoid absorption into the Red forces) scattered around, and many patches which combined the main colours. For example, when Moscow so foolishly lost control of Siberia it left pockets of Soviet power in certain cities like Irkutsk and Krasnoyarsk, some components of which went underground, awaiting their moment. The city of Omsk, on the other hand, became a capital for the anti-Bolshevik forces. In other words, a map of the Russian civil war resembles a political map rather than a military one.

Like red states and blue states in the US, there might be clusters but no clear line dividing all the red states from all the blue ones.

The partial exception to this was the territory held directly by the Bolsheviks which was, more or less, consolidated but fluctuating. The area 'controlled' by the Soviet Government included most of the Russian, Siberian and Ukrainian heartlands in late 1917, but by 1919 it retained only 10–20 per cent of the territory of the former tsarist empire. There were also pockets of opposition, some of it underground, within the territory it claimed to govern, and pockets of support beyond, but it was more contiguous than the areas dominated by the anti-Bolshevik forces, and this came to have a crucial importance for the civil war. A prime reason for the failure of the anti-Bolshevik crusade was that its only secure territory was that on which its armies stood. As they moved forward or back they left political vacuums or, worse, opponents, to take over.

But who were the forces involved in the conflict? Conventionally, the main forces are described as the Whites and the Reds. Some analysts, following Oliver Radkey, have identified a third, less committed group known as the Greens, not because they were eco-warriors but because they were rural, largely peasant or peasant-oriented independents. For current purposes, while the existence of less committed groups will certainly be acknowledged, they will be seen to gravitate around the White–Red axis rather than maintain their independence. This will also point up a key feature of both Whites and Reds – they were politically broad coalitions rather than narrowly identifiable parties.

The Whites extended from proto-fascists on the right, through Kadet liberals to SRs, even some Left SRs, and a handful of Mensheviks and former Bolsheviks. However, the great bulk of them were tsarists turned Russian nationalists. In sociological terms, they were dominated by senior officers of the defunct imperial army. They also had support from a broad spectrum of displaced members of the former ruling class, though not all such people could stomach siding with the former oppressors. Some White armies had very capable politicians in tow. Perhaps the most notable was the former Marxist turned liberal, Peter Struve, who was a member of the council of Denikin's Volunteer Army in South Russia more or less from its inception in 1917 and in 1919 was its representative in Paris. Later, he assisted the publication of its newspaper and was Wrangel's Foreign Minister as 'the cause' imploded in 1920.

The political headquarters of the White movement as a whole was essentially in Paris, which was hardly the most convenient arrangement given the complexities of communication during the world and civil wars. However, it was towards the Allies negotiating in Paris that the White movement looked for support. In a sense, the lobbying at Versailles undertaken by White political figures, of whom Miliukov was the most eminent, prefigured the Cold War (Mayer 1967). The Russian question came to be one of the most important issues facing the peace conference, and Germany was, in part, a beneficiary in that the most draconian plans for dealing with the defeated enemy were not implemented by the victors for fear of completely bankrupting central and eastern Europe and making it a prey to the newly-emerging 'disease' of communism. Instead, while Germany was severely punished, a sort of predecessor to the Iron Curtain, a so-called '*cordon sanitaire*' (infection control zone) was set up.

Miliukov's book *Bolshevism – an International Danger*, which is largely forgotten and unread today, was a first clarion call to Cold War, except that what the Whites were seeking at Versailles was assistance in a hot war (Burbank 1986). They wanted intervention by significant military forces from France and Britain. Some western politicians were convinced. The British Secretary of State for War, Winston Churchill, tried to persuade his government to send 250,000 troops to 'strangle bolshevism in its cradle' as he memorably put it. The saner and more pragmatic counsel of Prime Minister Lloyd George prevailed. He argued that Britain was already politically unsettled and sick of war. There were not enough troops out there keen on taking on such a task. Smaller forces were deployed, initially to retrieve supplies, briefly to sustain the eastern front, and, in theory, to repay the debt for the support given by imperial (i.e. White) allies during the world war.

In practice, imperial ambitions also played a part. For example, British Indian troops pushed up from the south to the Caspian Sea and very briefly, for a single month in fact, held the city of Baku in August–September 1918. Baku was the Russian Empire's largest oil city and BP (the British Petroleum company) had had significant interests there before the war. French imperialism motivated intervention forces in Odessa and the Black Sea region. Russia's immediate neighbours were not slow to take advantage of the weakness of the centre. Finland held on to whole of the territory of the former Grand Duchy of Finland and aided ethnically-related Karelian separatists in a broad swathe of ill-defined borderlands. Turkey 'retrieved' lost provinces after Russia's Caucasus Army collapsed. After the terrible Armenian massacres, the core territory of Armenia itself was threatened and only a miraculous mobilisation of the tiny nation preserved the remnants of its homeland at the battle of Sardarapat and enabled it to declare its independence (28 May 1918). In 1918, Japan also started nibbling at disputed territories on the mainland and among the islands, especially Sakhalin, where it remained until 1925. Troops from the United States briefly occupied Archangel in the north and Vladivostok, partly to pre-empt further Japanese expansion. In 1920 Poland launched a speculative attack in the western Ukraine but was beaten back and almost destroyed, except that the opposing Soviet forces made crucial political and strategic errors (see Chapter 9 for more details). Intervention, then, was crucial to the White 'cause' but, in practice, was perhaps less help than it appeared. Intervention was never sufficient to be militarily decisive, but was prominent enough to tarnish the appeal of the Whites, who were easily portrayed by their Bolshevik opponents as pawns in the imperial struggles of the great powers. After all, how could nationalists be seen to be dependent on the supplies and armies of foreign, including traditionally hostile, powers?

It should not be forgotten that the Reds, too, were a coalition. In the interlude between the first and second civil wars, that is, the spring and summer of 1918, the new authorities had tried to wipe out further pockets of opposition. The suppression of the Constituent Assembly effectively destroyed the remnants of the old right, such as the nationalists, as well as the Provisional Government centre, including mainstream SRs and the Menshevik right. As a result, there was not much organised opposition left, but, as the battle lines were drawn up in 1918, many individuals from the former opposition worked with the Bolsheviks as the lesser evil. Most of the staff of key administrative and economic institutions, like the Supreme Council of the National Economy (*Vesenkha*) were non-Bolshevik and included many former opponents, including the critical diarist N.N. Sukhanov.

In addition, a new form of opposition began to grow within the party itself: this became known as the Left Communists. It emerged in protest at the supposedly compromise direction of policy adopted by Lenin after the collapse of his first plan for the transition to socialism. Left-wing critics within and beyond the party were especially disappointed that revolutionary war had been given up in the light of the Treaty of Brest-Litovsk; that workers' control had been subverted and one-person management was being revived; that the party was spreading its tentacles ever more widely and that workers' voices were being increasingly stifled. The dominant ideology emerging at the heart of the Soviet Government seemed to combine production at any price (productionism) and socialism in one country at the expense of world revolution.

Lenin perceived the new danger from the left and in April opened up a political assault on Left Communism which he described as 'an infantile disorder'. Bitter polemics ensued but Lenin, as we shall see in more detail, was not deflected one iota from his new course. Indeed, he widened the attack. On 11–12 April mass arrests of anarchists and other independent leftists took place in Petrograd and Moscow. The centre of anarchist influence was, symbolically and ironically, the villa owned by the former tsarist police chief, Durnovo, the author of the brilliant memorandum of February 1914. The assault on the House of Anarchy on Malaia Dmitrovka ulitsa in Moscow cost 40 dead and wounded among the defenders and 12 Cheka agents killed.

Such attacks were very risky. To justify them, Lenin pointed to 'anti-Soviet' activities conducted by the anarchists. However, nothing was more likely to provoke such activity than repression. The discontented leftists saw the growing repression as part of a wider set of anti-revolutionary tendencies of the Bolsheviks. Their former allies, the Left SRs, were strengthened in their conviction that the Bolsheviks were abandoning the path of revolution. Some of them took the Brest-Litovsk Treaty to be proof that, after all, the Bolsheviks were agents of the Kaiser, and they began to point the finger at the German ambassador, Count Mirbach, whom they considered the real ruler of Russia. Opposition on the left escalated, fuelled by repression and repression escalated fuelled by opposition. Terrorism re-emerged, targeting Bolsheviks and their allies. On 20 June, a leading Petrograd Bolshevik Commissar, Volodarsky, the head of local propaganda, was assassinated by a Left SR. From 6 to 22 July a series of Left SR attempted uprisings, signalled by the assassination of Mirbach, flared up and were repressed. Nonetheless, on 30 August, the head of the Petrograd Cheka, Moisei Uritskii, was killed by an SR assassin. Even worse, on the same day, Lenin was also shot and severely injured by an SR sympathiser. These acts set off a fierce Red Terror in which hundreds, or even thousands, of Cheka prisoners were massacred by the panic-stricken authorities in a fashion reminiscent of the September massacres in the French revolution. Almost as a side-issue to this, the Imperial family had been executed in Ekaterinburg on the night of 16–17 July.

There were two further highly threatening sources of opposition. One was the emergence of a multitude of peasant revolts in response to the 'triple whammy' of spring 1918, when, through committees of poor peasants, conscription and the grain monopoly, the Bolsheviks tried to get control of the countryside for the first time rather than leave it to its own devices (Figes 1989). The other was increasing worker protests at declining living standards and rising unemployment. Taking all these phenomena together, there was a veritable perfect storm of opposition to the new government. On the face of it, in summer 1918, it appeared to be going the same way as its Provisional Government predecessor. Collapse appeared to be only a matter of time.

The civil war, which was in the process of apparently fading away even before the death of Kornilov on 13 April, began to flare up again at the same time as the internal crisis was threatening Lenin's power. Seen from this perspective, the second civil war could be seen to have saved the Bolsheviks. As the common external enemy, the Whites, gained a new lease of life – thanks, not least, to the Czechoslovaks – the ultra-left and other more moderate forces, including many peasants, realised that the whole revolution would fail if the Whites prevailed. Rather, as the Whites became identifiable only as anti-Bolshevik, so a broader Red identity, based on being anti-White, began to emerge. Many of those who had major differences with the Bolsheviks had to suppress those differences in the light of their even greater opposition to the Whites. Thus the Reds began to include workers opposed to the return of employers; peasants who hated landlords more than they hated communists; Mensheviks and SRs who wanted Soviet democracy not a renewed imperial autocracy and many others. Perhaps most unexpectedly, there were even some nationalists, like General Brusilov, who eventually, after being imprisoned by the regime, came to assist it, notably in its fight against Poland. Such people were rarely converts to the Bolshevik cause. By and large, they helped organise the Red Army since it was, at least, Russian, as opposed to the Whites, who seemed to be bringing Russia's enemies and imperial rivals into the country. Even anarchists turned to support the Reds as the lesser evil. The whole irony was caught by Victor Serge who recounts that, in 1919 when Petrograd was under imminent threat from the White army led by Iudenich, which had advanced via Estonia, every potential source of resistance was called on. The party even armed anarchists, two of whom, in a supreme irony, found themselves guarding the printing works of the newspaper *Pravda* which had been in the forefront of denouncing anarchism. When the time came to return them to prison once the crisis had passed, one of their Bolshevik guards opened the car door and told them to escape. 'I was a fool wasn't I?' he asked Victor Serge. 'But you know, all the same I am glad of it.' (Serge 1963: 93–4.)

It should be emphasised, particularly in the light of Radkey's identification of independent 'Greens', and Eric Landis's more recent and innovatory studies, that many, almost certainly most, of those who fought for the Reds were not Bolsheviks and knew little about Bolshevik objectives. Rather they were the continuation of the popular movement of 1917, defending almost exactly the same programme – land redistribution, Soviet democracy, industrial revival and some sort of workers' control/supervision of production – as they had in 1917. As the Whites threatened, so the popular movement leaned towards the Bolsheviks. As the White threat weakened, after 1919, so it began to reassert its own principles distinct from those of the Bolsheviks. Indeed, the crisis of spring and summer 1918 could be interpreted similarly. In the first wave of revolution from October to March there was a common fight against the common enemy. As that enemy appeared to be vanquished in the heartlands and confined to the periphery, so the various strands of the popular movement began to assert themselves in opposition to what they saw as Bolshevik betrayal of the revolutionary programme, not least in their catastrophic attempts to coerce peasants into handing grain over to the state in exchange for worthless tokens. This ill-conceived policy visited arbitrary repression on the peasants and, as a first line of defence, they tended to move out of or conceal crops which were to be requisitioned. The result was a further catastrophic decline in grain output and procurement by the authorities. In the end, the Bolsheviks were forced to give in to this pressure and allow limited market relations to return. But it was only in 1921 that Lenin recognised the need to do this. The peasants had inflicted a serious defeat on the Bolsheviks, but it did not come cheap. While the Whites threatened, the peasants' protests were relatively muted. After the White defeat, they became dangerous to the regime. But first, the Whites had to be defeated. (Lih 1990, Landis 2008 and Read 1996: 228–38 and 258–82 discuss armed requisition and its consequences.)

The Second Civil War

Siberia and the Urals

On 18 November the Czechoslovak forces remaining in Russia finally dropped out of the Russian conflict. Their attempts to return to Europe had been rendered unnecessary by the armistice of 11 November. The First World War had come to an end. There was no Western Front to which they could return. During the months they had been trying to extricate themselves from a conflict that had been thrust upon them they had enabled major events to evolve in Siberia and the Urals. By negating the weak authority of the Bolsheviks they had allowed a spontaneous upsurge in the power of the Bolsheviks opponents.

A number of tendencies emerged but, initially, two were the most important. One, centred on the SRs, gathered together the remnants of the party's representatives to the Constituent Assembly and invited other groups to join them in setting up a Committee of Members of the Constituent Assembly, known as the *Komuch* from its Russian acronym. It settled in Samara in the Volga region, one of the most westerly points held by the Czechoslovaks. Incidentally, the complexity of the situation is illustrated by the fact that there was a second short-lived Komuch government of the Kama region in August and September 1918 in Izhevsk in the Urals. The second major grouping was a more typical 'White' force of former officers and Kadet and Nationalist political sympathisers which was based in Omsk, a city on the mighty Irtysh river in western Siberia along the Trans-Siberian Railway. Both groups proclaimed themselves as governments in June 1918, Komuch on the 8th and the provisional Siberian Government in Omsk on the 29th.

At that point, the fledgling Bolshevik enforcement squads – the Red Army and the Cheka – were tied up with conflicts in their heartland with the anarchists and the Left SR 'uprising'. They soon had to face the Frankenstein's monster Trotsky had inadvertently created in the East, because, on 6 August, less than three weeks after the capture of Yaroslavl' from the SRs, a force of Czechoslovaks and Samaran SRs captured the key Volga city of Kazan'. This presented a clear threat to Moscow and had to be resisted, not least because substantial state gold reserves had been transported there for safety during the war. Bolshevik defeat in the area also opened the way to a rare occurrence in the revolution, a worker rebellion against the Bolsheviks, led by employees of the State Ordnance Factory in the town of Izhevsk. The Bolsheviks had pulled most of their followers and forces out of the town to take part in the struggle for Kazan (Swain 1996; Retish 2008: 179–88).

In its first major campaign the Red Army recaptured Kazan' on 10 September. At the same time, the Komuch had called a State Conference (8–23 September) to bring together the two Siberian 'governments'. It proclaimed a Napoleonic style 'Directory' of five members including one general, two SRs and two Kadets, who proclaimed themselves to be the Provisional All-Russian Government. The conference had convened in the Siberian city of Ufa, which was just as well because the former stronghold of Samara was captured by the Red Army on 8 October, causing the Directory to flee even further and seek the protection of the White military forces in Omsk on 9 October. The improbable alliance of White officers and socialist SRs did not last long. On 18 November, the White leader in Siberia, Admiral Kolchak, arrested the SR members of the Directory, dissolved the Komuch and proclaimed himself Supreme Ruler, a title eventually upheld by the émigré politicians in Paris, at the expense largely of General Denikin, who was serving the White cause in Southern Russia and Ukraine. The suppression gave the Constituent Assembly the unique experience of having been suppressed by both Reds and Whites. On both occasions, the suppression had caused little by way of direct repercussions on the suppressors, a poignant symbol that real power at that time flowed outside the forces of parliamentary democracy, which lacked serious roots in Russian society.

South Russia and Ukraine

For the moment, the fight for Siberia remained literally frozen as the harsh winter months came around. This was fortunate for the Bolsheviks because a whole new phase of civil war was spinning into view as international events began to take hold. On 11 November, an armistice was declared on the western front. Though it did not officially surrender, Germany had thrown in the towel in the First World War. This had colossal repercussions for the former eastern front. Just as the Czechoslovak forces had created a protective umbrella under which the anti-Bolshevik forces in Siberia could emerge, so the Austro-German occupation of Ukraine had done the same. Under the occupation, a variety of political forces of varying strengths had survived. The result was a highly complex network of parties, factions and armies. The withdrawal of the occupiers in late November and December left a massive power vacuum and changed the balance of forces in the area. German and Austrian protégés left behind were now cruelly exposed to opposition and reprisal. Groups, including the Bolsheviks, who had been kept at bay by the superior power of the occupying armies, now swooped down, each trying to pre-empt the other. Focus in the civil war switched from the Urals and western Siberia to South Russia and Ukraine. In the initial scramble for power the group around Hetman Skoropadsky, who had been the German's puppet ruler of Ukraine, was ejected from Kiev by another nationalist group led by Symon Petliura, who had not been tainted by collaboration. Opportunism was not confined to local forces. On 14 December,

French forces landed in Odessa and took control of the region. The initial skirmishing was brought to an end in January and February as Soviet armies returned to fill the vacuum. On 3 January the Red Army entered Kharkov, in eastern Ukraine. On 6 February 1918, Soviet troops recaptured the chief target, Kiev. However, far from bringing stability and an end to the civil war, these conflicts were merely the hors d'oeuvres for a complex and decisive set of battles in 1919.

Unforgettable 1919

In 1952 a film was made entitled *Unforgettable 1919*. Khrushchev, in his Secret Speech, claims it was a favourite of Stalin's in the last months of his life. He watched it time after time. If true, this is hardly surprising, not least because the film shamelessly exaggerated Stalin's role. Even so, 1919 was, for the Reds, an unforgettable year. It was the year of decision, the point at which internal and external forces were at their strongest in opposition to the Soviet Government. In mid-1919, the Soviet Government controlled only some 10 per cent of the territory of the former Empire. It was confined to an area of European Russia, plus a thin finger of territory stretching down the Volga to Astrakhan and on to its estuary in the Caspian Sea. Crucially, this territory, though small in area, was rich in population and in war materials left over from the First World War. It was also the centre of the railway network and, writing after the event in 1929, the situation in 1919 was brilliantly characterised by Winston Churchill. 'The ancient capital lay at the centre of a web of railroads ... and in the midst, a spider. Vain hope to crush the spider by the advance of lines of encircling flies.' (Mawdsley 1987: 275; Read 1996: 197.) However, at the time, no one could be sure of the outcome in such a volatile situation, but what was clear, and this is why Stalin, a key participant in some of the events, looked back on it with such nostalgia, was that the Bolsheviks had, against all the odds, taken on the remnants of old Russia and their powerful international backers, and emerged victorious. It was not for nothing that one Bolshevik writer, Lev Kritsman, entitled his account of these years *The Heroic Period*. From the Bolshevik perspective that is exactly what it was. We will look at the armed struggle in this decisive and utterly confusing year before getting some idea of the war's terrible human cost.

In 1918, the crisis in the east and that in the south had threatened at different moments. In 1919, the two areas were equally threatening, and a lesser, but still dangerous, front was added in the Baltic region. But at the same time, as we have mentioned, the territorial divisions were not relatively neat, like an international war. Each of the participants was fighting not only the armed external enemy but an internal battle against opponents within their own base territories. It was this, as much as anything, which gave the struggle its immense complexity, especially in Southern Russia and Ukraine.

However, it was from Siberia that the first threat came. On 13 March, Kolchak's troops occupied Ufa. From there they continued to advance out of Siberia and across the Urals. For six weeks they advanced and presented a growing threat. Had he succeeded in linking up with White forces elsewhere, such as the North where some remnants of British intervention were still deployed, the Bolsheviks would have faced a re-energised enemy. However, Kolchak's forces overstretched themselves and, by 26 April, they had pushed too far and were defeated. They were sent scurrying back to their stronghold in Omsk.

Many followers were already aware that the White cause was as good as lost. Some of them were even secretly contemplating switching to the Bolshevik side. In his unpublished memoirs *Belyi Omsk* (*White Omsk*) the Kadet politician N.V. Ustrialov (1890–1937) expressed a growing disillusion which even preceded the reversal in the Whites' military fortunes. He and those like him were sick of the ineffectiveness and squabbling of the Siberian White leadership and, as nationalists, were embarrassed at their dependence on foreigners. By comparison, the Bolsheviks were Russian and increasingly powerful. Several of them also thought that the more extreme features of Bolshevik socialism would 'normalise' under pressure of everyday life and problems (Read 1990: 190–191). Ustrialov eventually quit the Whites and worked for the Soviet Union as a manager of the Soviet-controlled Chinese Eastern Railway in Harbin, North China.

However, that was not the perspective of the other substantial White force, the so-called Volunteer Army in South Russia. The Soviets were advancing, from the fall of Kharkov and then Kiev to the Red Army, and its eventual occupation of Odessa on 6 April, in the wake of a French retreat as they realised what kind of effort would be needed to hang on. This, plus the fall of Simferopol', a leading Crimean city, on 10 April, pointed to a next step which would be to attack the Volunteer Army itself. On 15 February, Ataman Krasnov, former Kornilovite spokesman and nominal chief of the Cossacks of the Don territory, had resigned as head of the Cossack Don Army opening its way to fusion with the Volunteer Army under the more capable, energetic and less politically committed General Denikin, who began to prepare an offensive.

That offensive began on 19 May. That alone gives us pause for reflection. This was less than a month after the breakdown of Kolchak's offensive in the east. The failure to make the two offensives simultaneous was a crucial and elementary error. How can it be explained? There are a number of factors to take into account. In the first place, communications between the two armies were tenuous at best. The continued Bolshevik hold on Astrakhan prevented direct, overland links. There was a dangerous route across the Caspian and one pair of brave envoys attempted to use it, but were intercepted and executed. Other than that, telegrams had to go around the world via Paris and the Pacific to reach each other.

However, poor communications is only part of the story. The two leaders, Denikin and Kolchak, were also in partial competition with each other. They were in an unacknowledged race to reach Moscow first. The winner would be in the driving seat to organise and lead a new, probably dictatorial, military government, though, again, neither side would admit such ambitions entirely openly. Each left the eventual form of government to speculation. Both also toyed vaguely and improbably with ideas of a new Constituent Assembly or similar institution to draw up a new system of government. Cynically, when they were strong, Kolchak, Denikin and allies and successors like Baron Wrangel', did not pay much attention to such issues, but as their movements eventually weakened, deathbed conversion to democracy was more pronounced.

The final component was over-confidence. The Whites misunderstood and under-rated their Bolshevik enemy, considering them nothing but a German-implanted alien force. They believed the Russian (and Ukrainian and other peoples) were groaning under the Bolshevik yoke and looking to be liberated. It was thought by many that they would only have to advance to be welcomed joyously. Whatever the true picture of the aspirations of the Russian people, it was soon clear that they did not see former landowners, aristocrats, Imperial officers and financiers and factory owners as liberators. There were, as we shall see, other reasons for White failure, but the overweening confidence, mutual rivalry and misunderstanding of the size of their task were among the most important. Had Kolchak and Denikin attacked simultaneously they would have deprived the Bolsheviks of a key asset – the use of the railway network to squash each of the advancing flies one by one. Even so, Denikin's offensive came close to success.

The offensive began on 19 May. The Volunteer Army rolled out of Rostov and headed north. On 25 June they took the Bolsheviks' eastern

Ukrainian stronghold of Kharkov and advanced rapidly into Russia itself. Five days later, Denikin's forces captured the cities of Tsaritsyn and Ekaterinoslav. The Volunteer Army then moved to consolidate its position on its western flanks by dominating Ukraine. On 23 August the Bolsheviks were driven out of Odessa and, in one of his biggest achievements, Denikin's army became the sixth since late 1917 to make a 'triumphal' entry into the battered city of Kiev. This victory opened the way to the main goal, an offensive towards Moscow. On 14 October, White forces took Orel, only 220 miles from the capital.

Denikin was helped by the fact that his advance was a signal for another, much smaller, White army under General Iudenich, to advance out of the Baltic States where it had been forming under the protection of Estonian independence. Although small it was a threat, not least because the Estonian border was only 100 miles from Iudenich's objective, Petrograd. The Army of the North West marched forward on 11 October and by 22 October was in the suburbs of the revolutionary city. For once, two White armies were attacking simultaneously and had succeeded in challenging Bolshevik power in its very heartland. Had Kolchak also been part of the attack the outcome might have been different.

However, a key factor in Denikin's success was that significant Red forces were still engaged in mopping up in eastern Russia and western Siberia. As Denikin broke out from the south, the Red Army was retaking key points in the Urals and further east. On 9 June Ufa was recaptured, followed by Perm (1 July) and Chelyabinsk (25 July). Once the Urals were secure, the main focus of Soviet power turned towards the Volunteer Army, which advanced out of Orel along the Moscow road towards Tula. Here, the most decisive single battle of the civil war was fought. Concentrating as much of their remaining forces as they could, the Red Army was victorious. Failing to advance and being defeated drove the Volunteer Army into a headlong retreat. On 20 October, Orel was recaptured by the Reds.

The momentum had shifted decisively, and in the following months the Reds advanced to annihilate their enemies. The war was virtually over by the end of the year. The roll-call of Red victories was impressive. On 22 October Iudenich's troops were defeated on the outskirts of Petrograd. On 9 November Ekaterinoslav fell, not to the Red Army, however, but to the partisan army of the anarchist Nestor Makhno who was, at that moment, allied to the Soviet Government. On 14 November, Kolchak's capital, Omsk, was recaptured by the Red Army. On 17 November Kursk was captured and Denikin's remaining forces began to disintegrate. In a dagger to the Volunteer Army's heart, the campaign continued into Kharkov (12 December), Kiev (16 December), Ekaterinoslav (30 December) 'liberated' from the hands of Makhno, and Tsaritsyn (3 January 1920). If anything, these campaigns rather than autumn and winter of 1917/18 mark a true 'triumphal march' of Soviet power. But 1919 did not see the complete ending of the war. There were major flurries in 1920, of which the most important was the Polish invasion of Ukraine in summer. We will complete the roll-call of events and then turn to asking how and why the war turned out as it did before moving on to the question of what it was like to live through it.

The defeats had wrecked the Whites. On 4 January 1920 Kolchak was fleeing eastwards through Siberia and 'abdicated' in favour of the already defeated Denikin. In early February his luck ran out and he was captured by Red forces and, on 7 February, executed by the Revolutionary Committee in Irkutsk. On 8 January, Denikin's political capital, Rostov, was captured. With the writing on the wall, foreign backers of the Whites bailed out and started making accommodations with the now permanently established Soviet Government. On 16 January, the Allied Blockade of Soviet Russia was lifted. On 2 February, Iudenich's erstwhile protectors in Estonia signed a peace treaty with Russia. The final collapse of the Whites proceeded apace. Soviet armies pushed rapidly into South Russia, Eastern Ukraine and the Crimea. On 17 March 1920, Ekaterinodar was occupied by the Red Army. By 27 March they reached Novorossiisk. This precipitated Denikin's resignation. He was replaced by General Baron Wrangel' who was recalled from a two month exile in Constantinople to which he had sent by Denikin. However, Wrangel' and the Volunteer Army could do little but hole up as long as possible in the Crimea before being forced, in late autumn, to arrange the flight across the Black Sea to Turkey of as many of his troops, supporters and camp-followers as he could. In a campaign conducted by the Red Army and Makhno's partisans, the Whites were finally driven from Russian soil on 14 November. One of Makhno's lieutenants predicted that, now they were no longer useful to the Bolsheviks, they would be next. It did not take long. On 26 November, the Red Army turned on Makhno and his forces, too, were routed. Makhno and his last small band of followers were pursued by the Red Army until Frunze's forces eventually pushed them out of Ukraine in August 1921, sending Makhno into his final years of obscurity in Romania, Poland, Germany and, finally, France. He died in 1934 after working as a labourer in a Paris factory, perhaps telling tales of his past that his fellow-workers might well have considered exaggerations. They were not.

Wrangel's force had been allowed to live on borrowed time in the Crimea because a more serious threat had arisen in the form of the Polish attack. From the beginning of the Polish invasion on 24 April, until the final ending of hostilities on 12 October, the Red Army was forced to face its prime foe and leave Wrangel's rump government alone for the time being. But, eight days after the truce with Poland, on 20 October, Wrangel's bolt-hole was attacked and on 14 November the final evacuation took place. This was not the end of all conflict but the White threat was over. The remaining conflicts were about the periphery and minority nationalities and, along with some of the intricacies of the Polish war, will be examined later in this chapter. For the moment, we will reflect further on the reasons for the defeat of the Whites.

Why were the Whites Defeated?

The greatest asset of the Whites was their military training and experience. This was recognised even in one of the most successful, Stalin-era, propaganda movies, *Chapaev* (1934), a fable about how an heroic and enthusiastic but ill-disciplined group of partisans, led by the untutored Chapaev, were made into a formidable force by a pipe-smoking political commissar. At one point, the partisans quake as the disciplined and awe-inspiring Death's Head squadron of the Volunteer Army marches forward. Without doubt, the military expertise, particularly in the early stages, was on their side. In the next chapter we will examine some of the ways in which the Bolsheviks built up their own fighting skills, but for the moment it should be pointed out that the White superiority in this vital area also carried a cost. They had the skills because they were military men. But as we have seen throughout, from Danilov to Kornilov, many, though by no means all, Russian generals and subalterns lacked political finesse. The Whites were no exception. Politically, the movement was as incoherent and disorganised as it was militarily organised. What did they stand for politically?

Many right wing groups claim to be representing a silent majority and/or to be anti-political. Again, the Whites were no exception. According to Denikin, one of the chief virtues of his followers was that they were 'alien to politics' (Denikin 1973: 32). This was an absurd claim. Nothing is more political than civil war. But the fiction hid the severe problems the movement had in defining its politics. Denikin went on to say, contradicting the first part of his statement, that the

Whites were 'true to the idea of saving the Motherland' (Denikin 1973: 32). This glossed over a complete avoidance of discussion of what type of government this restored Russia would have. Were the Whites monarchists? Some of them were, but Russian monarchism was dogged by not having an obvious candidate for the throne. No one supported the restoration of Nicholas. His haemophiliac son was too ill and too young to be a figurehead. Grand Duke Michael had renounced his claim. The execution of the tsar and his family and of Michael left the succession very vague and no obvious contender emerged. Some of the Whites, however, claimed to be democrats. Miliukov and Struve were only two of many Kadet liberals who were forced uneasily into the White camp. They wanted a new constituent assembly, but most White leaders were not interested. The politicians formulated programmes but the White movement as a whole had no serious credo. It was too diffuse to do so. Would landowners agree to land reforms? No, in most cases. Employers wanted their factories back. Financiers dreamed of running their banks once again. But the White leaders, following their founding-figure, Kornilov, believed only by establishing their own power would 'order' and 'stability' return to Russia.

It was at this point that the silent majority often entered the incoherent political discourse of the Whites. The Russian people were, it was assumed, yearning for the selfsame stability and for liberation from the Bolsheviks. White officers believed that, as they advanced, so they would be welcomed by the population. One of them, General K.V. Sakharov, who fought alongside Kolchak, expressed it thus in his memoirs. If only the rear would support them, the road to Moscow would be opened up 'and then the whole people would come over to us ... The Bolsheviks and other socialist filth, would be destroyed – from the roots up – by the burning rage of the popular masses' (Mawdsley 1987: 280). Harsh experience did little, at first, to dampen such perceptions but, in reality, the population as a whole had little time for the Whites. The masses had serious differences with the Bolsheviks but they were savvy enough to recognise the Whites would not be an agent to deliver the popular programme, which was what, if anything, the masses still yearned for. In addition, the Whites were, to say the least, heavy-handed with local populations. While neither White nor Red Armies were blameless, and no one was very keen on having either of them around, the Whites built up the worse reputation. They tended to loot rather than requisition and to rampage rather than reconcile. By comparison, the Bolsheviks were an equally ruthless force but they were cold and directed and tended to avoid alienating ordinary people.

In short, the Whites had no clue when it came to politics. Sublimating everything into an ill-defined nationalism was no substitute for a real political message. Worse, their nationalism was seriously compromised in three ways. Most obviously, they were heavily dependent on foreign assistance, a glaring contradiction they could not hide. Secondly, and somewhat more important, the movements, insofar as they had bases, were in non-Russian territories, among Cossacks, Ukrainians, Estonians and others who wanted nothing to do with a revived all-Russian nationalism. White armies were barely tolerated in such areas and were even seen as an embarrassment because their very existence would draw Bolshevik attention like a magnet. The third, and most shocking, element of compromise arising from their nationalism was the horrifying anti-semitism of many Whites. While it was never official policy it was never effectively denounced either. Jewish populations in town and village which came under White control suffered grievously from pogroms. Precise figures are hard to come by but there is no doubt that White forces and their Ukrainian nationalist allies, conducted the worst massacres of Jews seen in modern Europe. Estimated figures for dead range from 50,000 to as many as 200,000 (Pipes 1994: 112), with one authority giving a figure of 115,000 in 1919 alone (Heifetz quoted in Read 1996: 309 fn. 34). This was Europe's first anti-semitic holocaust of the twentieth century and is, ironically, only concealed from view as a blight on twentieth-century history by its much worse successor, many of whose victims came from the same 'bloodlands' (Snyder 2010). Indeed, as one of them, Sakharov, boasted in 1924, 'the White movement was, in essence, the first manifestation of fascism' (Mawdsley 1987: 280). He had a point.

Between Red and White: The Makhno model

White political bankruptcy also had one other important feature. The Whites did not enjoy the essential requirement of an advancing army – a secure rear area. As an army advances, its main fighters go to the front, leaving only a thin screen behind to defend the areas of supply and communications. As Denikin's army, in particular, advanced, its long supply lines and weakly-defended rear were exposed. Enemies sprang up behind them like mushrooms. The most unified and menacing were the independent peasant armies of Makhno and Grigoriev in Ukraine. Being composed largely of peasants these armies enjoyed the key advantage of guerrilla fighters – the ability to blend into the background. Makhno's men were especially adept at this type of warfare. On one occasion they smuggled themselves into a White-held village in hay carts and, once they were in the centre, leaped out and attacked and killed the enemy before they could organise.

They could also produce mass armies when necessary, and Makhno's men inflicted a bitter defeat on a Volunteer Army reserve and supply train making its way to the front to support Denikin's drive on Moscow. It was intercepted at the crossing of the River Siniukha near the village of Peregonovka on 26 September 1919. Makhno's small force was outnumbered but they threw themselves on the Whites, for whom defeat and flight were not sufficient to save them. Makhno's horse-mounted peasants pursued them with ease and massacred nearly every one of the White officer/soldiers. They could be equally ruthless with each other. Another peasant guerrilla, Nikifor Grigoriev, had set out as a leftist loosely associated with the Reds and Makhno, but on 7 May 1919 he changed sides becoming an anti-Bolshevik, anti-semitic nationalist. Makhno inveigled him into a parley on 27 July. Accounts of what happened next differ but either the meeting degenerated into a shoot-out when Grigoriev drew his pistol and was shot, possibly by Makhno, or when Grigoriev and his bodyguard were preparing to speak Makhno arrested them and shot them on the spot. On another occasion he summarily executed an acquaintance from among his supporters for putting up a pro-Makhno but anti-Jewish banner.

Undoubtedly, Makhno's army was a serious threat to the White cause in Ukraine, and one French reporter even attributed Denikin's defeat to the constant harassment by Makhno rather than direct battle with the Red Army (Lincoln 1991: 327). While one might not agree with this statement, there is no doubt that despite only having a force averaging 15,000 men, Makhno played a big role in the civil war. Not only that, the relatively loose and population-dependent way of fighting was much closer to the initial Bolshevik policy of a citizens' militia than it was to the highly-disciplined and conventional structure of the Red Army. The example of Makhno thereby showed that the militia option might well have been viable and that the Bolshevik leaders' choice of a top-down army was selected for reasons of political preference rather than operational necessity.

Makhno's social organisation, too, was anti-authoritarian by comparison to the Bolsheviks. Makhno's formula was not perfect. His principles of self-organisation worked better in the traditionally communal-minded villages of central and eastern Ukraine than they

did in the small towns and industrial centres which came under his
control, where lack of authority led to disorganisation. Nonetheless,
Makhno's model deserves to stand as a credible alternative vision to
Lenin's centralised authoritarianism (Avrich 1973; Palij 1976; Malet
1982; Voline 1982; Skirda 2004; Arshinov 2005; www.mahno.ru; www.
nestormakhno.info).

But as far as the war in general goes, Makhno's army was only the
most effective of many oppositional groups that sprang up behind
the Whites. In every case, as White forces moved on, their enemies
would emerge from under cover. In cities, Revolutionary Committees,
like the one in Irkutsk which 'tried' and executed Kolchak, would
come into the open and take control. From this point of view the
Whites' failure was attributable to the fact that they only controlled
the ground on which they stood, a factor arising from their political
bankruptcy, resulting in an inability to produce anything resembling
a political programme that would attract the masses. It was exactly
here that the Bolsheviks, though by no means universally popular,
were able to mobilise sufficient support to get them through. Unlike
the Whites, they never forgot they were fighting a political war. The
Whites saw it almost exclusively in military and operational terms. In
many ways, this was a fatal flaw and, in itself, almost guaranteed defeat.
Despite the apparent closeness of success in summer 1919 it is hard
to imagine that the Whites could have held the populated Russian
heartlands. The White advances were like compressing a spring – the
more the spring was pushed down the more resistant it became and
the stronger the recoil when the grip was released. Victory was an illusory goal for the Whites. By challenging the Soviet system and taking
their attack to it they were, inadvertently, contributing to Bolshevik
survival. They were forcing the population into choosing Red over
White. In this struggle, the Whites could never have won.

Experiencing Civil War

In 2002, Donald Raleigh produced one of the most eye-opening
studies on the Russian civil war. Building on a fine pioneering study
of the Saratov peasantry in revolution, researched and produced
during the Soviet era, Raleigh returned to the region and wrote a
pathbreaking account of the city and province from 1917 to 1922. His
often harrowing analysis heads a multitude of first-rate local studies
(Raleigh 1985, 2002; Mawdsley 1987; Figes 1989; Hickey 1996; Karsch
2006; Badcock 2007; Retish 2008; Wright 2012). The result is that we

now have an immensely rich historiography and set of sources for the civil war years.

A number of key features have emerged. In the forefront, the scale of the humanitarian catastrophe of this period has been underlined. The human cost of the struggle was of the order of 10 million lives. Relatively few died of fighting. Among combatants there were about 350,000 battle dead. The real killers were epidemics – Spanish flu, typhus, cholera – and hunger, both the result of extreme social break-down. Even among combatants more, 450,000, died from illness than from military engagements (Mawdsley 1987). Among the population as a whole, around a million died from typhus and typhoid in the peak year of 1920. About five million died from famine in 1921–2. Socially, the struggle liquidated an entire elite of aristocrats, landowners, factory owners, financiers and many professional and educated people. About two million of them ended up in exile by 1922. While mass flight of the class enemy was welcomed by the Bolsheviks, those that fled took away with them many skills and much knowledge and managerial expertise, which the new authorities found very hard to replace. Economically, the balance sheet is hard to believe. In today's crisis a fall in production of 1 per cent or less is considered a recession and a crisis. Traditional calculations suggest that by 1921 output in key areas of industry was close to obliteration. For example, compared to pre-war levels, mining output was only 29 per cent; oil production 32 per cent; manufacturing as a whole was about 15 per cent; metal industries 10 per cent; cotton textiles 7 per cent and transport 20 per cent. Overall, industrial production was less than 20 per cent of what it had been in 1912 (Malle 1985; Davies 1994). These classical accounts have been augmented by a brilliant calculation of Russia's economic performance in the years of war, revolution and the New Economic Policy (Markevich and Harrison 2011). According to their findings 'Russia's national income fell below 1913 by nearly one-fifth in 1917, and more than three-fifths by 1921.' In the clinical terms of economic history the revolutionary and civil war period is characterised thus:

> There was urban, then regional famine. The February 1917 Revolution, which ended the monarchy, was sparked by urban food shortages. In October 1917 the Bolsheviks inherited a public and private distribution system in collapse. Despite falling harvests, procurement brigades stripped the grain-producing regions of food. Those who stayed in the towns were forced into a 'crisis mode of consumption.' In Petrograd in the spring of 1919, an average worker's daily calorie intake was below 1,600, less than half

the level of four years later. By the end of the war, money wages were apparently 4 percent of their pre-war level in real terms, with workers surviving on public and private inventories and barter.

While, as we have seen, the economy up to 1917 appeared to hold up better than previously thought, Markevich and Harrison unequivocally concluded that:

> economic decline through the Revolution and Civil War appears sharper than in previous accounts. Comparing 1917 with 1913, output per head fell by one-fifth in four years. Over the two years that followed, from 1917 to 1919, output per head halved ... Notably, output fell most precipitously *before* 1919, when the Red and White armies clashed most fiercely. The decline was concentrated in the sectors subject to nationalization; half of the decline in large-scale industry over the entire period took place in 1918 alone. This suggests strongly that the confrontational policies of 'war communism', with widespread state confiscation of property and rule by decree, caused greater disruption than the fighting. Moreover, as the fighting died away, the economy stabilized at around 40 percent of pre-war output but did not at first recover. By 1920 with a command economy in place, the Bolsheviks were able to return large-scale state industry to a path of modest growth. But agriculture continued to struggle, because the policy of surplus confiscation under war communism gave peasants no reason to produce food above subsistence. A deadly game ensued between the farmers and the authorities over the true level of food reserves in the countryside. This game ended in the catastrophic famine of 1921. (Markevich and Harrison 2011: 687.)

They also point out that 'a notable feature of our results is that the famine of 1921 did not come out of the blue; it followed a run of disastrous harvests ... new research on the famine suggests that it actually began in the summer of 1920, and in some regions as early as 1919' (Markevich and Harrison 2011: 688, based on Adamets 2003 and following Ó Gráda 2007). And finally, they emphasise that:

> Postwar recovery began only in 1922, following the revolutionary government's decision to restore market relations and the private sector in small industry and urban-rural trade. The 'New Economic Policy' (NEP) was announced in March 1921 under crisis conditions of accelerating hyperinflation and famine;

recovery was marked only in the following year ... Strong at first, the recovery soon slowed to a single-digit pace. In April 1929 ... average incomes were still below the prewar level. In fact, Soviet GDP per head did not significantly exceed this benchmark until 1934. (Markevich and Harrison 2011: 688.)

The worst of the effects fell on the cities where flight to the country-side or death caused populations to fall disastrously. The former capital, Petrograd, suffered most. Its population collapsed from a peak of 2.5 million in February 1917 to 750,000 in August 1920. These figures are the most extreme. Petrograd was especially vulnerable for several reasons. First, it had to import the vast majority of its food, much of it from South Russia, which was under White control. Secondly, its industries were supplied with raw materials by sea, for example, coal from Newcastle in England. Blockade by Germany had interrupted this since 1914 but after 1918 the embargo was continued until 1920 by the allies in order to undermine the Soviet Government. Thirdly, armaments were a key part of Petrograd industry and demand slumped after the Treaty of Brest-Litovsk. Petrograd's factory proletariat fell from 412,000 workers in 1910 to 148,000 in 1920 (McCauley 1991). Finally, on 12 March 1918, the Soviet Government moved from Petrograd to Moscow, which became the capital. This removed another of Petrograd's main sources of employment.

Moscow suffered less, but even so its population fell from a peak of 1.8 million in 1915 to 1 million in 1920. Its proletariat also shrank, from 190,000 workers in 1917 to 140,000 by August 1918 and a mere 81,000 by January 1921 (Chase 1987). Overall, this amounted to major deproletarianisation of the Bolshevik heartland, a feature having not only sociological but acute political consequences. Other cities suffered according to their local situation. Kiev underwent an almost incessant ebb and flow of occupying forces and many of its problems came from being in the eye of the military hurricane around it. Of course, some peripheral cities saw hardly any disruption. Irkutsk, for example, was virtually self-supporting and self-governing irrespective of national conditions. Vladivostok was subjected to brief foreign occupation by United States troops, and later by Japanese, but otherwise carried on in its own way, at least until the moment of its re-integration with the rest of Russia in 1922. But with few exceptions, the impact of the civil war was devastating.

So severe were the conditions that the question is not just why did so many die but rather how did so many survive? The simple answer to this question is that many people moved back to the village. Almost all city dwellers had relatives in rural areas and many had land, wives, children in their native village. The village proved itself, as it had many times before in Russian history, to be the national safety net. A 'primitive' village like the typical Russian one is less vulnerable than the city because it is largely self-sufficient. Left to itself, the village had the skills, material resources and labour force to reproduce itself. It was much less dependent on networks of supply, communications and so on than cities and industries. Of course, conditions might be very harsh and living standards fall, but, as long as warriors or bandits did not intervene to loot it and the environmental conditions remained within normal parameters, the village could cope to a much greater degree than the town. The village was the redoubt in which Russia survived from 1918 to 1922/3. This is not to say the rural population did not suffer, far from it, but they were more likely to survive.

Generalisations and statistics are only part of the picture. Combining the new and the traditional historiography has vastly extended our knowledge of the sufferings endured in this dreadful period. One of the most penetrating eyewitnesses of the period was the independent Russo-Belgian revolutionary Victor Serge. Arriving in Petrograd in 1919 he described what he saw as 'a revolution dying', a phrase used by a Bolshevik activist in conversation with him (Serge 1963 71). He described the revolutionary city in graphic terms:

> We were entering a world frozen to death. The Finland Station, glittering with snow, was deserted. The square where Lenin had addressed a crowd from the top of an armoured car, was no more than a white desert surrounded by dead houses. The broad, straight thoroughfares, the bridges across the Neva, now a river of snowy ice, seemed to belong to an abandoned city; first a gaunt soldier in a grey greatcoat, then, after a long time, a woman freezing under her shawls, went past like phantoms in an oblivious silence. (Serge 1962 70.)

Petrograd, he concluded, was the 'metropolis of Cold, of Hunger, of Hatred, and of Endurance' (Serge 1962 71). In a short story, the writer Evgenii Zamiatin, whose great anti-utopian novel of 1922, *We*, inspired Huxley's *Brave New World* and Orwell's *Nineteen Eighty-Four*, wrote about the horrors of 1919 in Petrograd which was, metaphorically, partly post-apocalyptic and partly reverting to the stone age:

> Glaciers, mammoths, wastes. Black nocturnal cliffs, somehow resembling houses: in the cliffs, caves … One thing is clear: it is winter.

And you must clench your teeth as tightly as you can, to keep them from chattering: and you must split wood with a stone axe; and every night you must carry your fire from cave to cave, deeper and deeper. And you must wrap yourself into shaggy animal hides, more and more of them. (Zamiatin 1975 140.)

The central figures, an intelligentsia couple, trying to survive in their now almost bare apartment, are unable to keep up with what is required, and run out of fuel for the 'centre of this universe – its god, the short-legged, rusty-red, squat, greedy cave god: the cast-iron stove'. They die miserably, as tens of thousands had done in real life.

Intellectuals were particularly exposed to the conditions of the time, in that workers tended to have some prospect of work and a priority call on the meagre rations available and wealthier bourgeois had resources and property which could be traded for food and fuel. But intellectuals had nothing and were despised by many of the new rulers as an insidious class enemy. Some were able to get jobs in the still-functioning intellectual areas of writing, publishing, teaching and higher education, but even that was not necessarily sufficient.

An extraordinary example of this is to be found in the person of the historian and associate director of the Rumiantsev Museum, Iurii Vladimirovich Got'e, who wrote an extensive diary chronicling his life in Moscow during the civil war. He described in great detail the problems of the time, great and small, such as having to get official permission to undertake a railway journey, the neglect of the streets which were becoming overgrown with grass and weeds, the frustrations of trying to find supplies, being forced to 'loan' the family silver to the government and deciding it was better to pawn or sell valuables before they were, inevitably, confiscated. He also had to help his brother out of the clutches of the Cheka in Novgorod. In August 1918, he was informed by a friend of his brother's plight and the circumstances of his arrest. Many prisoners in Novgorod and elsewhere were being transferred out of Cheka control to be processed for release 'But then' his informant wrote, 'the events in Petrograd struck', that is the assassination of Uritskii and the shooting of Lenin on 30 August. As a result 'all the cases were hastily recalled to the Extraordinary Commission [that is, the Cheka] and on the following morning six persons were shot' (Got'e 1988: 466). He needed to get a railway pass for his journey to Novgorod. 'The passes for business trips were issued by a comrade-worker whose rudeness was unmatched by anything I had heard or seen. And since our office had not seen fit to put a number on the certificate given to me, they didn't give me the pass at all, and I lost another day', a particularly insupportable delay given his mission was to save his brother, who could have been executed at any moment. The ride to Novgorod, was slow and uncomfortable in a grossly overcrowded train. Surprisingly, Got'e tells us, its rigours were endured by the passengers not in the 'nasty and unpleasant way' he expected but in a spirit of being 'mutually well-disposed, meek and courteous', together with 'a hint of mockery at the state of things' (Got'e 1988: 195). Such were the oddities and inconsistencies of early Soviet Russia that 'My task in Novgorod', he wrote, was 'to liberate my brother; I achieved that quickly and, moreover, without great effort' (Got'e 1988: 195). It was almost easier for him to get his brother released, simply by vouching for his political reliability, than it had been to get his train pass.

The situation in Moscow and its surrounding region, while very difficult, was by no means as apocalyptic as in Petrograd. As late as summer 1918 his wife, Nina, who lived on the family estate in the country, which Got'e visited frequently, was still speculating on how they might share a state apartment with friends and whether there was any chance they might be able to retain a servant and find a French nanny for their son Volodia (Got'e 1988: 465). Even so, material hardships were already biting deep. Nina wrote: 'I am not eating any potatoes at all. I am on a diet of mushrooms, beans and kasha [a kind of porridge] which I have found on the estate. There is nowhere to buy meat; there are almost no eggs – only enough for Volodia, and I occasionally make fried eggs; the cows give little – they have stopped milking three of them. My spirits are low, like everyone else's.' (Got'e 1988: 466.)

By the standards of the following year, 1919, Nina's hardships looked like luxuries. Transport, economy and society were in mutual freefall. The collapse of the railway system brought the economy down. The collapse of the economy caused depopulation of cities and death from disease and hunger. Donald Raleigh's harrowing account of life in Saratov city and region shows not only the depth of the crisis and its deadly grip but also the often heroic and selfless efforts of some figures among the new local Soviet authorities to deal with it. It is impossible to convey the full horror in a few lines but some of the evidence stands out. Saratov was near the front line in 1919 and this was reflected in a collapse of public health. Rates of infectious disease rose from an already elevated 68.3 per thousand in 1918 to an extraordinary 122.2 in 1919. Terrible hygiene, poor nutrition including near absence of milk for babies and children, chronic shortage of doctors, cumulative exhaustion of the population all contributed so that in the

Saratov province the number of deaths from disease rose from 16,000 in 1918 to just over 200,000 in both 1919 and 1920. The 1921 figure fell back to 63,000 but the return of famine in 1922 pushed it back up to 123,000 (Raleigh 2002: 199–200). Animals were also affected. Cattle plague rates soared. 'By early 1921 the city's dumping ground where diseased horses were brought for slaughter had turned into a nightmare. With the coming of spring [i.e. when the thaw came] the unburned carcasses strewn about threatened to contaminate the city's water supply.' (Raleigh 2002: 200.) Bedbugs and lice were rife. Sexual licentiousness, partly arising from the massive increase in prostitution caused by the proximity of economically desperate women, men and children and an 'eager clientele' among garrison soldiers, caused rates of STDs to 'reach alarming proportions'; by late 1920, clinics were treating 10,000 cases per month (Raleigh 2002: 200).

Among the most heartrending victims were homeless children (*besprizornyi*). Described ironically in one local paper as 'the hope and pride of the revolutionary people' there were 'tens of thousands of local children and millions nationwide ... left homeless, destitute, neglected', who found themselves 'at the mercy of an impoverished and later depleted social system'. They were 'brutalized by poverty and disease, filth and neglect, undernourishment, substance addiction and physical and sexual abuse' (Raleigh 2002: 203). Many of them were forced to live on the streets, and turned to sometimes horrifyingly violent crime to survive. Some were in homes but:

> what would we encounter if we were to peer into the broken windows of a few children's homes? There was enough vile food to keep them alive from a calorific point of view, but no heat, blankets, soap or hot water. Some children had not bathed or changed their undergarments for five months. They suffered from scabies and lice ... Like the city itself, the homes were dingy, cheerless, overcrowded, in urgent need of repair, and staffed by unqualified personnel. (Raleigh 2002: 205.)

This was before economic restructuring in 1921 caused most of the homes to shut down and turn many of the children out, and before they were hit by the 1921/22 famine which, according to the leading authority on the issue, 'played a greater role in depriving children of their homes than did any other cause' (Alan Ball quoted in Raleigh 2002: 205).

These were by no means the only evils that afflicted Saratov. No brief account can do justice to them all. Many other problems were rampant across the province and the whole nation. Refugees, whom we encountered in graphic descriptions from 1915, became an almost permanent feature of the Russian landscape. Melancholy groups were being driven hither and yon by successive waves of fighting, by economic collapse, by food shortages and by famine. Other evils were more specific. Like many Russian cities and villages, in which many buildings were made of wood, the city of Saratov suffered from fires. There were 492 in 1920. But on a hot, dry, windy day, 31 July 1920, disaster struck. A fire broke out which burned for eight hours. It consumed 1,819 buildings and, possibly, 100 lives. In any case it left 25,000 people, one eighth of the total population, without a home. Not surprisingly, by early 1921 the authorities were blaming fires not only on neglect and incompetence but also on deliberate actions (Raleigh 2002: 193). A 'Stalinist' culture of wreckers, saboteurs and enemies of the people was already gestating.

It was the village that pulled Russia through its crisis. The myriad villages dotted over the landscape had travails of their own but, in the final analysis, they proved tough and unexpectedly resilient. It was deep in village culture, going back centuries, that the outside world brought little but trouble and, in the extreme circumstances of the time, this assumption stood them in good stead. They did what they had always tried to do in moments of crisis, they bunkered down, tried to repel almost all forces from the outside and concentrated on producing the food they needed for survival. It has to be remembered that most of the peasantry were subsistence producers who cultivated most of what they needed and traded little. Had Russian agriculture become more developed and more specialised the peasants, like their brothers and sisters in the towns, would have been dependent on trade and therefore on a set of collapsing networks of which transport was the most critical. In a sense, 'backwardness' saved the peasantry and the nation. We will look at aspects of national policies in the next chapter. Here we will concentrate on what it was like to live in the village from 1918 to 1922. We have a number of detailed studies which show graphically what they had to put up and how they lived through it.

In addition to perennial hazards – like climatic conditions, poverty, illness, crop and livestock disease – the civil war brought added burdens. Most obviously the combatant armies looked to the village to requisition (or often loot) food and horsepower and to conscript young men as soldiers. Within Soviet territory, the urban crisis stimulated panic measures in this direction which, for example, brought armed requisition squads into the countryside. The new regime also brought a host of locally powerful officials. Some were heroic and brilliant, others were incompetent but the worst were malevolent, turning their parishes (*volosty*) and counties (*uezdy*) into personal fiefdoms. Refugees could be a burden especially in areas of heavy fighting. Also, tens of thousands of armed deserters roamed around stealing and raping almost at will. They based themselves in remote corners of forests, hills and mountains emerging only to prey upon the locals. Peasants had little but their traditions, local solidarity, agrarian skills and traditional craftiness to protect themselves against these almost-biblical plagues.

One of the places about which we know most, thanks to the work of Aaron Retish, is Viatka in the Urals. The extent of its suffering in these years can be shown in a few indicative statistics. In one area of the province, numbers of cattle fell from 164,000 in 1916 to 108,000 in 1921 and 88,000 in 1922. For the same years the corresponding figures for bulls, was 12,000; 1,000 and an astonishingly low 500. Draft horses declined from 161,000 to 104,00 and 85,000. Grain output fell from 28 million *pudy* (1 *pud* equals 36 lb, or about 16 kg) to a catastrophic 4 million in the famine harvest of 1921, and still only just over 8 million in 1922 (Retish 2008: 243, figures rounded up and down). In another district, by 1922 35 per cent of households did not own a horse (Retish 2008: 242–3). Viatka province was 'devastated' between 1913 and 1920. The population of Viatka fell from 3.65 million to less than 2 million. 'Mobilization, famine, disease, flight and state terror ruptured family relations and destroyed whole households ... The disappearance of livestock and agricultural instruments made the peasant economy a hollow shell of what it once was ... There was a surge in divorce, family abandonment, and suicides.' (Retish 2008: 259–60) The result was that:

> Peasants witnessed their village wasting away. Beautiful homes fell into disrepair with broken glass panes, shuttered windows, and dilapidated roofs. Once-vibrant homesteads had sick, starving elderly and children struggling to survive. Fields returned to the wild and neighbours abandoned their homes to seek food elsewhere. Peasants sought answers in the political and civil order. Some rebelled against the regime, but most turned to those above them for aid. (Retish 2008: 262.)

In a coruscating judgement that would apply not just to Saratov but to most of Soviet Russia, Raleigh concluded that 'Economic ruin proved every bit as difficult to lick as the White armies. Industrial output in the Lower Volga region in 1921–22 amounted to just 30 per cent of its pre-war level.' Six devastating years had:

> brutalized [the] people, and brought them to the brink of physical exhaustion and emotional despair. Shortages of everything except enmity, cynicism, and contempt had unleashed people's vileness and exposed their vulnerability. The fierce struggle did not spare the regime itself ... Then, in 1921, famine ... seized hold of the city and province and kept it in its grip until the 1922 harvest was in. (Raleigh 2002: 206.)

While the only census of the period was not conducted until 1926, its conclusions on the demographic crisis were clear. Nationally the population in 1926 was 147 million when it was projected that it would have been 175 million without war and revolution, that is it was 28 million short. In Saratov province the population losses (that is actual decline plus an estimate of the consequences of a lowering of the birthrate) meant that between 1914 and 1922, it lost nearly 900,000 people, or 20 per cent of what its population would have been without the war. The dimensions of the crisis are staggering.

Our final major question is to ask how the Bolsheviks coped with crisis, contributed to it, survived and began to construct a new economic, social and political system on such ruined foundations.

Chapter 8: The Emergence of Bolshevik Order: Spring 1918–March 1921

By the time of the spring 1918 crisis between the signing of the Treaty of Brest-Litovsk and the Czechoslovak 'uprising' all the signs seemed to suggest that the Bolsheviks were following their Provisional Government predecessors down the road to political oblivion. Lenin's plans for transition were in ruins as workers went for nationalisation and workers' control, and the middle class, especially factory owners, managers and financiers, simply quit their posts and even moved to White areas or abroad. The financial and economic disarray of 1917 had become a downward spiral, sucking society down with it. The vital artery of Russian national life, the railway system, was plunging into chaos with universally disastrous consequences. Worker alienation and peasant indifference, once they had taken the land, were creating a political backlash. Bolshevik gains in the lower-level soviets began to be reversed, as rivals such as the Mensheviks and the SRs began to make advances (Brovkin 1983; 1987).

Lenin Modifies Marxism

The Bolshevik, now renamed Communist, Party had always been prone to splits based on ideological arguments. It was, first and foremost, an ideological party devoted to implementing Marxist principles with a kind of secular religious determination. They had fought other socialist parties on largely ideological grounds and, at times, had fought almost equally fiercely among themselves over certain ideological principles. In a sense, Lenin had long resembled a kind of fundamentalist Marxist ayatollah following a set of dogmas and fighting with friend and foe over nuances of interpretation and implementation. For a true Bolshevik, ideological rectitude was the supreme virtue, overriding everything, including personal feelings such as friendship. In Lenin's life, for instance, in 1903 he severed relations with his close friend Martov over ideology and, in 1917, welcomed his arch-critic Trotsky, back into the camp after more than a decade of denunciation since the ideological differences seemed to have disappeared. For a party so prone to enter into sometimes vicious factional polemics, it is no surprise that the pressures of early 1918 ensured that acrimonious divisions would emerge. Essentially, there was, on one hand, a left-communist faction which claimed the revolutionary programme of 1917 was being abandoned and, on the other, the bulk of the party, which clung to Lenin, who was moving from a centrist position to one further to the right.

One of the first major issues, sparked off by Brest-Litovsk, was 'world revolution'. The party had assumed that, without it spreading at least to Germany, the Russian revolution would fail. On 26 October, Trotsky had been unambiguous in his address to the Second Congress of Soviets: 'The Russian Revolution will either cause a revolution in the west, or the capitalists will strangle our [revolution]' (Bunyan and Fisher 1934: 136). The argument was rooted in Marxist dogma. Marx had argued that socialism could only come about in an 'advanced', that is, highly developed, capitalist country which had exhausted capitalism's extraordinary ability to find new ways to make profits and had ended up impoverishing its own workers who could not then provide a market for the system's goods. Of all the major European countries, Russia was the one that least fitted the Marxist prediction. Capitalism was still struggling to establish itself against a decaying feudalism, and the working class was massively outnumbered by the peasantry, a class doomed to disappear under capitalist conditions. So how could one be a Marxist in Russia? Only, Lenin had long argued, by cultivating two peculiarly Russian features of the movement. One was to put Russia's revolution in the context of an international struggle against imperialism. In fact, the global nature of imperialism, it was argued, gave renewed significance to struggles where it was weak. The chain of capitalism, Lenin argued, borrowing the phrase from others' polemics, could be expected to break at its weakest link. Trotsky's post-1905 theory of 'permanent revolution' had also argued that it was easier to combat the capitalist bourgeoisie in a place like Russia, where it was weak and immature, than to do so in Britain or the United States where it dominated the economy, the major political and social institutions and key opinion-formers like the developing mass press, which it imbued with its values.

The second Russian innovation was the need for a strong, centralised and highly politically conscious party to make up for the numerical weakness of the actual workers. Critics argued this led to the party 'substituting' itself for the historical role of the class. In 1904, Trotsky had gone even further when he was polemicising against Lenin: 'the organisation of the party substitutes itself for the party as a whole, then the Central Committee substitutes itself for the organisation and finally, the dictator substitutes himself for the Central Committee.' (Trotsky 1979.)

In the crisis of early 1918, it appeared that Lenin was weakening the commitment to immediate world revolution in favour of consolidating the situation within Russia. In particular, this involved the unexpected Bolshevik hijacking of the entire state apparatus, a process later known as totalitarianism, a term that still elicits controversy (Gleason 1998). This was a surprise to a party brought up on the view that the destiny of the state under socialism was that it would disappear. Lenin had only just completed a major pamphlet, *State and Revolution*, arguing that this was the case. However, the devastating effect of Brest-Litovsk seemed to entail the abandonment of thoughts of spreading the revolution in the near future. In its place, as we have seen, Lenin was arguing for something quite different, survival at any cost, including retreat to the Urals (see p. 129). He was developing a provisional theory of socialism in one country.

There was a third, completely unexpected, adaptation of Marxism to Russian conditions. It was one which only had resonance once the party was in power and was focused on the apparently devastated economy and society it had inherited. The fact that the following three years added previously unimaginable circles of hell to a situation which was already thought to be disastrous only strengthened its importance. The third innovation was the emergence of productionism. What was meant by this was that maximising economic output should be the first priority of the revolution. It was partly a pragmatic concession to the immediate conditions, which almost any government of the time would have to deal with, but for the Bolsheviks it was more than that. Obviously, it had to have ideological constraints in that the adopted measures had to be compatible with socialism, but it also had a vital ideological dimension. If Russia's economic 'backwardness' was an obstacle to its Marxist future, then overcoming that backwardness was an unavoidable first stage on the way to socialism. No one knew how long that stage would be because it could always be foreshortened, so it was argued, if the revolution spread. If it spread, comrades in the advanced capitalist countries would help the Russian revolution. In this way, the prominence of productionism was in inverse proportion to the success of revolution in the advanced capitalist countries. Given the absence of revolution in an advanced capitalist country, productionism became a permanent feature of the Soviet system and was, arguably, its central characteristic right down to the mid-1980s.

Lenin's second plan for transition: Socialism in one country

Lenin's own thoughts on the substitution of this second conceptualisation, replacing the failed 'optimistic' scenario of a 'gradual, peaceful and smooth' transition led by workers and Soviet supporters who 'would soon learn' the intricacies of producing and distributing goods, can be found in his writings of early spring 1918. The most important, a lengthy and at times turgid, tortuous exposition of them, was written in April and, to underline its importance, published simultaneously in the party newspaper *Pravda* and the state newspaper *Izvestiia* on 28 April. It was entitled 'Immediate Tasks of the Soviet Government'. Six theses arising from the article were also published on 9 May in the party newspaper for peasants, *Bednota*.

At the heart of the new discourse was the concept of 'iron proletarian discipline'. For Lenin the dictatorship of the proletariat was now confirmed by 'the historical experience of all revolutions' (Lenin 1967: vol. 2, 669). Does this prove Lenin was always insincere about his more consensual first transition plan? Maybe, but it was not unusual for Lenin to call on the testimony of history to support whatever line he was pursuing, even when he had made a similar call upon it to support an earlier and contradictory line. In any case, for Lenin there was no doubt what the new principles should entail. 'The general and summarising slogan of the moment', Lenin wrote in the theses which accompanied the article a few days later, was 'iron discipline and thorough exercise of proletarian dictatorship' (Lenin 1967: vol. 2, 683). His words could hardly have been more clear. 'Dictatorship, however, is a big word', he had warned, 'and big words should not be thrown about carelessly. Dictatorship is iron rule, government that is revolutionarily bold, swift and ruthless in suppressing both exploiters and hooligans. But our government is excessively mild, very often it resembles jelly more than iron.' (Lenin 1967: vol. 2, 670.)

Such dramatic and foreboding statements seemed almost out of place compared to the rest of the article, the prescriptions of which were mundane and undramatic. The priority of the moment, he said, was 'to concentrate efforts … on the most important and most difficult task of the socialist revolution, namely the task of organisation.' (Lenin 1967: vol. 2, 645) Revolutionaries were now exhorted to 'Keep regular and honest accounts of money, manage economically, do not be lazy, do not steal, observe the strictest labour discipline.' (Lenin 1967: vol. 2, 651.) Apart from the word 'labour', the slogans could have come from a Victorian moral primer. The chief task of revolution was no longer to fight at barricades, organise street demonstrations and dream of sweeping into western Europe, now 'The decisive thing is the organization of the strictest country-wide accounting and control of production and distribution of goods.' (Lenin 1967: vol. 2, 652.) These were, of course 'tasks' largely fulfilled by the market and by enterprise under capitalism. Easy for Lenin to pronounce such a slogan but it was totally unclear from his writings how it could be achieved. His emphasis on it was, nonetheless, correct from the Soviet point of view. Organisation was the banal but key task. Its objective was also spelled out. Without it 'there can be no thought of achieving the second and equally essential condition for introducing socialism, namely, raising the productivity of labour on a national scale' (Lenin 1967: vol. 2, 652).

It should first be noted that these were not aspects of socialism but 'essential condition[s]' for its 'introduction'. Raising productivity meant overcoming backwardness It was a means of constructing the arena in which emerging socialism would compete with capitalism. If, as Marx had argued, socialism could only be built in a condition of material abundance, then it was necessary to create that abundance of goods and then build socialism. Productionism had been born.

Some of the means Lenin proposed to achieve its goals were also rather ordinary but, nonetheless, very controversial. There should be a strengthening of one-person management in place of factory committees and workers' control. This was associated with a policy even more unpopular with the left, namely the reinstatement of as many former managers and technical specialists as could be attracted by much higher salaries than the wages of workers themselves. The old principle of not paying managers more than the wage of a skilled worker had been sacrificed, along with many others, on the altar of temporary expediency. As is so often the case, temporary became permanent.

There were many other such U-turns, some of which we will examine shortly, but one of the most spectacular and most illustrative of the 'new' logic that was developing was the adoption of Taylorist principles as a means of achieving productionist goals. Frederick Taylor had revolutionised capitalist industrial production through the 'scientific' study of labour. Examining the physical movements associated with labour had led to the introduction of the production line. Critics, including most socialists, argued that it was a form of super-exploitation and that it increased the alienation of the labour force from what they produced by restricting workers to simple, endlessly repeated acts, thereby turning them into mindless adjuncts of the machine. Nonetheless, Lenin seized upon it as a means for constructing socialism. While the actual tasks and experience of the individual worker remained the same, under socialism, Lenin argued, the process itself became positive. It helped emancipate labour by increasing productivity. The effects of tsarism and the hangover of serfdom meant that, in Lenin's words, 'The Russian is a bad worker compared with people in the advanced capitalist countries.' The people must 'learn to work'. It was necessary to apply 'much of what is scientific and progressive in the Taylor system' (Lenin 1967: vol. 2, 664). Associated with this there would also be re-introduction of piecework, a socialist form of competition and 'unquestioning obedience while at work to the one-man decisions of Soviet directors' (Lenin 1967: vol. 2, 683). For many workers, socialism was beginning to look like capitalism, and it is no wonder that Lenin defended his system as state capitalism. But that, too, brought forth a stronger state. Time and again he emphasised that 'Dictatorship presupposes a revolutionary government that is really firm and ruthless' (Lenin 1967: vol. 2, 683), and that it was necessary to use 'compulsion so that the slogan of the dictatorship of the proletariat should not be desecrated by the practice of a lily-livered proletarian government' (Lenin 1967: vol. 2, 664). 'The proletarian dictatorship', he wrote, 'is indispensable' while, on the other hand, currently 'our government is too mild' (Lenin 1967: vol. 2, 683).

Lenin's second plan for transition is most frequently referred to as 'war communism', but this name is misleading. The underlying principles of 'war communism' are to be found in 'Immediate Tasks of the Soviet Government' and associated writings. But the point of the new turn was that peace had been achieved, both what Lenin called the 'unstable' (Lenin 1967: vol. 2, 645) peace with the imperialists after Brest-Litovsk and victory in the civil war since 'in the main ... the task of suppressing the exploiters was fulfilled in the period from October 25 1917 to (approximately) February 1918' (Lenin 1967: vol. 2, 649). The new line was not, as its traditional name suggests, a formula for war-fighting but one to take advantage of the current 'respite' to 'heal the very severe wounds inflicted by the war ... and bring about an economic revival' (Lenin 1967: vol. 2, 646). Lenin was well aware that many political conflicts lay ahead, with monarchists, Kadets and 'their henchmen and hangers-on the Mensheviks and Socialist Revolutionaries' (Lenin 1967: vol. 2, 649), but also repeated several times that the back of internal opposition had already been broken. Only by succeeding in the new tasks of administration would Soviet Russia be strong enough to achieve not only 'a real increase in our country's defence potential' but also enable it to 'render effective assistance to the socialist revolution in the West, which has been delayed for a number of reasons' (Lenin 1967: vol. 2, 646).

Rather than a set of expedients to fight a war, the second transition was based on long-term principles, in fact ones that became the bedrock of the Soviet system. If we put them all together – iron discipline; ruthless dictatorship rather than a mild, jelly-like or lily-livered proletarian government; productionism; a nationwide system of accounting and control of the production and distribution of goods; building Soviet strength for future defence and to enable better assistance to foreign revolutions; one-person management; piecework; bonuses; one-party government; the menace of enemies all around and within; a postponement of world revolution – we end up with something normally thought of as Stalinism. While Stalin was very different from Lenin, and put his own personal, malevolent stamp on the Soviet system, it is nonetheless clear that rather than 'war communism', what Lenin had envisaged in these months was a prototype of 'socialism in one country'. He had enunciated certain key principles which were fundamental to the Soviet system right through to its demise. We will now turn to look at some of the institutions and policies which emerged to put these principles into practice in the period from April 1918 to March 1921. Coercion is often considered the key mode of 'delivery' of Bolshevik governance and we will look at this area first but, in the Bolshevik value system, mobilisation, 'winning over' the population, 'raising consciousness' was the ultimately decisive area.

Coercion

The Cheka and terror

The most notorious of all major Soviet institutions, and ironically one which most successfully survived the collapse of the rest of the system, was its political police, usually known as the 'secret' police, though its existence was no secret. The first such force was founded on 7 December 1917. Up to then the coercive instruments of the revolution had been the soviet-based Red Guards and the Military Revolutionary Committees. The new body, the Extraordinary Commission for Combating Counter-revolution and Sabotage, was known as the Cheka, an acronym derived from the first two words of its name in Russian. Its name also defined its role. It was set up as a 'temporary' body to act as a swift, determined and righteous dispenser of justice. Its head, Feliks Dzherzhinskii, was an unusual Bolshevik. He was a Jesuit-educated, Polish Catholic by origin. His revolutionary devotion and asceticism embodied the ideal of implacable revolutionary justice which was supposed to be at the heart of the Cheka. He followed the decades-old principle of large parts of Russia's radical intelligentsia that 'the good of the revolution is the highest law'. While by no means infallible, he pursued this objective with selfless zeal and total commitment. He was a kind of revolutionary saint. However, one such individual, or even tens or hundreds of them, were not enough. Like many agencies of the new state, the Cheka soon began to attract employees who were neither devoted to the cause nor morally scrupulous. As the role of the Cheka expanded it had to cast its nets wider and wider to gain recruits. It also began to bring back certain 'specialists' and managers from the tsarist political police system. In many respects, as a new agency of the fledgling state, it went through a similar evolution to most other government agencies. It started out with a small, devoted, more or less competent set of core leaders but, as its tasks and responsibilities increased exponentially, it became larger and larger in order to cope, and less and less 'pure' in terms of the personnel.

A few facts and figures about the number of chekists, as they were called, and the number of arrests and, worse, executions associated with them shows the main contours of its development. By mid-July 1918 it had 35 battalions in its Special Corps. By 1921 it had 31,000 'frontline' agents and commissars and a total of 143,000 employees, though budget cuts reduced this to 105,000 by May 1922. According to official reports it suppressed 245 'uprisings', mainly resistance to grain requisitioning, in 1918 and the first seven months of 1919. In these conflicts, 1,150 died on the Red side and 3,057 among the 'insurrectionists'. These figures only covered half the provinces of European Russia. In terms of executions, there had been 6,300 by the end of 1918 and 3,456 (excluding Ukraine) in 1919. Unofficially, figures are very much higher. One of the most extreme, calculated by Robert Conquest and presented to the US Senate Judiciary Committee in 1971 was of 500,000 executions and deaths in custody. This is unlikely to have been an underestimation (Leggett *et al.* in Read 1996: 206–217) Clearly, the commission was fulfilling its own job description as presented by Latsis, one of its leading figures:

> It was necessary to make the foe feel that there was everywhere about him a seeing eye and a heavy hand ready to come down on him the moment he undertook anything against the Soviet Government ... [The Cheka was] an apparatus for compulsion and purification [because] the masses of the people were still imbued with the old spirit. (Bunyan and Fisher 1934: 296)

In 1922, this 'temporary' and 'extraordinary' body had become such an ordinary and essential part of the system that it was reorganised on a permanent basis and given a new name, the GPU (The State Political Administration).

Perhaps surprisingly, the Cheka did not provoke as much controversy in the party as the other really important enforcement mechanism, the Red Army. All parts of the party seemed to see the need for a rapidly-acting and vigilant sword of justice to be swinging over the heads of counter-revolutionaries. The enemy were ruthless, they had to be paid back in kind. A 'lily-livered proletarian government' would be short-lived. The revolution had to be defended against its implacable enemies. In the words of the author of one of the most detailed comparative studies of revolutionary terror in France and in Russia 'The Furies of revolution are fuelled primarily by the inevitable and unexceptional resistance of the forces and ideas opposed to it' (Mayer 2001: 4). Whether one agrees with that judgment or not, it certainly has some truth in it, and would have been heartily endorsed by Bolsheviks of all kinds. However, there were many dissenting voices outside the party among not only, obviously, the right but many parts of the Soviet left. This was, not least, a response to the fact that the category of enemies of the people was rapidly expanded to include many Mensheviks, SRs and, of course, anarchists who were among the first on the left to feel the Cheka's bite in the Durnovo villa and elsewhere. Crudely speaking those within the circle defended by the Cheka supported it, those outside, who could be its victims, did not.

Unsurprisingly, critiques from foreign leftists, like the once-respected Karl Kautsky, who was reviled by Lenin for deserting the internationalist cause in 1914 and voting for German war credits, were easily brushed off, but they contained an important message.

Terror and abandonment of democracy threatened not only enemies but those who conducted such policies. Remarkably, the essence of such a critique of coercion had, as we have seen, been made by members of the party's own Central Committee within a few days of October. But Lenin was impervious to such criticism. Democracy would have been good, but in the circumstances it would only play into enemy hands.

However, there was one critic who hurt the Bolshevik leaders. In 1918, shortly before her brutal death at the hands of political thugs and from her prison cell in Berlin, the Polish revolutionary Rosa Luxemburg wrote a pamphlet, *The Russian Revolution*. While largely enthusiastic about the October revolution, Luxemburg enunciated a profound critique of the Bolsheviks' anti-democratic tendencies and their inclination towards terror and one-party government. Her critique was based on a plea for freedom, not as a desirable added extra but as an essential contribution to success.

> Freedom only for the supporters of the government, only for the members of one party – however numerous they may be – is no freedom at all. Freedom is always and exclusively freedom for the one who thinks differently. Not because of any fanatical concept of 'justice' but because all that is instructive, wholesome and purifying in political freedom depends on this essential characteristic, and its effectiveness vanishes when 'freedom' becomes a special privilege.

What was the consequence of the absence of freedom? Intellectual death:

> Without general elections, without unrestricted freedom of press and assembly, without a free struggle of opinion, life dies out in every public institution, becomes a mere semblance of life, in which only the bureaucracy remains as the active element.

She was also very quick to identify two other flaws in Bolshevism which needed to be addressed. First there was a tendency to dogmatism:

> The tacit assumption underlying the Lenin–Trotsky theory of dictatorship is this: that the socialist transformation is something for which a ready-made formula lies completed in the pocket of the revolutionary party, which needs only to be carried out energetically in practice. This is, unfortunately – or perhaps fortunately – not the case.

And in a summary of her views, including strong support for wha
they were attempting, she pointed out Bolshevism's tendency to
identify its own particular way of doing things as a universal mode
ideal for all:

> Everything that happens in Russia is comprehensible and repre
> sents an inevitable chain of causes and effects, the starting poin
> and end term of which are: the failure of the German proletaria
> and the occupation of Russia by German imperialism. It would be
> demanding something superhuman from Lenin and his comrade
> if we should expect of them that under such circumstances the
> should conjure forth the finest democracy, the most exemplary
> dictatorship of the proletariat and a flourishing socialist economy
> By their determined revolutionary stand, their exemplary strength
> in action, and their unbreakable loyalty to international socialism
> they have contributed whatever could possibly be contributed
> under such devilishly hard conditions. The danger begins only
> when they make a virtue of necessity and want to freeze into a
> complete theoretical system all the tactics forced upon them by
> these fatal circumstances, and want to recommend them to the
> international proletariat as a model of socialist tactics. When the
> get in their own light in this way, and hide their genuine, unques
> tionable historical service under the bushel of false steps forced
> on them by necessity, they render a poor service to international
> socialism for the sake of which they have fought and suffered; for
> they want to place in its storehouse as new discoveries all the distor
> tions prescribed in Russia by necessity and compulsion – in the last
> analysis only by-products of the bankruptcy of international social
> ism in the present world war. (Luxemburg 1961.)

Her measured remarks were met by stinging rebukes from Lenin and
Trotsky. In response mainly to Kautsky's criticism but implicitly to
Luxemburg as well, the latter defended Bolshevism:

> It is only possible to safeguard the supremacy of the working class
> by forcing the bourgeoisie accustomed to rule, to realize that it is
> too dangerous an undertaking for it to revolt against the dictator
> ship of the proletariat, to undermine it by conspiracies, sabotage,
> insurrections, or the calling in of foreign troops. The bourgeoisie,
> hurled from power, must be forced to obey. In what way? The
> priests used to terrify the people with future penalties. We have
> no such resources at our disposal. But even the priests' hell never

stood alone, but was always bracketed with the material fire of the Holy Inquisition, and with the scorpions of the democratic State. ... The Russian White Guards resemble the German and all other White Guards in this respect – that they cannot be convinced or shamed, but only terrorized or crushed.

The man who repudiates terrorism in principle – i.e., repudiates measures of suppression and intimidation towards determined and armed counter-revolution - must reject all idea of the political supremacy of the working class and its revolutionary dictatorship. The man who repudiates the dictatorship of the proletariat repudiates the Socialist revolution, and digs the grave of Socialism. (Trotsky 1975: 175.)

The Red Army

If the party, by and large, accepted the Cheka, the principles on which the Red Army was founded evoked considerable argument (von Hagen 1984, 1990; Benvenuti 1988). The *April Theses* could hardly have been clearer. 'Abolition of the police, army and bureaucracy', Lenin had written. Instead, there would be a militia, that is the population would be armed and would defend itself, a concept deemed to be democratic by many left-wing parties. The point was that if the people held the weapons there would be no army to be used by the rulers to oppress them. In the first months of Soviet rule, the policy was carried out to the letter. The tsarist army had fallen apart, with great encouragement from above (Wildman 1988).

It was not so much the decision to remake an army that evoked criticism in the party but the way in which it was done and the principles according to which it continued to evolve. The first defence forces of the Soviet revolution had been, like most of its institutions, somewhat amateurish and ramshackle. Informal Red Guard units plus a core of pro-Bolshevik military units, like the Latvian Riflemen and Kronstadt sailors, coalesced, usually in support of Military Revolutionary Committees, not only in Petrograd and Moscow but in many major centres. However, the leaders of the revolution, especially Trotsky who was the party member supervising the process of building a new army, soon came to the conclusion that informal and militia-style units were not enough and turned to a version of conventional principles of military organisation. Ranks were reinforced, even to the return of insignia for senior officers. Rank-and-file committees were abolished or marginalised. Like many 'democratic' innovations which had been needed against tsarist oppression, they were declared 'unnecessary' since the proletarian state was devoted to the welfare of the masses. This even stretched to the death penalty itself which was re-introduced in August 1918. Trotsky himself put it into practice in a famous incident at Sviazhsk on 18 August 1918 when he had twenty deserters shot.

Other developments also antagonised the party left and powerful military groups outside the party such as the Kronstadt sailors. In particular, the policy of recruiting expert 'specialists' (spetsy) from the old regime was energetically pursued in the military sphere. As a result, former Tsarist officers came flooding back into the new Red Army. In total some 15,000 to 20,000 were recruited. Initially, they comprised 75 per cent of the officer corps, but by 1920 it was about 33 per cent. Some of them, like Brusilov, joined up freely because they saw the Bolsheviks as Russia's only hope of protection, even though he had no sympathy with revolution. Others, like the Latvian Vacietis and Mikhail Tukhachevsky, who had risen from the lower ranks, were more whole-hearted supporters. But they were in a small minority. Most of the rest joined out of necessity, that is they had no better means of support, while others were more directly coerced, through threats to themselves and sometimes to their families. Of course, it was an obvious political risk to have such people in important positions. The Cheka took a particular interest in surveillance of spetsy in all walks of life, and continued to do so for decades to come.

However, the Bolsheviks developed a new type of personnel, partly derived from Provisional Government predecessors – political commissars. There were about 6,400 at the end of 1918 (Read 1996 210). As their name suggests they were political officers who supervised the ideological rectitude of soldiers and officers. This largely entailed putting on political education classes for the troops. It has been pointed out that the army was a key point at which the party and the population came together and political training in the military was seen as a crucial element in winning over the population, especially peasants who comprised the bulk of the army and were otherwise difficult to get together for purposes of political education (von Hagen 1984). Their other main task was to keep a close ideological eye on the spetsy, to ensure they were reliable and were not engaged in activities which were potentially harmful to the Bolshevik cause. They, like other key party officials, had close contacts with the Cheka and could call them in where they suspected ideological subversion and other disloyal behaviours.

The party left in particular hated the way the army was going. It was beginning to resemble the old army in structure and even, thanks to specialists, in terms of personnel. Many party leftists continued to support the militia idea. The debate came to ahead at the 8th Party Congress. The resolution which was passed on 20 March 1919, entitled 'On the Military Question', was resoundingly dismissive of all criticism of the army. Its arguments also revealed the new logic being used to cover a whole series of policy U-turns, not only that on military construction. Having been clearly committed in 1917 to replacing a standing army with a guerrilla-style militia the resolution took a completely different line: 'To preach the doctrine of guerrilla forces as a military programme is tantamount to recommending a return from large-scale to cottage industry.' (McNeal 1974: vol. 2, 76.)

The law, the constitution and the justice system

Before moving on to the attempts of the Bolsheviks to win over the population we need to note one other important feature of coercion. What was it, in terms of rules and regulations (rather than ideology, which is examined in the next section) which was being enforced? One of the targets of a thorough revolution such as that in which the Bolsheviks were engaged was to completely undermine the law and constitution of the previous system. It was inconceivable that, at any level, they would operate within the compass of tsarist law. All well and good, but that does present a massive problem. In the long term, the new system would produce its own laws and so on but that would take time, thought, personnel and education of the population and of those charged with implementing the law, such as the regular police force and the judiciary. Even universally recognised crimes such as murder and theft were complicated when there was a bitter civil war which, on one hand, entailed killing on a mass scale within and outside regular battle and, on the other, the mass of the population was being encouraged to expropriate those who had anything to be taken. The Bolshevik slogan 'Loot the looters' was hardly a suitable basis for a legal system.

In some ways the apparently larger task, producing a constitution, proved easier than the 'secondary' task of setting up a legal system. Given the absence of real, contestatory political institutions after the dispersal of the Constituent Assembly, it was a much simpler matter of getting a committee together, circulating drafts for approval, re-drafting them in the light of comments received and then promulgating the legislation through the already more-or-less tame Soviet governmental bodies. We have already encountered the preamble to the constitution, the Declaration of Rights of the Working and Exploited People. The Constitution itself was promulgated on 10 July 1918. It was a very technical document, as such things usually are, but it did embody certain principles of which the most important was that the centre controlled the periphery with little countervailing force.

As far as implementing everyday law was concerned the situation remained fluid. The Party Programme of 22 March 1919 stated the situation thus:

> The Soviet power, abolishing all the laws of the overthrown government, ordered the judges elected by the soviets to carry out the will of the proletariat in compliance with its decrees, and in cases of absence or incompleteness of such decrees, to be guided by socialist conscience.

The concluding phrase is remarkable. The gaps in actual statute (written) law were to be plugged by the 'socialist conscience' of the judges. For this system to work it would have needed characters with near-perfect knowledge and wisdom to staff it. As in every other area we have encountered, demands for qualified revolutionary personnel far exceeded supply. The new legal system of People's Courts had many admirable features, in theory, in that it was to draw ordinary people into its operation and be free and accessible to all on an equal basis. But like many other Bolshevik aspirations, it was easier to define such fine principles than it was to implement them in the intended manner.

The emerging Bolshevik legal system also spawned a new set of organs of political justice, as opposed to the People's Courts which focused on criminal law. These were Revolutionary Tribunals, inspired by French revolutionary precedents. Their task, in effect, was to judge cases brought by the Cheka (Rendle 2011).

Mobilisation

While coercion is often seen by historians and other observers to be the key element in the construction of the new order, for the Bolsheviks themselves, and Lenin in particular, 'winning over' the population and mobilising them for the revolutionary struggle was much more important in the long term. It was success or failure in this sphere that would define the revolution. As we know, now that it has run its course, many reasons have been put forward to explain its collapse. However, the most important underlying factor was that the party failed in the crucial objective of 'winning over' the population as a whole. By the 1980s it was hard to find a real Marxist in the Soviet Union (Read 2001 explores this question). But it was not only the long-term shortage of Marxists that was important. Time and again we have seen new institutions being set up, all of which needed personnel with practical skills and who were politically trustworthy, people who were, in later Maoist terminology, both Red and expert. They were in chronically short supply. It pointed to the fact that the system lacked the most important ingredient for building Bolshevism – Bolsheviks. Its first task was to create them. But that was yet another challenge for the hard-pressed and tiny minority of experienced and committed Bolsheviks. How could the party break out of the vicious circle of ever-expanding demands for its expertise leading to it thinning out and being diluted by undesirable influences? The battle for purity and ideological rectitude began inside the party itself and it became increasingly alarmed about how to deal with the problems of dilution.

The party in transition

The history of the Bolshevik Party has been told many times (Schapiro 1955, 1963; Service 1979; Sakwa 1988) but we need to remind ourselves of several key features. Lenin, in 1902, wrote a pamphlet entitled *What is to Done?* which became very controversial. In answer to his own question, Lenin was urging the party to throw off its small-scale structure and turn itself into a regular political party like the German Social Democrats, insofar as that was possible in Russian conditions. The party could not be an open one because, as Lenin strikingly put it, the difficulty with an open party would be that, while it 'is supposedly most "accessible" to the masses ... [it] is actually most accessible to the gendarmes and makes revolutionaries most accessible to the police' (Lenin 1967: vol. 1, 196). However, it should have a permanent centre of full-time revolutionaries and a membership noted for commitment. 'The task', Lenin argued, 'is not to champion the degrading of the revolutionary to the level of an amateur, but to *raise* the amateurs to the level of revolutionaries.' (Lenin 1967: vol. 1, 201.) Again using the image of raising levels upwards, Lenin underlined the point. It was necessary to raise 'the workers to the level of revolutionaries; it is not at all our task *to descend* to the level of "the working masses" as the Economists [a rival group] wish to do' (Lenin 1967: vol. 1, 205) For the time being, it would have to remain conspiratorial.

The degree to which the party split with the Mensheviks and the issues at stake have often been exaggerated. In the eyes of most grass-roots members there was little difference, and even at higher levels there were constant efforts at reunification. The main obstacle was always Lenin. In effect, he moulded the party to reflect loyalty to him above all other factors. He did not undertake this in a megalomaniac way, but through equating true ideology, strategy and tactics largely with his own opinions on these matters. This had the effect of turning the party into an instrument for the implementation of his will and his ideas. While it was small and dominated by café intellectuals, that was possible. As it emerged into full-blown revolution after February 1917 it was more difficult.

Prior to February, Lenin had spent only a couple of years at liberty in Russia. The rest of the time he had been in exile in Siberia (1896–1900) and then abroad, in London, Paris, Zurich and Geneva, apart from a brief return to Russia from late 1905 to early 1908, though much of that time he lived in autonomous but not independent Finland, beyond the reach of the Russian police. Even in 1917, he only returned from Switzerland on 6 April and was in hiding in Finland from 8 July to around 7 October. This was a not untypical c.v. for a Russian revolutionary, so much of the leadership of the party was conducted in western Europe via secondary, mediated contact with Russia itself.

From February, however, this relatively small, intimate group began to expand. Estimates vary but it is generally accepted that before February the party had about 10,000 members. By October it had about 250,000. While it was obviously good to be attracting greater support, for a party like the Bolsheviks, in which ideological rectitude and a developed class-consciousness were assumed to be the essential foundation, to have 25 members at the end of the year for every one at the beginning imposed a massive strain on that expectation. Party members were supposed to embody advanced proletarian conscious-ness or, more directly, to know what the Bolshevik movement – with its complex philosophy not only of world revolution but also its noble, if distant, vision of the transformation of human nature – was all about. We have already noted that only a handful, even of party leaders, knew what the party stood for. Let us recall that Sukhanov had pointed this out. His observation was spot-on. Members and supporters were flocking to Bolshevism because it took on the popular programme of peace, bread, land and all power to the Soviets, but reserved the true meaning of these slogans to itself. After October, the membership peaked at 400,000 by the end of the year. By March 1919 it had fallen to 350,000. In successive years it reached 611,000 and 732,000 in March 1921 (Rigby 1968: 52).

The intake in these years caused new anxieties for the leaders. Many of the new recruits were identified as bandwagon-jumpers, people who joined up because the party was in power and because many party members lived more privileged lives than those outside the party. Many joined to get, or retain, a job. In party terminology, these groups were characterised as 'careerists' and 'bureaucrats' and the party soon turned its attention to the task of weeding them out. However, the problems went far deeper. If the majority of actual party members were not Bolsheviks in the true sense, what about the rest of the country! From this point of view, the heart of the Bolshevik enterprise was to realise the vision of, at most, a few thousand experienced party members in a country of, once peace returned, 125 million. The task of 'winning over' the masses would not be easy. Of course, there was the halfway house achieved in October of garnering mass support by adopting the policies of the masses and of adopting productionism and so on shortly after, but, in the eyes of Lenin, Trotsky, Stalin and other leaders, the point was to move on from there to full scale construction of the socialist world.

This was, to say the least, a daunting task. As we have seen, in so many areas there were demands for reliable Bolsheviks to run the secret police, the judiciary, the ministries, the economy, education, the factories and so on. Above all they were called upon to become leaders in the civil war. In 1919, for instance, 650 of the 1,100 pioneer graduates of the party's elite school, the Sverdlov University, were mobilised (Read 1990: 137). The risk was that many of the most reliable and most committed party members died within a year or two of taking on their responsibilities. There just were not enough 'Reds' to go around. Incredibly, even some 20 per cent of political commissars were not party members! Where could the leadership start?

The fact that it was necessary to start with the party itself told its own story. If the population was to be infused with the Bolshevik dream, it had to be infused into the party first, so that they could be its evangelists. In the demanding circumstances of civil war, the process of spreading the idea of revolution was subject to the same pressures of lack of appropriate resources and personnel. There were no teaching and learning aids, no teachers and, arguably, no authoritative account of Bolshevik principles. Party newspapers filled the gap in the early days and were the focus of propaganda, policy announcements and articles and speeches by Lenin and other party leaders. These were consumed avidly by the faithful and were also the focus of party meetings. Indeed, these were the classic instruments of Bolshevik propaganda in 1917, including the prominent use of slogans. Lenin also referred to propaganda by decree, meaning that many of the measures introduced by the Bolsheviks were sometimes more valuable as pointers to their ideology than as instruments to change the actual situation.

It was only in 1919 that systematic efforts began to be made to set up new institutions and to provide more programmatic materials for study within and beyond the party. The Sverdlov University was opened on 1 June 1919 in Moscow, based on an amalgamation of the Central Party School and the Proletkul't influenced Proletarian University (see p. 191), which was effectively swamped within the new institution. Its first intake of worker Communists arrived, eager to find out what exactly it was they were supposed to believe. The course was short and very intensive. There were 1,500 hours of lectures in each year of the two-year course. It was not immune from the general pressures, and a constant source of complaint from its managers was that high-profile lecturers often failed to turn up because of other pressures. Bukharin missed one of three he was supposed to give and even its head, V.I. Nevsky, missed three of the six assigned to him (Read 1990: 137–138).

A major step forward on the propaganda front was taken at the 8th Party Congress. As early as April 1917, Lenin had called for a new party programme to be drawn up, not least because both warring branches of the RSDLP mother party, Bolsheviks and Mensheviks, shared the same one, dating back to 1898 and 1903. It had taken two years but, on 22 March 1919, a new programme was eventually published. It was a very detailed document, outlining party objectives in all spheres from world revolution to crèches. As such, it is a very illuminating document, even more so since it was accompanied by an explanatory book written by two leading party intellectuals, Bukharin and Preobrazhensky. Its purpose was encapsulated by its title, the *ABC of Communism*. It was intended to be a simple primer of revolutionary ideology, a secular, radical catechism. It's hard to say how far it succeeded. Certainly the programme and the *ABC* were widely distributed and widely discussed in party meetings and reading groups. One might doubt how far they enlightened the simple, poorly-educated workers since some of the sections were more suitable for a doctoral thesis than a piece of popular education. It also included dream sequences, imagining a world in which producers did not ask for recompense for their output and consumers did not pay for what they took. One simply deposited what one wished to in the communal warehouse and took out what one wanted. (Bukharin and Preobrazhensky 1969: 116.)

The fragility of the party leadership's ideological hold over even its own membership is highlighted by its constant concern over the quality of its members. The dilution of the required political consciousness by 'bureaucratism' and 'careerists' was already causing deformations according to the ideologically rigorous. Little did they know that by the end of its life the Soviet Communist Party would be composed almost entirely of careerists, and the ideologically correct would be marginalised. The language of the Decree on Party Organisation was unambiguous. 'Numerical growth of the party is progressive only to the extent that healthy proletarian elements of town and countryside are brought into the party ... All party organisations are under orders to keep careful track of their composition.' (McNeal 1974: 83.) Signs of weaknesses were already making themselves known: 'Many party members assigned to state tasks are becoming cut off from the masses to a considerable extent and are becoming infected with bureaucratism.' (p. 84.) 'Unhealthy symptoms are observable within party organisations as well ... there is an extensive influx into the party of elements that are insufficiently communist and even of outright hangers on. The RKP [Russian Communist Party] is in power, and this inevitably attracts not just the best elements, but also careerist elements to its ranks.' (p. 89.) The solution was 'a thorough-going *purge* of both soviet and party organisations'. (p. 89.)

Concern was such that, later in the year, the party embarked on the first of a series of procedures for which it became notorious, though the procedure itself is widely misunderstood. The procedure was called a *chistka* in Russian, a cleansing, but it has become better known by another term, purge. As the name suggests, the idea was to cleanse the party of unhealthy elements. It was done by decreeing that every party member would have to surrender her or his party card and undergo review of their activities before they were re-admitted. Those whose record was suspect were not allowed back. Not surprisingly, given the endless pressures on party personnel and the dire shortage of expertise in all areas, it was not long before many of them were re-admitted because in many cases no one else had the necessary skills to replace them.

It should be pointed out that the underlying problem was a practical consequence of the theoretical criticism that the October revolution was 'premature', that it had occurred before its preconditions, notably an exhausted capitalism and a large, class-conscious proletariat had evolved. The party leaders could never admit that, underlying the plethora of problems of personnel, lay the fundamental contradiction of their revolution. They were being forced to construct the conditions, after the revolution, that should have been in place before it, which should have been the preliminary foundation of their revolution. Ironically, in 1922, in one of his last articles entitled 'Better Fewer, but Better', Lenin was still grappling with the same problem and still proposing the same inadequate solution, implied in the title. Trotsky, too, for all his tendency to structural historical analysis and his awareness of bureaucratic distortion, never put the two together to admit the elitism and prematurity of the revolution were the prime causes of its bureaucratisation. Supervisors, and supervisors of supervisors, were filling in for absence of appropriate class consciousness.

Before leaving the topic of the party we should note that, in 1919, an international version was set up in the form of the Communist International, frequently called by its abbreviated name, Comintern. Its aim was to guide and co-ordinate efforts to achieve international revolution. In our period it had little practical importance, though it was, in the 1920s and 1930s, a significant player on the international scene. However, we can make a number of points about its existence up to 1922. First, it was a rallying point for revolutionary sympathisers from around the world. This had two significant consequences at this early stage. One was that it helped organise foreign disruption of the efforts of the interventionist powers in the civil war. The most successful of these was the 'Hands off Russia' campaign conducted in Great Britain which confirmed Lloyd George in his reluctance to send large numbers of troops to Russia. Secondly, Comintern became the incubator of fledgling Communist Parties in Britain, France, Germany and elsewhere. However, it was only in 1921, as attention was freed up by the end of the civil war, that Comintern began to be regularised. When the Bolsheviks were desperate, in 1918 and 1919, they were more or less prepared to accept assistance from anyone inclined to give it. After the war was over, however, Lenin began to realise that, unlike the Russian Communist Party itself, Comintern had attracted supporters from a wide range of left-wing political tendencies. In true Leninist fashion, the urgent task became the establishment of unity and 'democratic centralism'.

With this in view, though its actual first Congress had taken place in 1919, its real founding conference was convened in Moscow in

August 1920. It coincided with the Soviet advance on Warsaw which evoked some excited anticipation among the delegates until news of the defeats filtered through. However, its main task was to regularise the programme and to set up conditions for admission to the organisation. Twenty-one such conditions were enacted of which, again revealing the Leninist imprint, 14 involved splitting existing socialist parties. In a sense, this was to distinguish international 'Mensheviks' from 'Bolsheviks'. Presciently, Rosa Luxemburg had identified the underlying tendency which was embodied in the Comintern even though she had been murdered in January 1919, long before the Second Congress took place. As we have seen, she warned Lenin that 'the danger begins only when they make a virtue of necessity and want to freeze into a complete theoretical system all the tactics forced upon them by these fatal circumstances, and want to recommend them to the international proletariat as a model of socialist tactics' (Luxemburg 1961 quoted above p. 178). It would be hard to imagine a better summary of the aims and objectives of the emerging Comintern, and of the risks of its tactics, which, as Luxemburg clearly feared, might end up weakening the world revolutionary movement by imposing a 'one size fits all' approach to revolution based on the Bolsheviks' own experience. To follow the consequences of this would, however, take us well beyond our period.

Spreading the message beyond the party: Education, religion, propaganda, science

Obviously, if the party was finding it difficult to educate itself, when it came to getting the message across to the 125 million non- members the problem was even more acute. Considerable resources were devoted to this area, and at first sight it seems odd that this was done, given the exigencies of civil war. But it was done for two reasons above all others: first, the issue was very important to them; and second, in areas like education they had little choice. A new, revolutionary government could not allow the tsarist education system to continue, not least because of the centrality of religion and the church in the curriculum and organisation. A decree forbidding the involvement of clergy in education was passed on 24 December 1917, followed by the official separation of church and state on 20 January/ 2 February 1918. This opened up a war with religion in general and the Orthodox Church in particular which had a significant side-effect of perhaps unnecessarily antagonising part of the population which adhered to religion.

When it came to cultural and educational matters, and even prop-aganda, the Bolsheviks had plenty of helpers. One of the jewels of nineteenth-century Russia was its intelligentsia. In the sciences and the arts, Russian practitioners began to make a name for themselves. Mendeleev, Vernadsky, Tchaikovsky, Tolstoy, Dostoevsky and many more developed world-wide reputations in their respective fields ranging from chemistry to literature. But there was also a narrower and more specifically Russian meaning to the term, a meaning that included a moral sense of duty to the poor and to the uneducated. Lenin, Trotsky, Bukharin and other intellectual leaders of the party had been moulded in this way. So had most of their politi-cal opponents like Martov, Miliukov, Sukhanov and many others. After October there were many such intellectuals who committed to the revolution, though not specifically to the Bolsheviks. The spirit of the moment was caught in Alexander Blok's brilliant poem *The Twelve* which depicts twelve, foul-mouthed, hard-drinking, Red Guards on patrol in Petrograd 'Each one like a jailbird on the run' (Blok 1974: 117). Unexpectedly, at the end of the poem, a shadowy figure of Jesus appears at their head, symbolising that like Christianity, a world-shattering movement would be constructed on the basis of flawed human clay. Blok was expressing a form of traditional intelligentsia populism, a belief in the great destiny of the ordinary Russian masses. This was the impulse that was behind the commitment many intellectuals made to the revolution. Great artists and poets such as Marc Chagall, El Lissitzky, Vladimir Tatlin, Vladimir Mayakovsky and many others created a wave of exciting creativity around the revolution. They contributed to propaganda boats and propaganda trains which were fitted out and roamed the country. New ideas and innovatory artistic movements of many kinds associated themselves with the revolution. Mayakovsky produced propaganda posters. Tatlin dreamed up artefacts from gigantic monuments to new styles of furniture and clothing appro-priate to the new way life. Pioneering filmmakers like Dziga Vertov produced newsreels of the civil war. Our fleeing revolutionary of August 1914, Vassilii Kandinsky, became an important figure in one of the key, innovative artistic institutions of the day, *Vkhutemas* (The Higher Artistic and Technical Workshop) which brought together artists, designers and technologists. Like many others he found the growing constraints on artistic freedom too much and left for Germany in 1921, where he became a major figure in the German equivalent of *Vkhutemas*, the Bauhaus. Chagall became Commissar

or Art in his home town of Vitebsk and was in charge of decorating
the streets for major festivals. Reaction to his efforts was often one
of bewilderment.

> On October 25th my multicoloured animals swung all over the
> town, swollen with revolution. The workers marched up singing
> the International. When I saw them smile, I was sure they under-
> stood me. The leaders, the Communists, seemed less gratified.
> Why is the cow green and why is the horse flying through the
> sky, why? What's the connection with Marx and Lenin? (Chagall
> 1965: 137.)

This was an issue for all the avant-garde who attached themselves to
Bolshevism. They believed they were producing art for the people
but the people, in many areas, did not have a clue about what the
art was intended to mean. One group, associated with a Bolshevik
dissident named Alexander Bogdanov, focused around the task of
creating a new proletarian culture. They argued that previous dominant classes – the feudal aristocracy, the bourgeoisie – had forced
their cultural values on the society they ruled through law, the
church, customs, habits and, more recently, the media. It therefore
followed that the proletariat needed to develop its own culture, free
of the distortions induced by former bourgeois power. They set up
'laboratories of culture' to develop a proletarian culture based on co-
operation, collectivism and comradeship to replace the individualism
and competition of bourgeois capitalist culture. The organisation,
known as Proletkul't, was seen as trouble-making. In particular, Lenin
objected to its claims to autonomy and, in 1920, clipped its wings.
For the remaining period of its life it was a simple worker-education
organisation without broad pretensions to remake culture – a task
which had to be left to the party (Biggart 1989, 1998a, b; Mally 1990;
Read 1990).

This was, eventually, the fate of nearly all the avant-garde. But in
the immediate aftermath of the revolution the Soviet leaders had
no alternative but to recruit such people since there was no alternative. Many pro-Red posters of the civil war came from the hands of
artists who were scarcely Bolshevik in any respect other than possess-
ing a general sympathy with the masses and hope, like that of Blok,
that something extraordinary could be cut from the crude cloth
of the Russian people. However, it would be hard to say how many
Bolsheviks were created through their efforts.

A more immediate and practical issue also brought advanced intellectuals and the party into contact and conflict, education. October
occurred after the academic year had started and, by and large,
schools and universities continued as best they could, making their
way around issues like the exclusion of clergy from the process and
meeting the ever-increasing shortages with whatever resources they
could to, for example, keep buildings heated. It seems to have dawned
on the Education Ministry – now the Commissariat of Enlightenment
under the leadership of Anatoly Lunacharsky who was a writer, essay-
ist and playwright as well as Communist bureaucrat – only in early
summer 1918 that something should be done to create a revolutionary and socialist education curriculum and system. Quite a tall order
given the school year was only three months away. The immediate
problem was that there was no agreement on what the system should
be. Some very radical proposals for centring the system on labour
were discussed. Among the proposals were putting the concept of
labour at the heart of all aspects of the curriculum; linking schools
and factories from a very early age; teaching in either ten-day or
7/7 cycles and allowing local communities a free hand in running
schools. Possibly to the relief of future generations of schoolchildren
and partly under the influence of Lenin's wife Nadezhda Krupskaya,
a more moderate set of proposals was adopted. Krupskaya pointed
out that there needed to be breaks in the school year and that the
more radical proposals were unworkable. Who would teach it? How
could the new ideas be passed on to the current teaching staff?
Where would textbooks and other materials come from? In a society
descending into civil war the project smacked of fantasy. Defenders of
the radical line denounced this response as 'pedagogic opportunism'
and argued that even if they could not be implemented immediately,
it was important to have them established as a signpost for future
development. The plea was to no avail and the moderate line carried
the day (Read 1990: 100–104).

It was not only schools that were targeted. The tougher nut of
higher education also had to be cracked. Perhaps surprisingly, the
Bolsheviks showed more respect and less certainty when dealing with
the academy, perhaps because most of them were themselves former
students. University autonomy was not terminated until 1922, and as
such it outlasted the old regime's army, landowning class, financiers,
capitalists and other apparently more formidable foes. And it was
not because they were considered unimportant, quite the reverse.
Bolshevism had grandiose ideas for the development of science and
for the development of the individual human personality. In the final
sentences of his book of 1923, *Literature and Revolution*, Trotsky, rather

oddly, echoed Nietzsche in his vision of the human, or superhuman, future:

> Man will make it his purpose to master his own feelings, to raise his instincts to the heights of consciousness, to make them transparent, to extend the wires of his will into hidden recesses, and thereby to raise himself to a new plane, to create a higher social biologic type, or, if you please, a superman.
>
> It is difficult to predict the extent of self-government which the man of the future may reach or the heights to which he may carry his technique. Social construction and psycho-physical self-education will become two aspects of one and the same process. All the arts – literature, drama, painting, music and architecture will lend this process beautiful form. More correctly, the shell in which the cultural construction and self-education of Communist man will be enclosed, will develop all the vital elements of contemporary art to the highest point. Man will become immeasurably stronger, wiser and subtler; his body will become more harmonized, his movements more rhythmic, his voice more musical. The forms of life will become dynamically dramatic. The average human type will rise to the heights of an Aristotle, a Goethe, or a Marx. And above this ridge new peaks will rise. (Trotsky 1960: 126.)

Even in the straitened times of war, considerable effort was expended. Initially, the Bolsheviks had three key objectives. First, the academy should be opened up to everyone irrespective of class. To achieve this, in 1919 they set up the first Workers' Faculties. These took promising young adults of humble background, gave them a two-year full-time crash course in the basics and then launched them into university degrees. Academics protested that they were undermining academic standards because their levels of achievement were below those of the regular students. The Workers' Faculty students were enthusiastic and they were also seen by the party as a fifth column to infiltrate the universities. They were given fast-track access to academic councils and soviets and conducted class warfare against the 'bourgeois professors'. Second, they needed skilled personnel for administration and production. Third, they wanted a more socialist curriculum. However, for the time being the universities retained a degree of autonomy.

The need for a third plan for transition

Overall, the years of civil war were the most intellectually diverse of the entire Soviet period. This was partly because of inexperience of the authorities, partly through lack of consistent policies and partly because of the priorities of the period which left some questions unsolved as attention was focused on more critical areas. However, two pressures emerged which brought about a new attempt at stabilisation and control. As the civil war wound down, the White bogeyman was no longer effective in scaring the Bolsheviks' critics among the masses and the left. Instead, the last flames of the popular movement began to flicker. Peasants inflicted a significant defeat on the party which had to abandon forced grain requisitioning in the face of their protests. This also meant that transition number two had gone the way of its predecessor. The end of the civil war, the political opposition and the crisis in grain procurement opened the way for transition plan number three, Lenin's final personal throw of the dice as, from autumn 1922, he became increasingly ill, eventually to the point of not being able to participate in day-to-day government. In 1921 and 1922, Lenin re-established the structure of the economy and tightened up the political and intellectual dictatorship. He also presided over the restructuring of the state and the emergence of the Soviet Union. In doing so he brought the revolutionary period to its end. It is to these processes that we now turn.

Chapter 9:   The End of the Revolution?
January 1921–December
1922

Internal and External Crises 1920–21

As the war against the Whites wound down, so the pressures which had been contained because of it began to re-assert themselves. Popular and party discontents began to re-emerge. Fortunately for the Bolsheviks, much of the energy behind them had been dissipated by the years of attrition. Hunger, disease and constant war had taken their toll. The economy, especially industry, had hit rock bottom. Nonetheless, the last flickering flames of opposition to the new Soviet system were a serious threat, because the party and state were as exhausted as the population.

Internal uprisings 1920–21: Western Siberia, Tambov, Kronstadt

Back to 1917' was a key theme in almost all the final protests which emerged both in Soviet society and in the Communist Party. It was not unreasonable. The Bolsheviks had made broad, libertarian-sounding promises in 1917. They claimed that the emergency situation needed harsh but temporary measures. It followed that, as the emergency began to recede, there should be some return to the original ideals. The logic was not lost on the leaders and followers of the final round of discontent. Nor was it lost on Lenin. In effect, aspects of transition number two, of Plan B, were no longer appropriate to the new situation of extreme collapse and peasant resistance. It was a moment of decision. A new direction was needed. What path would Lenin and

the Communist Party leadership choose? Would they tighten up revo
lutionary discipline or relax it to release economic entrepreneurship
and restore the economy? What direction would Lenin's third and
final attempt to develop a successful path of transition take and would
it be any better than its failed and outdated predecessors?

From 1920 to 1922, questions and answers emerged. In the proc
ess the revolution – at least in the sense of the active participation
of the popular movement motivated by the popular programme of
peace, bread, land and all power to the soviets – came to an end. The
Bolsheviks achieved complete and unchallenged power at this time
but still very much as the strongest of the weak given the feeble state
of the population and the fragility of the economy. They were also
exposed to foreign attack, but once again most potential enemies
were also suffering and those that tried to take advantage of Russia's
apparent defencelessness, such as Poland, found it impossible to gain
much advantage.

Not surprisingly, it was among the peasantry that the first postwar
protests emerged. They were still suffering from the effects of grain
requisitioning, a system often deemed to be an emergency response to
wartime collapse. However, since the moment the Soviet Government
had established a grain monopoly in spring 1918, it is hard to see
what other legal mechanism for exchange there was. An illegal black
market emerged without which the situation would have been even
worse. But the black market was not sufficient. Peasants resented
requisitioning for the simple reason that they received practically
nothing in return for handing over grain. In conditions of war, peas
ants were somewhat more tolerant of this system as they had become
accustomed to supporting their sons in the military in this way. In
peacetime, however, it was simple robbery. Receiving worthless tokens
for non-existent industrial goods was not real payment.

There had been thousands of small acts of resistance to the requi
sitioning squads but the first major postwar outbreak came in western
Siberia. The immediate cause was the extension, in January 1921, of
requisitioning to include all seed grain. Obviously, the peasants would
be left with nothing to sow and there would be no 1921 harvest, with
predictable consequences. The peasants had no trust that the requi
sitioned seed grain would be redistributed among them to prevent
such a catastrophe. Rebellion broke out in the Ishimsk district and
spread rapidly to the whole of Tyumen' province and then to Akmola
Omsk, eastern Cheliabinsk and Ekaterinburg provinces. The head
quarters was established in Tobolsk. From the Urals to Kazakhstan
some 100,000 rebels were fighting the Soviet Government. They had

only the loosest of programmes. Free trade in grain and land was uppermost. The demand for free, democratic soviets echoed the popular programme of 1917. Anarchists and Left SRs were among the leading forces but the insurgency was largely composed of self-organised local groups, increasingly adept at guerrilla warfare in their own difficult and remote terrain. They also had many Red Army veterans involved as well as local Cossack communities. The Soviet Government used every tactic of ruthless terror and village-burning to undermine the insurgency but it was only in December 1921 that the Communist military command was able to announce the elimination of all 'banditry'. In fact, isolated groups continued the fight into 1922 but by then the main force had long been defeated, its leaders arrested and executed (Heath 2010).

Other uprisings echoed these key features. The next largest was the Tambov rebellion. Tambov province is a rich, black earth zone whose proximity to Moscow, less than 300 miles away, had led to it being scoured time and time again by requisitioning squads. Being more geographically restricted it was also more politically focused. Its acknowledged leader was Alexander Antonov, an SR by background. A rise in the 1920 requisition requirement from 18 to 27 million pudy (1 pud = 36 lb, approximately 16 kg) created the background. The flashpoint which set it off occurred on 19 August 1920 when a particularly violent requisitioning squad hit the town of Khitrovo, provoking a backlash. By October, some 50,000 peasant fighters supported the rebellion. In January 1921 rebellion spread to Samara, Saratov, Tsaritsyn and Astrakhan on the Volga. By then, some 70,000 peasants supported the rebellion. The political leadership, focused on a group called the Union of Toiling Peasants, issued an appeal for support, calling on its followers to fight for basic principles of overthrowing Communist oppression and restoring the Constituent Assembly, with an interim administration comprising all parties which had fought against the Communist oppressors. The Union wanted to implement the Assembly's programme for the socialisation of all land. It supported co-operatives to supply primary needs of townspeople; called for workers' control and state supervision of production; privatisation of small enterprises and workshops; state ownership of heavy industry; equality of all without class distinctions; national self-determination; an end to the civil war; restoration of relations with foreign powers; mobilisation of Russian and foreign capital for reconstruction; and freedom of speech, press, conscience, association (*soiuz*), and meeting. Again, the programme of 1917 resonated though, somewhat surprisingly, soviets were not mentioned (Landis 2008).

After the Polish War (see pp. 201–2) came to an end the full force of the government could be turned on the rebels. Some 100,000 Red Army troops under Tukhachevsky and special Cheka units were deployed to end the rebellion. Reports suggest 50,000 people were interned in seven concentration camps where the death rate may have been as high as 10 per cent per month. Poison gas was used to kill rebels hiding deep in near-impenetrable forests. By the end of 1921 the rebellion was broken but, as in western Siberia at the same time, scattered groups held out for some time into 1922. Antonov and his brother Dimitrii were killed near Borisoglebsk in a firefight with the Cheka, during an attempt to capture him on 24 June 1922. They were buried outside the walls of the monastery of Our Lady of Kazan'. According to some sources around 240,000 people may have died in the course of the rebellion from fighting, internment and repression (Sennikov 2004).

It was not only peasants who were protesting. In the winter of 1920/21 there were many strikes in large and small cities and enterprises. Most of them were direct responses to the terrible conditions of disease, hunger, low living standards and unemployment. In Petrograd the disturbances were driven by severe shortages of food and fuel. By December, coal from the Donbas was not arriving, oil supplies fell to one-third of what was required and, of 18,000 freight cars of wood ordered to make up the gap, only 3,000 made it through exceptionally heavy January blizzards. The authorities allowed 225 buildings to be dismantled for firewood in January and February. The Petrograd Soviet ordered the closure of all factories and mills from 19 to 23 January as a fuel-conservation measure. Things got worse. By mid-February workers rations had been cut by a third, and 93 of the largest factories had been closed. Real wages were at about 10 per cent of 1913 values and the price of bread had risen 1,000 per cent in 1920. In January and February 1921 the price of key commodities, sugar, potatoes and rye bread, almost tripled (Semanov 1973: 26–31; 35). Hyperinflation was taking off: in 1918 a gold rouble was worth eight paper roubles. In February 1921, 10,000 paper roubles equalled a gold rouble. By May 1922 it was 240,000 to one (Got'e 1988: 422; 435; 452). Not surprisingly, large demonstrations and strikes began. On 24 February 2000 workers took to the streets. The escalating protests were met with great harshness by the fearful authorities. According to one eye witness, the anarchist Alexander Berkman, the workers were weak from hunger, 'overawed' by the authorities and ultimately 'crushed with an iron hand' (Berkman 1922: 8; Lincoln 1991: 493).

However, the most iconic and most painful of rebellions was the one that took place in March 1921 in the naval base and city of

Kronstadt, situated on an island in the Gulf of Finland some 12 miles (20 kilometres) from Petrograd. It embodied worker, peasant and sailor protest as well as a last-gasp attempt to return to the political and social principles of 1917. Indeed, Kronstadt was a microcosm of the wider revolution in the period from February 1917 to March 1921. As we have seen, Kronstadt was in the forefront of revolutionary action in 1917. Sailors were among the first to respond to the February Revolution. They had also declared Soviet power in their city in May, long before Petrograd itself. Kronstadt sailors had provided the force to overthrow the Provisional Government twice. They were rebuffed by revolutionary leaders, including Lenin, in the July Days but had proven decisive in October. They were the greatest revolutionary powerhouse of 1917. But they were not Bolshevik. Some were, but the majority were closer to direct-rule anarchists than to the party of Lenin. After October this posed a problem for the new government. How could they tap into the much-needed revolutionary zeal of the Kronstadters as well as keep them under control as a potentially hostile force? Since many Kronstadters were peasants, one mutually beneficial policy was for the party to encourage Kronstadters to return to the countryside as evangelists of the revolution. This was a role the Kronstadters eagerly took to and there are many instances of them aiding the transfer of land in Russia's villages in the period from September 1917 to February 1918. They also participated in large numbers in the hit squads associated with Military Revolutionary Committees in the first months of the revolution. As such, they were a major force behind the 'triumphal march' of Soviet power. Since, while this was going on, Lenin had been urging soldiers and sailors to return home with their weapons, many of them never returned to their Baltic base. However, there were still large numbers left in Kronstadt who were considered suspect by the Bolsheviks.

Step by step, the party extended its control over the city in 1918 and 1919. Fedor Raskolnikov was appointed commissar and he soon made it clear that he did not consider himself subject to the authority and decisions of the daily meeting of the Kronstadt Soviet in Anchor Square. Tension also grew in protest at the alleged luxurious and elitist lifestyle of Raskolnikov and his partner Larissa Reisner, which contrasted with the increasingly difficult circumstances of the ordinary workers and sailors in Kronstadt. Despite the differences, the relations between the new government and the Kronstadters reflected that of other parts of the country. Namely, once the civil war began the differences were put to one side and a left-wing rainbow coalition was formed. Many Kronstadters fought valiantly on the Red side in the civil war. However, again reminiscent of wider society, as the civil war wound down, old agendas returned. In particular, the Kronstadters resented the loss of Soviet freedom. When they heard that a major strike movement was underway in Petrograd, they determined to assist it. The Soviet Government was well-informed about all this, since the Kronstadters planned in public, and it was determined to avoid conflict with Petrograd workers and Krondstadt sailors at the same time. They quickly settled with the workers and prepared for a final showdown with Kronstadt.

The main programmatic statements put out by the Kronstadters make poignant reading. Their main objection was to the Bolshevik monopoly of power enforced by the Cheka. They did not, as is persistently alleged, call for 'Soviets without Communists' but for equality for all Soviet-oriented parties and freedom for left-wing political prisoners. In particular, they pointed to the infiltration of all factories, schools universities and enterprises by controlling party cells which gave the Communists a highly privileged position from which to influence Soviet elections. They maintained a class basis in their demands and called for rights for working people but not for the bourgeoisie. They opposed forced grain requisitioning, defended the free market in individually produced products and handicrafts, and denounced the road-block detachments which prevented peasants from bringing produce to sell to the under-nourished inhabitants of many cities.

Once again, the demands were highly reminiscent of the popular programme of 1917. That, however, did not guarantee a hearing from the Bolsheviks. Lenin and Trotsky resolved to crush the uprising. Propaganda suggested that the rebellion was inspired by White Guard influences from nearby Finland but this was nonsense. Lenin knew that and, in a franker assessment of the situation described it as 'the flash that lit up reality better than anything else.' (Lenin 1960–70: vol. 43, 138; Avrich 1970: 3). At the Tenth Party Congress he said 'In Kronstadt they did not want either the White Guards nor our movement' (Lenin 1967: vol. 3, 574). The rebellions as a whole, and Kronstadt in particular, are often described as attempts at a Third Revolution, supporting the programme of 1917, including Soviet power, but without the Communist monopoly. Lenin was rejecting any such concept and, with Trotsky alongside, ordered a ruthless repression of the rebellion.

The first assault was underprepared and failed. It was only a brief reprieve. A week later, Trotsky ordered a second infantry assault across the ice of the Gulf with 50,000 men, a third of whom were party members, rising to 70 per cent in the spearhead units (Getzler

1983: 243) The city was captured. Some thousands of prisoners were taken and, for six weeks, Cheka execution squads went to work, killing hundreds of them. The irony of the situation was not lost on one anarchist observer who pointed out the Communists were celebrating the fiftieth anniversary of the Paris Commune of 1871 at the same moment as they were suppressing Kronstadt. They even renamed one of the rebel ships the *Paris Commune* (Getzler 1983: 244).

The Communists had taken on the role of suppressors of popular democracy. Their reason for doing so was perhaps best described by Victor Serge, whose conscience was much troubled by the incident. He had great sympathy with the Kronstadters but, in the final analysis, he believed they had to be defeated because any weakening of the revolution would only serve its enemies. 'Kronstadt had right on its side. Kronstadt was the beginning of a fresh, liberating revolution for popular democracy: "The Third Revolution" ... However, the country was absolutely exhausted ... If the Bolshevik dictatorship fell, it was only a short step to chaos and through chaos to a peasant rising, the massacre of the Communists, the return of the émigrés, and in the end, through the sheer force of events, another dictatorship, this time anti-proletarian.' (Serge 1963: 128–129.) It was not the last time Soviet repression would be justified in such terms. He was horrified by the force of the repression from Lenin and Trotsky's 'disgusting' ultimatum – 'Surrender, or you will be shot down like rabbits' – to the actual assault, which he considered to be a 'ghastly fratricide' (Serge 1963: 130).

War with Poland April–October 1920

But danger did not come only from the home front. In 1920, smouldering skirmishes with Poland turned into full-scale war. The underlying cause was the vagueness of boundaries and, even, countries in the area between Poland, Lithuania, Russia, Belarus and Ukraine. Ephemeral governments came and went according to the fortunes of war. The Soviets themselves set up a Lithuanian–Belarussian Republic (Litbel) as a protectorate, but it lasted only a few months (27 February to 17 July 1919). It was in the spring and summer of 1920 that decisive clashes occurred.

As with many aspects of Polish–Russian relations the war has a Polish-oriented explanation and a Russian-oriented one. Supporters of Polish action argue that the war was essentially defensive, with the Polish leader, Pilsudski, taking a bold decision to secure Poland's historic frontiers and to strengthen potential allies against one of its traditional foes – Russia. In this interpretation it is also claimed that Pilsudski was defending central and western Europe from Communist expansionism. From the Soviet perspective, the war was seen as an attempted land-grab by Pilsudski, timed to take advantage of Soviet Russia's internal weaknesses and distractions. Pilsudski was thought to be establishing a 'greater Polish' empire at the expense of Russia and Ukraine. Hoping to take advantage of the chaos and the weakness of Soviet Russia, as well as sensing a final opportunity was presenting itself before Soviet Russia turned a corner from getting economically and militarily weaker and more stretched into becoming stronger and more consolidated, Pilsudski persuaded the Polish government to agree to an invasion of western Russia and western Ukraine.

The course of the war gave some credence to both sides. The first thrust was made by Poland, which attacked south and east with a view to taking Kiev and incorporating much of the western Ukraine, such as L'vov, into the new Poland. The Red Army rebuffed the assault and, as it advanced, dreams of spreading the revolution developed. In a miniature model of post-1945 policies, a pro-Soviet government of communists and sympathisers was set up in a small, Soviet-controlled, provincial town, with a programme supposed to appeal to Polish peasants and workers against their 'bourgeois' rulers (Croll 2009). It had some success, but its coercive core, especially towards the peasants, and the depth of Polish nationalist feeling, meant it had little effect in its brief life. However, before the tide turned against Tukhachevsky and the Red Army and Budenny and the Red Cavalry, Moscow believed the moment of revolutionary war had begun. Victory at Warsaw would open the road to Berlin. But the Soviet forces made crucial errors, became separated from each other and were defeated at Warsaw in mid-August. They were forced into a headlong retreat as rapid as their advance. Major fighting ceased in October with both armies in more or less the same situation they had been in before Poland's attack. On 18 March 1921 the Treaty of Riga regularised frontiers and relations between Russia and Poland. Neither side had achieved its deeper objectives. Defeat opened up the eyes of the Soviet leadership to their country's continued vulnerability.

Lenin's Third Plan for Transition: The Adoption of the New Economic Policy and the Tenth Party Congress

The multiple crises following the end of the war against the Whites showed that Lenin's second transition strategy was also in tatters

In particular, forced requisitioning had been a disaster. It had driven the peasants to produce less and less: they reasoned that whatever they had would be taken, so why produce it in the first place? The weakness of the agrarian economy was highlighted in the famine of 1921–2 when several million people died after a drought in the Volga region tipped the enfeebled agriculture of the area over the edge. A wave of starving people set off looking for food:

> Now typhus had got to our village. Over the roads coming from the south emaciated people struggled northward in search of food. Many passed through Ostrovsky, leaving behind them lice and typhus. They were a ghastly sight; skeletons over which withered skin was stretched. One could not guess whether they were young or old. Dirty rags covered them. ... They hoped to live on the charity of the villages through which they passed; but everywhere the doors were closed to them because of typhus ... Wearily the unfortunates trudged along the endless frozen roads. They tore bark off the trees and ate it; dug roots from under the snow. They told terrible stories of women eating their new-born babies, of bodies dug up in cemeteries, also eaten. Their cattle, they said, has all died during the summer from a plague which swelled them into huge balloons and killed them in a few hours, rendering the flesh uneatable. (Bashkiroff 1960: 184–5.)

This was only the most extreme example, and malnutrition was claiming victims throughout these years. Ironically, the famine came after measures had been put in place to replace the scourge of requisitioning but they had not had time to work through the system. The industrial economy was also at a disastrously low ebb. This had had its effect in demoralising workers and pushing them into the desperate strikes of 1920 and early 1921. It was time for Lenin to have a third attempt at developing a viable system of transition to socialism.

The outcome was a policy that has gone down in history under the name of NEP, the New Economic Policy. Since its most dramatic aspect was a partial restoration of the market it was unpopular with the party left who said it was really the Old Economic Policy or that NEP stood for New Exploitation of the Proletariat (an acronym that, like the original, works as well in Russian as English). In some ways the title is, indeed, misleading. Traditionally NEP was considered to be a moment of apparent opening up of the system, of a limited 'liberalisation'. However, NEP ultimately comprised a complex and interacting set, not just of economic, but also political and cultural

WAR AND REVOLUTION IN RUSSIA, 1914–22

measures which, taken as a whole, were far from being open, liberal or democratic.

The central plank of the new policy platform was a change in the requisitioning system. Instead of the arbitrariness of forced requisitioning, the state would take a predetermined proportion of each household's output in the form of a tax in kind, that is, in produce rather than money. The part not taken in tax could be disposed of by the household. The big implication here was that, once the needs of the household itself had been supplied and the tax paid, there might well be a surplus left over which could be sold legally on the market. Thus, the new system allowed a partial restoration of the market. This was a clear victory for the peasants over the ideological schemes of the party. From the time of its introduction in 1921, to the onset of collectivisation in 1929, the peasantry existed under conditions for which they had striven for decades, even centuries. They had rid themselves of landowners and, in the new circumstances, the commune enjoyed a last flourishing. Traditional peasant self-organisation insulated it against the feeble intrusion into the countryside of Soviet institutions. Both party and soviets remained weak. In early 1919 there were only 54,900 peasant members of the party out of a total rural population of 130 million (Pershin 1966: 127). It was indicative of the slow pace of rural change in the 1920s that even in 1928, on the eve of collectivisation, there were still only 250,000 rural members of the party.

The return of the market was not limited to peasant communes, however. In a broader acknowledgment of the, to say the least, prematurity of its ambitious policies, the Soviet Government reduced direct state involvement in the economy. Small-scale services, such as shops, restaurants, artisanal and craft workshops and so on, were allowed to operate as independent co-operatives. For the moment, neither they, nor peasant households, were allowed to employ labour. The outcome was a new flourishing of such institutions. The state retained control of larger industrial enterprises as well as taxation, all foreign trade and other major strategic and infrastructural elements, such as rail and water transport. They constituted what Lenin referred to as the 'commanding heights' of the economy. Naturally, the left of the party was unhappy to see the retreat from socialist principles but, for the time being, it was widely recognised that there was no alternative.

The adoption of the tax in kind was announced to, and adopted by, the party at its Tenth Congress in Moscow, which was taking place at almost exactly the same time as the Kronstadt rebellion. Indeed, many of the delegates left for Petrograd to take part in the final assault on the rebels. The congress also considered and passed resolutions bolstering the new strategy. There had been a number of disputes in the party about the way the revolution was developing, and several of them came to a head at the congress. Two aspects of worker participation had been causing controversy.

The role of trade unions in the Soviet system had been one such area. Greatly differing views existed. Some supported a division into spheres, according to which the trade unions should become the managers of the economy, with the party managing politics and Proletkul't managing the cultural sphere. Lenin had no time for that. The party, he argued, must remain supreme over all other institutions. The decree passed at the congress defined unions as 'schools of communism', that is, they should be an interface between party and worker, socialising the workers into the new scheme of things. There was no reference to the traditional function of unions as representatives and defenders of workers' interests. Lenin had long argued that it was not necessary to defend workers against the workers' state since it embodied their interests. The topsy-turvy logic of the new system did not end there. As we have seen, socialism had turned Taylorism from a hated system of super-exploitation into a tool for achieving worker liberation. In an extreme example of the logic, Trotsky and others argued that labour should be 'militarised', that is, effectively conscripted and directed from task to task by the state. Fortunately, this frightening prospect of super-control by the state was not realised, although the disbandment of a number of military units as the war wound down, was postponed and they were transferred to economic tasks like felling trees and rebuilding railways and roads.

The tendency for the party to interpret the will of the workers was the source of the second problem the congress faced with respect to working-class issues, the so-called Workers' Opposition. Led by Alexandra Kollontai, the movement had bemoaned the marginalising of actual workers in the life of the new Soviet state. They were being increasingly subject to a party and state bureaucracy which was not composed of them, was not representative of them and certainly was not accountable to them. They proposed that workers should play an increasing and independent part in the life of party and state. In their main programmatic statement they called for an increase in the power of workers in the party at the expense of an all-enveloping bureaucracy which 'binds the wings of the self-activity and creativeness of the working class: ... deadens thought, hinders initiative and experimentation in the sphere of finding new approaches to production' (Read 1996: 279). Lenin's response in the congress was unequivocal. The group was denounced as an 'anarcho-syndicalist deviation' and it was completely condemned. The congress went further. It passed a decree condemning the existence of any sub-groups, known as 'fractions', in the party. It was the duty of every member of the party to implement party policy once it was adopted, not question it and lobby against it. Theoretically, opposition and debate were possible before decisions were made but even this area became difficult. Ironically, enthusiastic supporters of the measure, like Trotsky, found a few years later that their own activity was severely hampered by these very rules. In the hands of Stalin they became a weapon for the leadership majority to repress the minority.

The congress also took up one more important reform of the party which, like the other two, reinforced centralisation. It set up Control Commissions. Their role was to enforce ideological and behavioural rectitude within the party. This was quite extraordinary. It was a clear admission that even the party itself could not be trusted to toe the correct political line. It also embodied another interesting principle. Only long-serving party members could belong to the Central Control Commission. In this way, the party was trying to objectify correct political consciousness. In Leninist theory, it had been assumed that workers would naturally adopt the correct consciousness. This assumption had proved to be optimistic and, as we have seen, much of the focus in party work was on inculcating that consciousness. It had to be achieved or the revolution would fail. But in the interim, a whole range of supervisory institutions, whereby the minority with the correct consciousness could rule on behalf of the as-yet unenlightened majority, were being spawned by the revolution. Among the most important were the Cheka, the Worker-Peasant Inspectorate which supervised state institutions and the party Organisation Bureau. To some extent all of them were substitutes for correct political consciousness. The result was a system which resembled a theocracy, a government of the supposedly spiritually enlightened, rather than a democracy. Its leaders' claim to rule rested on the correctness of their ideas, not the mandate of their citizens (Read in Brovkin 1997).

If ideological discipline was tightening within the party, it is certainly the case that it was also tightening in wider society. The harsh suppression of the rebellions was one aspect, but there were others. There were proposals in early 1921 to shoot surviving Menshevik leaders but once Lenin was apprised of the situation their lives were spared (Serge 1963: 129–30). On the other hand, the remnants of the

SR party faced the first political show trial in 1922 and the defendants were sentenced to death, in defiance of international opinion. However, the sentences were suspended and they spent long terms in prison (Jansen 1982; Krasil'nikov *et al.* 2002; Finkel 2008). Effectively, Soviet Russia was thereafter not only a one-party state but a one-party society. A number of individual members of other parties joined the Bolsheviks while others worked alongside them in the economic, cultural, scientific and technical institutions, contributing to the reconstruction of the country.

Clamping Down On Culture

In the field of culture, tighter ideological discipline was also the order of the day. The partial suppression of Proletkul't in 1920, was an assertion that Lenin would not put up with claims for autonomy in this area. The draft resolution he imposed on the Proletkul't Congress was unequivocal:

> Adhering unswervingly to this stand of principle, the All-Russia Proletkul't Congress rejects in the most resolute manner, as theoretically unsound and practically harmful, all attempts to invent one's own particular brand of culture, to remain isolated in self-contained organisations, to draw a line dividing the field of work of the People's Commissariat of Education and the Proletkul't, or to set up a Proletkul't 'autonomy' within establishments under the People's Commissariat of Education and so forth. (Lenin 1960–70: Vol. 31, 316–317.)

The insistence on party leadership exercised through state institutions was a model for wider cultural intervention. Unsurprisingly, it was followed by extensive broader encroachment. In particular, the censorship apparatus was expanded and made permanent. Some control over publishing had taken place since 1918 through manipulation of scarce paper supplies and other indirect means. The first censorship was set up in 1919 as a function of the State Publishing Committee but it was separated and regularised in 1922 under the name *Glavlit* (The Main Administration for Literary and Publishing Affairs), which it retained until its abolition by Gorbachev in 1987. In 1922 it covered not just publications but many areas of intellectual life. By 1923, music and theatre were also subject to its permanent censorship. Finally, in September 1921, the last remnants of university autonomy were brought to an end and a new university statute defined the aims of the Soviet university:

1. The creation of specialists for all branches of the RSFSR [Russian Soviet Federative Socialist Republic].

2. The preparation of scientific workers to serve in the scientific and scientific-technical and productive institutions of the Republic and in particular in higher education institutions themselves.

3. The diffusion of knowledge among the broad worker and peasant masses whose interests should be in the forefront of all the activities of higher education institutions. (F 2036.1.595 quoted in Read 1991: 180.)

To accompany the crackdown, some 200 intellectuals were expelled. The list made arbitrary distinctions between those who left and those who stayed on. Also rather inexplicably, the Academy of Sciences was not brought under equivalent party control until the end of the decade. Nonetheless, the message was unequivocal. The party was the sole arbiter of intellectual life. While the parameters of permitted activity remained wider than they were in the 1930s, there was undoubtedly a closing down of many areas compared to the surprisingly wide range of surviving intellectual schools and activities in the civil war years (Read 1991; Finkel 2008).

Not surprisingly, the party also took action against its old bête noire, religion. The party programme had warned against direct pressure on believers: 'it is necessary carefully to avoid offending the religious susceptibilities of believers, which leads only to the hardening of religious prejudices' (Mc Neal 1974: vol. 2, .65). In practice, throughout its history of persecution of religion, this principle was often forgotten by party members. As part of the institutional reform of 1921–2, religious affairs became the concern of the Antireligious Commission of the Central Committee under the leadership of Emelian Yaroslavsky. It had formerly been under the oversight of *Glavpolitprosvet*, the party's political education body which had been transferred from the Education Ministry to the newly-formed Central Committee *Agitprop* (agitation and propaganda) department in 1920. In the ideological and political crackdown of 1921–2 the Orthodox church was an obvious target. Its head, Patriarch Tikhon, an outspoken opponent of Communism, was arrested. Trotsky's call for him to be executed was opposed by Lenin who did not want to make a martyr of him. Similar considerations were behind the postponement of his trial, scheduled for 11 April 1923, but he did remain in jail for the time being. The moment of reconstruction and the call for citizens to hand over valuables for famine relief in 1921–2 was expanded into a campaign for the church to hand over its valuables, notably chalices, vestments and other items used in church ritual. Believers and clergy protested at the heavy-handedness and, in the town of Shuia the process was stopped temporarily by popular protests. More subtly, the authorities followed a divide and rule policy, giving greater scope to a breakaway renovationist Living Church group which was less hostile to the revolution. The Living Church, however, did not establish deep roots among believers, not least because of its clear association with the authorities. It was also undermined by the dramatic release of Patriarch Tikhon from jail in June 1923 and his startling declaration of a cessation of hostility towards the state (Luukanen 1994). There matters largely remained until a new cycle of heating up of antireligious policy began from about 1928 onwards.

Lenin's Last Reflections, 1920–22

In his speeches to the Tenth Congress Lenin's tone had been sombre. Despite the great achievements of defeating the old ruling class, fending off foreign enemies and securing the Communist Party in power, Lenin did not allow any trace of jubilation or triumphalism to enter his speech. Instead, he concentrated on difficult tasks ahead. He even went so far as to say that the opposition of the enemy would, in some respects, be more dangerous than it had been before. He also pointed out that, while the international imperialist enemy had run out of energy for the time being, this was only a temporary lull and, perhaps sooner rather than later, a new onslaught would be inevitable. Already, the system was showing that it needed external enemies to validate internal authoritarianism. Like many party leaders, he called for harmony, using the word several times. It was recognised by everyone as a lightly-veiled call for all opposition within the party to cease and for it to be replaced by obedience, never a likely virtue for most red-blooded revolutionaries! Even more ominously, showing how little he had learned from Rosa Luxemburg's prophetic chiding, Lenin referred to the discussions within the party as a 'luxury' and, a second time for emphasis, as 'an amazing luxury'. Even given the surrounding circumstances this was an extraordinary term for a person who considered himself to be a democrat to use. For most socialists, like Luxemburg, discussion was necessary, even essential. Without it a party, even a revolution, risked suffocation.

But the strategy of the third transition was clear. While certain economic controls had to be loosened to allow the economy to recover, ideological and political constraints had to be tightened up. In some ways the two were interlinked. Economic relaxation opened a potential for class enemies, such as traders and middlemen, to re-emerge. The retreat might give succour to critics from the Menshevik and SR parties who believed they had been proved correct in opposing the 'premature' revolution. Therefore, political and intellectual repression was necessary. However, others would argue that it came from deeper within the logic of the Bolshevik revolution. The politically conscious advanced guard of workers and party members was a small minority and to hold on long enough to win over the majority would require dictatorship. Unfortunately, the vicious circle in which the Communists were caught was that, far from helping win over support, the dictatorship drove a wedge between them and much of the population. In the long run, the dictatorship held on, but the conscious ideals eventually all but vanished and the system collapsed.

In his final assessments of the revolution Lenin showed no awareness of the underlying difficulties. Nor did his fellow-leaders such as Trotsky. It was clear to both of them that the revolution was being swallowed up in bureaucracy. In his very last article, revealingly entitled 'Better Fewer, But Better', Lenin seemed to think that reducing the size of the central committee would be enough to start solving the problem. Neither he nor Trotsky, who built his political platform on denouncing the bureaucratisation of the revolution, ever admitted the problem arose from the very essence of the Bolshevik revolution. If an elite was to run the country and the masses were not to be trusted until they were suitably conscious politically, then a bureaucratic and unaccountable dictatorship of the conscious minority was inevitable.

In two other articles, Lenin also showed satisfaction with the new transition and refuted its critics. In 'On Co-operation' he argued that the balance of private versus public interest characteristic of NEP would allow the revolution to advance. The masses, especially the peasants, would, he argued, soon see that the public, collective interest would make them better off than sticking to individual private interest. A 'cultural revolution' would enable them to modernise their daily practices and outlook and bring them over to socialism. In the other article, 'Our Revolution', he defended the Bolshevik method of revolution. Critics claimed that, in Marxist terms, the revolution had taken place before the prerequisites of proletarian rule had evolved. In defence of October, Lenin replied that they had established the excellent prerequisite of a proletarian state and ruling party. On that base, they could, he argued, go forward and build socialism. Clearly, Lenin was enthusiastic and believed that the third attempt at transition was going to be the definitive and successful one. It did, at least, last longer than the others but Lenin himself did not survive long enough to see it torn apart by Stalin at the end of the 1920s.

The Birth of the Soviet Union: 31 December 1922

The adoption of NEP and the measures taken to consolidate the new situation left one crucial issue still to be resolved – the nationalities. The civil war had seen unprecedented fluidity with national and ethnic administrations and even mini-states, coming and going. Some, like Ukraine, were substantial entities, others, like Tatarstan, were small and weak. The conflicts had not entirely ended with the defeat of the Whites or even with the Treaty of Riga in March 1921. There were still unresolved border disputes with the other states in the Baltic region. Elsewhere, the situation in the Caucasus was still fluid. It was only in February 1921 that Georgian independence was reversed when the Red Army entered the capital Tbilisi. Even so, the area remained volatile until the repression of a major uprising in 1924. The conquest of Georgia opened the way to the formation of the Transcaucasian Federation in March 1922 which also included the no-longer-independent Armenia and Azerbaidzhan. In Central Asia, Soviet Russia overthrew all alternative governments but had to face 'banditry' for some years to come in the form of an Islamic guerrilla resistance known collectively as the Basmachi Movement. It was not definitively suppressed until 1934. Further east, it was only on 25 October 1922 that Soviet troops entered Vladivostok. Japanese forces remained in Kamchatka and also Sakhalin and other disputed islands until agreement was reached in 1925. The last White holdout in the Far East was only defeated on 17 June 1923 when Pepelyaev, the last Kolchakite general, surrendered with the remains of his force of around 500 after defeat near the remote Siberian outpost of Okhotsk. Remarkably, his death sentence was commuted and he was eventually released from prison into civilian life in 1936, but was re-arrested while working as a carpenter and executed in the Great Purge.

Despite the local settlements, the post civil war Russian Federation remained a loose patchwork of ethnicities with a variety of statuses.

As such, it presented great organisational problems to the Bolsheviks. In the first place, the Bolsheviks were internationalists who believed the concept of a nationality was outdated and secondary to questions of class. Nonetheless, they were obviously aware of the power and reality of various forms of nationalism and national aspirations. They could not ignore the fact that there were over 150 different national and ethnic groups with a similar number of very diverse cultures and languages. The problem was also compounded by another structural issue. Out of the total population of around 125 million, somewhere between two-thirds and three-quarters were either Russians or closely related Ukrainians and Bielorussians and the somewhat more distant but still Slavic, Poles. This meant that the diversity really expressed itself within the 20 per cent or so minority of the population. Of these, Jews, at about five million, were the only group above around two million. Thus the diversity was accompanied by small numbers attached to each group. In terms of culture they covered many of the main anthropological groups of modern and semi-modern humanity. Almost all the great religions were represented. There were Christians of Orthodox, Lutheran, Evangelical and Roman Catholic traditions. There were also intermediate groups like Armenian Catholics and the Uniates of western Ukraine who combined Orthodox liturgy with acknowledgement of the Pope. There were Sunni and Shia Muslims mostly living in Central Asia, the Middle Volga and beside the Caspian Sea. There were Jews mainly in the west but also in enclaves throughout European Russia. There were German protestant settlements on the Volga and Greek Catholics in the Crimea. In the Far East there were Buddhists and animists. In terms of ways of life, for sure there was modern industry and agriculture with cities and villages, but also there were herders, nomads, igloo-dwellers, traditional miners, foresters, fishing people, whale-hunters and mountain peoples. In the Bolsheviks' own eyes all these peoples had to be drawn into the great enterprise of building socialism. In less grandiose terms they also had to be governed and administered.

The party left had a rather simplistic view of what party nationalities policy should be. As internationalists they wanted simply to denounce nationalism as a bourgeois construct of no great importance and remain true to class-based analysis instead. A sizeable portion of the party seems to have had a great deal of sympathy with this view. The party itself, especially the leadership, was disproportionately composed of national minorities. Many were Jews, Trotsky, Kamenev and Zinoviev being the most prominent. Dzherzhinskii was Polish, Stalin and Ordzhonikidze were Georgian. Latsis and Vacietis were

Latvian. Ksenofontov was Greek. The rank-and-file also included Armenians, Azeris, Uzbekhs, Kazakhs, Tadzhiks and many others. All shared the experience of being deeply opposed to the right-wing nationalist movements in their own ethnic homelands. Paradoxically, however, some believed a degree of national independence was necessary to prevent minorities being swallowed up by the most hated of all the empire's nationalisms – Great Russian Chauvinism. Thus there were embedded ambiguities of outlook, even before policy came to be formulated.

In 1913, Stalin, whose status as a Russified Georgian gave him a certain prominence in the field, not to mention a particular personal perspective, was sent to Vienna to study the national question and, in particular, to confront the Austrian Social-Democratic view of the question which revolved around national autonomy. Roughly, what the Austro-Marxists argued was that rights of the nation should be attached to people not to a geographical area. For instance, Czechs would have complete cultural autonomy but that would be guaranteed within the multi-national state, not within a separate state. While in Vienna, Stalin wrote the as-yet definitive outline of Bolshevik policy in an article entitled 'Marxism and the National Question'. The main points were that, in the feverish wave of rising nationalism in pre-war Europe 'Social-Democracy had a high mission – to resist nationalism and to protect the masses from the general "epidemic"'. For Stalin, it was indisputable that 'A nation has the right freely to determine its own destiny. It has the right to arrange its life as it sees fit, without, of course, trampling on the rights of other nations.' Therefore, 'it follows that Russian Marxists cannot dispense with the right of nations to self-determination. Thus, *the right of self-determination is an essential element* in the solution of the national question. *National autonomy* does not solve the problem.' So what did?

The complete democratization of the country is the *basis* and condition for the solution of the national question ... The only correct solution is *regional* autonomy, autonomy for such crystallized units as Poland, Lithuania, Ukraine, the Caucasus, etc. The advantage of regional autonomy consists, first of all, in the fact that it does not deal with a fiction bereft of territory, but with a definite population inhabiting a definite territory. Next, it does not divide people according to nations, it does not strengthen national barriers; on the contrary, it breaks down these barriers and unites the population in such a manner as to open the way for division of a different kind, division according to classes. Finally; it makes it possible to utilize the natural wealth of the region and to develop its productive forces in the best possible way without awaiting the decisions of a common centre – functions which are not inherent features of cultural-national autonomy. Thus, *regional autonomy is an essential element* in the solution of the national question.

In more pragmatic terms Stalin answered his own question: 'What is it that particularly agitates a national minority?' He continued:

A minority is discontented not because there is no national union but because it does not enjoy the right to use its native language. Permit it to use its native language and the discontent will pass of itself.

A minority is discontented not because there is no artificial union but because it does not possess its own schools. Give it its own schools and all grounds for discontent will disappear.

A minority is discontented not because there is no national union, but because it does not enjoy liberty of conscience (religious liberty), liberty of movement, etc. Give it these liberties and it will cease to be discontented.

Thus, *equal rights of nations in all forms (language, schools, etc.) is an essential element* in the solution of the national question. Consequently, a state law based on complete democratization of the country is required, prohibiting all national privileges without exception and every kind of disability or restriction on the rights of national minorities.

That, and that alone, is the real, not a paper guarantee of the rights of a minority.

The task was:

organization on the basis of internationalism. To unite locally the workers of all nationalities of Russia into *single, integral* collective bodies, to unite these collective bodies into a *single* party – such is the task. It goes without saying that a party structure of this kind does not preclude, but on the contrary presumes, wide autonomy for the *regions* within the single integral party. (All quotes from Stalin 1913. All emphases in original.)

In 1916, Lenin added his voice to the dispute in an article entitled 'The Socialist Revolution and the Right of Nations to Self-Determination'. As the title implied, Lenin repeated the significance of self-determination. But, like Stalin, he interpreted it in a way which seems to have negated the central right of self-determination, that is, secession. As one commentator has put it:

> Lenin explicitly argued that the right to secede ought in itself to be sufficient to persuade national minorities of the security of their national rights in a democratic state. While supporting the right of nations to self-determination, the Bolsheviks would not necessarily argue in favour of the right of secession being exercised. In any case in a socialist state, the clear economic and political advantages of remaining part of a larger state combined with the guarantees provided by the right to secede and the natural international class unity of the proletariat would ensure that, in most cases, national minorities would choose to remain within the larger state. (*Encyclopedia of Russian History.*)

Both Lenin and Stalin acknowledged that, given Russia's diversity, a one-size-fits-all policy would be impossible. The precise circumstances of each nationality, its stage of historical development, needed to be taken into account. Indeed, the first Soviet constitution of 1918 and the 1919 Party programme continued to acknowledge these points. The latter included a clause which stated:

> The All-Russian Communist Party regards the question as to who expresses the desire for a nation for separation, from an historical-class point of view, taking into consideration the level of historical development of any given nation: whether the nation is passing from medievalism toward bourgeois democracy or from bourgeois democracy toward soviet or proletarian democracy, etc. (McNeal 1974 vol. 2: 61)

Nonetheless, by 1922 the administration of revolutionary Russia was inconsistent to the point of being a mess. Borders were only now being defined in an internationally accepted way. A rag-tag set of administrative models of local and national governance were in conflict. The very name of the country – the Russian Soviet Federative Socialist Republic – was problematic. The prominence of the term Russian smacked of the cardinal sin of Great Russian chauvinism and, despite admonishments from the centre, many Russians were involved in heavy-handed dealings with smaller nationalities with which they had little sympathy. Ironically, one of the worst cases involved Stalin and his mistreatment of fellow Georgians (Lewin 1968). Federation was also an unpopular word. Bolshevik policy had been anti-federal, though it was hard to draw a consistent line since party policy, as in the extracts above, opposed decentralisation and over-centralisation. Federalism implied excessive decentralisation. There was also a deeply structural flaw running through the administration. Ever since 1917, as the Kronstadters among many others had pointed out, the Communist Party and the Soviet state were becoming closely inter-related. The two structures paralleled each other at nearly all key levels. But they were not equal in authority nor were they complete mirror images in terms of actual power relations. The Ukraine, the Transcaucasus and Belarus republics and various ad hoc autonomous republics set up within the RSFSR had the power to take decisions separately from Moscow. However, the dominant force in each subgroup was the party and that was firmly under the control of the Politburo and the Central Committee in Moscow. Thus, any independent measures in the sub-groups would be reversed through central party control, which outranked the state institutions. During the civil war, when improvised policies were enforced by a variety of party, state and military bodies, there was no time or opportunity to deal with the problem. However, in facing a period of greater stability, the muddle had to be sorted out, though it was easier said than done.

Stalin, as leading expert on the issue, took the lead. He proposed incorporating all the subgroups as autonomous republics within the RSFSR. In other words, there would be a clear hierarchy from centre to locality. However, Lenin, who was ailing at this point and not able to fully participate in the debates, was able to modify this proposal which, in theory at least, seemed to risk institutionalising Great Russian chauvinism. Instead, Lenin proposed incorporating the major sub-groups as federal republics on an equal basis with Russia. The republics, including Russia itself, would also have certain 'autonomous' territories within, where special considerations, of language and education, for example, would prevail. To avoid pejorative connotations of federalism, the new state was described as a union and, to avoid the appearance of Great Russian chauvinism, no existing nationality was named in the new state's title. It was called the Union of Soviet Socialist Republics. Its constitution was agreed on 30 December 1922 and it came into existence on 31 December 1922. In 1925 it was modified by the assignment of full republican status to the Central Asian lands of Uzbekistan, Kazakhstan, Turkmenistan, Tadzhikistan and Kirghizia.

It would take us beyond the scope of our present study to pursue the consequences of the setting up of the USSR, but it is worth pointing out that it maintained the key points from the earlier discussions. It permitted secession in theory but not practice. It appeared devolved, but most power remained at the centre. The areas in which nationalities flourished were exactly those of language, schooling, culture which Stalin had pointed out back in 1913. This issue of cultural protectionism had become known as *korenizatsiia* (meaning literally 'rootedness', implicitly 'indigenisation') and it remained an aspect of Soviet cultural policy until the collapse of the USSR. (There is a very rich literature on Soviet nationalities policy of which some highlights are: Lenin 1964; Subtelny 1989; Levin 1990; Simon 1991; Carrère d'Encausse 1992; Suny 1992, 1994; Slezkine 1994; Pipes 1997; Smith 1997; Chulos and Piirainen 2000; Martin 2000, 2001; Suny and Martin 2001; Hirsch 2005.)

The proclamation of the Soviet Union, along with developments at, around and arising from, the Tenth Party Congress seemed to mark a final emergence from the directly revolutionary period. The new constitution formalised Bolshevik power over one-sixth of the globe's land surface. A potential superpower had emerged from the wreckage of tsarist autocracy and imperialist war. For the moment, it was weak (but to make the point yet again, so were its rivals and the least weak is the strongest). The priority was stability and reconstruction of the industrial economy and the fragile urban networks that had been smashed over the years of world war, revolution and civil war. The population was, largely, subdued by exhaustion and famine. While 1922 was the last great famine there were tens of thousands of deaths from malnutrition every year through the 1920s [comment by V.P. Danilov at CREES seminar Birmingham]. The need was for social stability and economic growth. NEP provided a framework for both. Civil, cultural and personal life began to flourish again. Shostakovitch was not being entirely ironic when he called a ballet about the period 'The Golden Age' because for many it was. Further transforming upheavals initiated by the party were stalled by Lenin's illness and death and the ensuing succession crisis. The way in which this golden moment crumbled as Lenin's third transition strategy also fell apart is another story. By 1923, the people's revolution and the other components of the multiple revolutions since 1917 had, to all intents and purposes, been played out. From then on, only the Bolshevik revolutionary strand survived to evolve further.

Conclusion

One of the most resonant phrases in discussion of the Russian
Revolution for over a decade has been that it was part of a 'continuum
of crisis'. The phrase was popularised by Peter Holquist (Holquist
2002). His point was to draw attention to the wider linkages which
had been instrumental in bringing the revolution about. It was not
just a Russian Revolution but in gestation and effect was part of wider
European and global processes.

In Holquist's own words:

> Contemporaries and subsequent analysts telescoped Russia's path
> through the common European deluge (1914–21) into its period
> of revolution. As a result, Russia has largely fallen out of the general
> story of the Great War and twentieth-century European history. Yet
> re-inserting the Russian experience is crucial for understanding
> the First World War in general. Russia's 1917 revolutions exerted
> a reciprocal impact upon the European wartime ecosystem. The
> Russian Revolution served as a major precipitant for the wartime
> 'remobilisation' after 1917 that took place across Europe. It had an
> equally great impact on the politics of war aims and peacemaking
> (Holquist 2002: 2.)

There is a great deal of truth in Holquist's argument, but a number of
observations could be made about it. First, even Russia's immense role
in the Second World War was ignored and is still under-recognised by
many in the west, so it is hardly surprising it was also marginalised in
the history of the Great War. This was the outcome of many factors
which have left Russia more peripheral in the western imagination
made it a country which is always 'unknown', 'mysterious', 'a riddle
wrapped in an enigma' (Winston Churchill) and so on, rather than

he outcome of something specifically connected to 1917. Second, periodisation of the revolution has always been variable. True, numerous accounts focus on 1917, notably Wade (2005) or 1917–21 such as Williams (1987) or White (2001). But many others have very different periodisation, for example Figes chose 1891–1924 (1996), Read has 1914–21 (1996) Pipes' two volumes cover 1890–1919 and 1919–1924 (1990 and 1994) and Service's brief account focuses on 1900–1927 (1986). These are only a few examples, there are many more. The importance of the Russian question in peace-making in 1919 and international relations beyond had already been noted, not least by William Appleman Williams (1988) and Arno Mayer. (1967) Third, while this is hardly Holquist's intention, the phrase has sometimes been used to 'flatten' the history of Russia in this period so the revolution is diminished in relative importance and the war elevated. This is comparable to certain tendencies in the historiography of the French revolution which, compared to classical views, have questioned the degree to which the revolution was revolutionary.

As Holquist himself shows in the core of his volume, which recounts the revolution as it happened among the Don Cossacks, any attempt to suggest the revolution was not of immense significance to Russia and the world flies in the face of reality. The revolution had an enormous impact on the social, political, cultural and economic life of Russia. The entire elite was swept away. Capitalism and the market disappeared or were severely curtailed. Ancient cultures and institutions – as fundamental as religion and the family – were subjected to massive transformative pressures. No aspect of Russian society was untouched. The only real qualification to this is that the peasantry, though they benefitted from the land redistribution, resisted a good deal of those transformative pressures until the ultimate storm of 1929–30. Nonetheless, no revolution better deserves the name.

Of course, this is not to deny the influence of the war on the revolution. Without August 1914 the revolution as we know it would not have taken place. Most likely some other form of revolution would have happened. By 1900 the autocracy, clearly had the mark of death upon it. But it would have been a very different revolution, perhaps a 'bourgeois' revolution based on property, capitalism and parliamentary democracy. We will never know. The war, however, did, indeed, profoundly shape the revolution. The defining context was the economy. The downward economic spiral of 1914 to 1921 was cataclysmic and ensured, more or less, that a harsh regime of severe rationing, authoritarian leadership and terrible shortages of almost everything, was, if not essential or unavoidable, at least probable. But war, alone, was not necessarily sufficient to bring about revolution. The potentially revolutionary nature of Russia was analysed, argued over and often promoted by its restless intelligentsia and embodied in its multiple (though maybe not of themselves fatal) crises of economic and social 'backwardness' (the Russians own term for the situation) contained within an anachronistic and oppressive political autocracy which looked to the distant past for its inspiration and legitimacy. The fusion of the two forces – wartime collapse and revolutionary inevitability – were what gave the Russian Revolution its depth and distinctiveness. In that sense it certainly was a 'continuum of crisis'.

One could make the caveat that Russian history over centuries has been and continues to be a continuum of crisis but one could also, by focusing on 1914–22 make a slight amendment to Holquist's phrase. One might call it a 'continuum of crises'. One of the fundamental features which Holquist, and the post-1991 generation of historians of the regions and provinces have brilliantly exposed, is that there is not just one revolution but multiple revolutions taking place. Many nationalities, regions and localities had their own revolutions and we have been able to sample them in the course of the present study. But there are also social revolutions of class transformation, cultural revolutions, gender revolutions, economic revolutions, political revolutions and so on. Many of these processes were inter-related but to lump them all together would be to miss the complexity, contradiction and diversity of these revolutions. Writing in 1996 the present writer stressed that 'it is vital to remember that the "Russian" revolution was not one revolution but many, conducted by various nationalities and classes in a kaleidoscope of combinations and with a whole series of outcomes' (Read 1996: 283). There seems little reason to do anything other than suggest that the weight of research since that time has amply supported that conclusion. Indeed, one of the most active schools of post-1991 historiography has adopted the phrase 'kaleidoscope of revolutions' as its key self-description and is producing important fruits of its work under this title.

In the manner of Lenin (and, by coincidence, I am writing this in April) let us summarise the main points of the revolution in the form of theses.

1. Before 1914 Russia had deep, potentially revolution-inducing social, economic, political and cultural problems. Society was beginning to change fairly quickly in many respects, but the state

dominated by Nicholas II, was more intent on preserving its traditional autocratic nature than in adapting to and absorbing change. This created enormous potential for explosive conflict.

2. Involvement in war catalysed existing problems, making some of them worse, and added problems of its own. Most such problems were related to the economy of wartime and, in the forefront was inflation, which bore heavily on the living standards of the urban working poor. The peasantry were less directly affected, though peasant sons comprised the bulk of the army. Military defeat precipitated political crisis which first peaked in August 1915, and also the ongoing social crisis of refugees and displaced persons.

3. The elite elements, mostly associated directly or indirectly with the Progressive Bloc set up in the Duma in August 1915, who took action in the February Revolution, aimed to nip revolution in the bud. They wanted to prevent it from threatening their property and social position. Nicholas II was the sacrificial lamb. His abdication would, it was hoped, placate the masses.

4. Popular activity in February was largely limited to Petrograd at first but, in the absence of firm opposition and then the startling news of the fall of the tsar, a chaotic but powerful mass movement – a popular movement like that of the French Revolution – quickly emerged. Soldiers, sailors, workers and peasants rapidly organised themselves in their localities in committees and soviets. The only quasi-national equivalent was the Petrograd Soviet. Far from containing the revolution, the February revolutionaries in the Duma had unleashed an immensely powerful force which soon swept them away.

5. The revolutionary energy released in 1917 was immense and ubiquitous. Although the Russian revolution was central, a cascade of multiple revolutions or a kaleidoscope of revolutions, were unleashed affecting class, gender, ethnicity, nationality and so on. A host of nations were born. Some remained independent (Finland, Poland); some were brought back under Russian control fairly quickly (Central Asia, Georgia, Armenia, Azerbaidzhan) and were incorporated in the USSR when it was founded on 29–30 December 1922. Others (Latvia, Lithuania, Estonia) were only re-incorporated after the outbreak of war in 1939.

6. While millions took part in rebellious activities in 1917, the decisive forces, more often than not, were soldiers and sailors rather than workers and peasants. They had the weapons to enforce their will more successfully than their civilian brothers and sisters. This element of the revolution has yet to be fully explored by researchers.

7. The Kornilov affair was crucial in destabilising the Provisional Government and, in particular, Kerensky's strategy of trying to maintain national unity in the face of the enemy at the gates. In a sense, the Kornilov affair was the first step in what became a civil war. Kerensky's failure to recognise that the rapidly polarising situation required him to choose a side, rather than stand in a now-deserted centre, precipitated his downfall.

8. The rise of the Bolsheviks after Kornilov was rapid and decisive. They benefitted from their 'wild card' position as an opposition – that is they could criticise extensively without the responsibility of implementing policies – and their rise was intimately connected with the rise of a desire for 'All Power to the Soviets' within the popular movement. The overthrow of the Provisional Government was not a simple coup. It was linked to a broad nationwide process. Mass land redistribution had already begun. The domination of the new Soviet Government by Bolsheviks was, however, more of a political coup.

9. Bolshevik dominance in and after October brought the 'wrong' leadership to the fore. The revolutionary pressure of the masses was for the popular programme of peace, bread, land and all power to the soviets, a programme closer to that of the SRs than the Bolsheviks. The latter were astute in adopting it but their aims were very different. They were ideologically driven to 'construct socialism' as a worldwide process based on transforming human consciousness and values. The knot tied here between the masses and the Bolsheviks constituted the tragedy of the revolution. Actual mass aspirations for practical improvements, self-government and self-organisation on a day-to-day basis found no firm national leadership. The new national leadership of Bolsheviks had a utopian agenda unknown to most of the masses before October. For the Bolshevik leadership, the promises of October – i.e. the popular programme – were not an end but only a beginning.

10. Lenin believed the civil war had been by and large won by April 1918. The new strategy for transition to socialism embarked upon by Lenin at that time was envisaged as a peacetime process aimed at reconstruction from the ruins of war and civil war. It had numerous 'Stalinist' principles of dictatorship and socialism in one country. To call it 'War Communism' is highly misleading. At the time it was thought of as the standard form of transition to socialism, applicable universally, not a set of war-induced

contingencies. In the longer term of Soviet history it was NEP that was the aberration. When it was replaced, Stalin reverted to many aspects of Lenin's 1918 strategy as the definitive path.

11. Arguably, the civil war helped the Bolsheviks retain power by establishing a clear choice – support the Bolsheviks and revolution or the Whites and counter-revolution. Many opponents of Bolshevism were forced to drop their opposition and support them as the lesser of two evils. The re-emergence of significant popular protest as the White threat receded in 1920 and 1921 confirms this effect. From this point of view the Whites, who at best had little chance of winning the civil war, unwittingly aided the Bolsheviks in their attempts to secure power. Closely connected to this, the civil war against the Whites concealed within it a more significant war between the Bolsheviks and the masses. The war against the Whites was the protective cover under which the Bolsheviks were able to crush many popular aspirations and freedoms in the name of military and political necessity.

12. Lenin and the Bolshevik leadership had three moments of relatively open choice in this period. The first was to take power in the first place. The second, very brief one, came at the end of the first civil war in April 1918, the third in March 1921 at the end of the second civil war and after the worst of the popular protests (apart from Kronstadt) had been suppressed. On both second and third occasions Lenin's choice was for greater centralisation, discipline and control rather than for a reversion to democracy, a multi-party socialist system and self-government as the masses wanted. The fact that, in 1921, concessions had to be made to the peasantry, who had defeated Bolshevik plans especially in the form of forced requisitioning of agricultural produce, does not detract from this observation. The 'anomaly' of concessions to the peasants was 'rectified' in a particularly brutal way through collectivisation at the end of the decade.

The Russian Revolution was, then, an infinitely complex phenomenon, or perhaps better, an infinitely complex set of intertwined phenomena. It was generated by a wide spectrum of powerful forces and it exploded in 1917 into a process with world-wide repercussions which are still with us. It was, indeed, a continuum of crises. However, it was also affected by the fatal knot of October. On the basis of a popular revolution seeking to establish popular democracy, self-government and social justice an ideological leadership came to power which believed those things could only be obtained in a certain way, based on the overthrow of capitalism on a global scale. Each of these revolutions impeded the other. The Bolsheviks prevented the emergence of popular democracy as envisaged by the masses in 1917. Mass scepticism and indifference held back the soaring utopian ambitions of the Bolsheviks. In the end, the Bolsheviks failed in their attempts to win over the masses for their version of socialist construction. As is usually the case, history had eluded the best efforts of those who wished to control it.

Select Bibliography

Abraham, Richard, *Alexander Kerensky: the First Love of the Revolution*. New York: Columbia University Press, 1987.

Acton, Edward *Rethinking the Russian Revolution*. London: Bloomsbury Academic 1990.

Adamets, Serguei *Guerre civile et famine en Russie: Le pouvoir bolchévique et la population face à la catastrophe démographique de 1917–1923*. Paris: Institute d'études slaves 2003.

Akhapkin, Iu. (ed) *First Decrees of Soviet Power*. London: Lawrence & Wishart, 1970.

Ali-uulu, Masud 2009 http://centralasiaonline.com/en_GB/articles/caii/features/2009/08/12/feature-03

Anweiler, Oscar *The Soviets: The Russian Peasants', Soldiers' and Workers' Councils 1905–1921*. New York: Pantheon, 1974.

Arshinov P. *History of the Makhnovist Movement*. London: Freedom Press, 2005.

Ascher, Abraham *The Revolution of 1905 vol 1 Russia in Disarray*, Stanford University Press, 1988; *vol 2 Authority Restored*. Stanford University Press, 1992.

Ascher, Abraham *P.A. Stolypin: the Search for Stability in Late Imperial Russia*. Stanford University Press, 2001.

Atkinson, Dorothy *The End of the Russian Land Commune 1905–1930*. Stanford University Press, 1983.

Avrich, Paul 'Anarchism and Anti-Intellectualism in Russia,' *Journal of the History of Ideas* Vol. 27, No. 3, pp. 381–90, 1966.

Avrich, Paul 'The Anarchists in the Russian Revolution,' *Russian Review* Vol. 26, No. 4, pp. 341–50, 1967.

Avrich, Paul *The Russian Anarchists*. Princeton University Press, 1967.

Avrich, Paul 'Russian Anarchists and the Civil War' *Russian Review* Vol. 27, No. 3, pp. 296–306, 1968.

Avrich, Paul *Kronstadt, 1921*. Princeton University Press, 1970.

Avrich, Paul *The Anarchists in the Russian Revolution*. London: Thames and Hudson 1973.

Badcock, Sarah 'An Analysis of the Inability of the Provisional Government to Prevent the Bolshevik Seizure of Power and the Failure of Kerensky's Coalition Politics in 1917'. unpublished PhD thesis Durham 1998.

Badcock, Sarah 'Women, Protest and Revolution: Soldiers' Wives in Russia in 1917' *International Review of Social History* 49, pp. 47–70 2004.

Badcock, Sarah *Politics and the People in Revolutionary Russia: A Provincial History.* Cambridge University Press, 2007.

Bashkiroff, Zenaide *The Sickle and the Harvest.* London: Neville Spearman, 1960.

Basmanov, M.I., Gerasimenko, G.A., Gusev K.V. pod obshcheĭ redaktsieĭ V.A. Dinesa *Aleksandr Fedorovich Kerenskiĭ.* Saratov: Izdatel'stvo gos. Ekon. Akademii, 1996.

Benvenuti, Franco. *The Bolsheviks and the Red Army, 1918–22.* Cambridge University Press, 1988.

Berkman, A. *The Kronstadt Rebellion.* Berlin: Der Syndikalist, 1922.

Berkman, A. *The Bolshevik Myth.* New York: Boni and Liveright, 1925.

Bernshtam, M.S. *Nezavisimoe rabochee dvizhenie v 1918 godu: dokumenty i materialy.* Paris: YMCA-Press 1981.

Biggart, John Alexander *Bogdanov, left Bolshevism and the Proletkul't 1904–32* (electronic resource). University of East Anglia 1989.

Biggart, John, Dudley, Peter and King Francis (eds) *Alexander Bogdanov and the Origins of Systems Thinking in Russia.* Aldershot: Ashgate, 1998a.

Biggart, John, Gloveli, Georgii and Yassour, Avraham (eds) *Bogdanov and his Work: a Guide to the Published and Unpublished Works of A.A. Bogdanov (Malinovskii).* Aldershot: Ashgate, 1998b.

Blok, A. 'The twelve', in: *Selected poems,* (trans by Jon Stallworthy and Peter France). Harmondsworth: Penguin, 1974.

Bogdanov, A.A. 'Fortunes of the Workers' Party in the Present Revolution' *Novaia zhizn'* 19 (26 January) and 20 (27 January) 1918, unpublished translation by J. Biggart for The Study Group on the Russian Revolution, January 1984.

Bogdanov, A.A. *Voprosy sotsializma: raboty raznykh let.* Moscow: Politizdat, 1990.

Bone, A (trans.) *The Bolsheviks and the October revolution: minutes of the Central Committee of the Russian Social-Democratic Labour Party (Bolsheviks) August 1917–February 1918.* London: Pluto Press, 1974.

Bonnell, V. *The Russian Worker: Life and Labor Under The Tsarist Regime.* Berkeley: University of California Press, 1983a.

Bonnell, V. *Roots of Rebellion: Workers' Politics and Organizations in St. Petersburg and Moscow 1900–1914.* Berkeley: University of California Press, 1983b.

Bonwetsch, Bernd 'Rußland, Oktober 1917: Hegemonie des Proletariats oder Volksrevolution? Bemerkung zur sowjetischen Historiographie seit Anfang siebziger Jahre', *Osteuropa* 1990, 39, pp. 733–747.

Bradley, J. *Muzhik and Muscovite: Urbanization in Late Imperial Russia.* Berkeley: University of California Press, 1985.

Brinton, M. *The Bolsheviks and Workers' Control, 1917 to 1921: The State and Counter-Revolution.* London: Solidarity 1970.

Brooks, Jeffrey *When Russia Learned to Read: Literacy and Popular Literature, 1861–1917.* Princeton University Press, 1985.

Brovkin, V.N. 'The Mensheviks' Political Comeback: The Elections to the Provincial City Soviets in Spring 1918', *Russian Review* Vol. 42, No. 1 (Jan.) pp. 1–50, 1983.

Brovkin, V.N. *The Mensheviks after October: Socialist Opposition and the Rise of the Bolshevik Dictatorship.* Ithaca and London: Cornell University Press, 1987.

Brovkin, V.N. *Behind The Front Lines of the Civil War: Political Parties and Social Movements in Russia, 1918–22.* Princeton University Press, 1994.

Brovkin, V.N. *The Bolsheviks in Russian Society: the Revolution and the Civil Wars.* Princeton University Press, 1997.

Browder R.P. and Kerensky A.F. (eds) *The Russian Provisional Government 1917: Documents,* 3 vols. Stanford University Press, 1961.

Brown S. 'Communists and the Red Cavalry: Political Education of the Konarmiia in the Russian civil war', *Slavonic and East European Review,* 73, 1 (Jan 1995) pp. 82–99.

Bryce, Viscount *The Treatment of Armenians in the Ottoman Empire in 1915–16.* HMSO London 1916 (available at: http://net.lib.byu.edu/~rdh7/wwi/1915/bryce/).

Brym, Robert and Economakis, Evel 'Peasant or Proletarian? Militant Pskov Workers in St. Petersburg, 1913', *Slavic Review* 53 1 (Spring 1994) pp. 120–139.

Bukharin N. and Preobrazhensky, E. *ABC of Communism.* Harmondsworth: Penguin, 1969.

Bunyan, J. and Fisher, H.H. (eds.) *The Bolshevik Revolution 1917–18: Documents and Materials.* Stanford University Press, 1934.

Burbank, Jane *Intelligentsia and Revolution: Russian Views of Bolshevism 1917–22.* Oxford University Press, 1986.

Bushnell, John *Mutiny amid Repression. Russian Soldiers in the Revolution of 1905–1906.* Bloomington: Indiana University Press, 1985.

Calleo, David *The German Problem Reconsidered 1870 to the Present.* Cambridge University Press, 1978.

Carr, E.H. *The Bolshevik Revolution 3 vols.* Harmondsworth: Penguin, 1968.

Carrère d'Encausse, H. *Lenin: Revolution and Power.* London: Longman, 1982.

Carrère d'Encausse, H. *The Great Challenge: Nationalities and the Bolshevik State, 1917–1930.* New York: Holmes & Meier Publishers, 1992.

Chagall, Marc *My Life.* London: Peter Owen, 1965.

Chaianov, A. *Ekonomicheskoe nasledie A.V. Chaianova* (ed. Tonchu, E.A.). Moscow; Izdatel'stvo Dom TONChU, 2006.

Chamberlin, W.H. *The Russian Revolution,* 2 vols. New York: Grosset & Dunlap, 1965.

Channon, John 'The Bolsheviks and the Peasantry: the Land Question During the First Eight Months of Soviet Rule', *Slavonic and East European Review* 6 4 October pp. 593–624 1988.

Channon, John 'The Landowners', in R. Service (ed), *Society and Politics in the Russian Revolution* pp. 120–146. Basingstoke and London: Macmillan, 1992.

Channon, John 'The Peasantry in the Revolutions of 1917', in E.R.Frankel *et al.* (eds) *Revolution in Russia: Reassessments of 1917.* Cambridge University Press, 1992.

Chase, W.J. *Workers, Society and the Soviet State: Labor and Life in Moscow 1918–29.* Urbana and Chicago: University of Illinois Press, 1987.

Cherniavsky, M. *Prologue to Revolution. Notes of A.N.Iakhontov on the Secret Meetings of the Council of Ministers, 1915.* Englewood Cliffs, New Jersey: Prentice-Hall, 1967.

Chulos, Chris J. and Piirainen, Timo, eds *The Fall of an Empire, the Birth of a Nation.* Aldershot: Ashgate, 2000.

228   SELECT BIBLIOGRAPHY

Claudin-Urondo, C. *Lenin and the Cultural Revolution* tr. B. Pearce. Sussex New Jersey: Humanities Press, 1977.
Cohen, S. *Bukharin and the Bolshevik Revolution: a Political Biography (1888–1938)*. Oxford University Press, 1973.
Cohn, Norman *Warrant for Genocide*. London: Serif, 1964.
Coquin, F.-X. and Gervais-Francelle, C. (eds) *1905: la première révolution Russe*. Paris: Publications de la Sorbonne, 1986.
Crisp, O. *Studies in the Russian Economy before 1914*. London: Macmillan, 1976.
Crisp, O. and Edmondson, L. (eds) *Civil Rights in Imperial Russia*. Oxford University Press, 1989.
Croll, Kirsteen Davina 'Soviet–Polish relations, 1919–1921'. PhD thesis, available as pdf, University of Glasgow 2009.
Daly, J. and Trofimov, L. *Russia in War and Revolution, 1914–22: a Documentary History*. Indianapolis and Cambridge: Hackett, 2009.
Daniels, R.V. *The Conscience of the Revolution*. Harvard University Press, 1960; Boulder, CO: Westview Press, 1988.
Daniels, R.V. *Red October: the Bolshevik Revolution of 1917*. London: Macmillan, 1968.
Daniels, R.V. (ed) *A Documentary History of Communism* 2 vols. Hanover and London: University Press of New England. 1984.
Danilov, V.P. *Rural Russia under the New Regime*. Bloomington: Indiana University Press, 1988.
Davies, R.W. (ed) *From Tsarism to the New Economic Policy: Continuity and Change in the Economy of the USSR*. Ithaca: Cornell University Press, 1990.
Davies, R.W. (*et al.* eds) *The Economic Transformation of the Soviet Union 1913–1945*. Cambridge University Press, 1994.
Davis, Mike *Late Victorian Holocausts: El Nino Famines and the Making of the Third World*. London: Verso, 2001.
Denikin, A. *The White Army* (trans by Catherine Zvegintsov). Gulf Breeze: Gordon Press, 1973.
Diakin, V.S. *Samoderzhavie, burzhuaziia i dvorianstvo v 1907–1911gg*. Leningrad: Nauka, 1978.
Dowling, Timothy C. *The Brusilov Offensive*. Bloomington: Indiana University Press, 2008.
Dune, Eduard M. *Notes of a Red Guard* (Trans and ed by Diane P. Koenker and S.A.Smith). Urbana and Chicago: University of Illinois Press, 1993.
Durrenberger, E. *Paul Chayanov, Peasants and Economic Anthropology*. London and Orlando: Academic Press, 1984.
Edmondson, L. and Waldron, P. (eds) *Economy and Society in Russia and the Soviet Union, 1860–1930*. London: Macmillan, 1992.
Eklof Ben and Frank Stephen P. (eds) *The World of the Russian Peasant: Post Emancipation Culture and Society*. London: Unwin Hyman, 1990.
Eklof, Ben and Frank, Stephen (eds) *The World of the Russian Peasant*. London: Unwin Hyman, 1990.
Elwood, R.C. (ed.) *Reconsiderations on the Russian Revolution*. Slavica, 1976.
Encyclopedia of Russian History, by the Gale Group, Inc. At http://www.answers.com/topic/soviet-nationalities-policies#ixzz1bm LBFWzk
Engelstein, Laura *The Keys to Happiness: Sex and the Search for Modernity in fin-de-siècle Russia*. Ithaca and London: Cornell University Press, 1992.
Ezergailis, A. *The 1917 Revolution in Latvia*. Boulder, CO: Westview, 1974.

Farson, Negley *The Way of the Transgressor*. London: Harcourt, Brace, 1940.

Ferro, M. 'The Birth of the Soviet Bureaucratic System', in R.C. Elwood, ed., *Reconsiderations on the Russian Revolution*. pp. 100–132, Slavica, 1976.

Ferro, M. *October 1917. A Social History of the Russian Revolution*. London: Routledge & Kegan Paul, 1980.

Ferro, M. *The Russian Revolution of February 1917*. London: Prentice-Hall, 1972.

Figes, O. *Peasant Russia, Civil War: the Volga Countryside in Revolution, 1917–21*. Oxford University Press, 1989.

Figes, O. 'The Red Army and Mass Mobilization during the Russian Civil War 1918–20', *Past and Present* 129 pp. 168–211 1990.

Figes, O. *A People's Tragedy: the Russian Revolution 1891–1924*. London: Pimlico, 1996.

Finkel, Stuart *On the Ideological Front: the Intelligentsia and the Making of the Soviet Public Sphere*. Princeton University Press, 2008.

Fitzpatrick, S. *The Russian Revolution*. Oxford University Press, 1982.

Fontenot, Michael James 'Alexander F. Kerensky: the Political Career of a Russian Nationalist'. unpubl PhD thesis. Ann Arbor, Michigan: University Microfilms International, n.d. 1981 printing.

Frank, Stephen P. and Steinberg, Mark D. (eds) *Cultures in Flux: Lower-Class Values, Practices, and Resistance in Late Imperial Russia*. Princeton University Press, 1994.

Frankel E.R. *et al.* (eds) *Revolution in Russia: Reassessments of 1917*. Cambridge University Press, 1992.

Frenkin, M. *Russkaia armiia i revoliutsiia 1917–1918*. Munich: Logos, 1978.

Frenkin, M. *Zakhvat vlasti Bol'shevikami v Rossii i rol' tylovykh garnizonov armii: podgotovka i provedenie oktiabr'skogo miatezha 1917–1918 gg.* Jerusalem: Stav, 1982.

Galili, Z. *The Menshevik Leaders in the Russian Revolution: Social Realities and Political Strategies*. Princeton University Press, 1989.

Gaponenko, L.S. (ed.) *Revoliutsionnoe dvizhenie v Russkoi armii 27 fevralia–24 oktiabria 1917 goda: sbornik dokumentov*. Moscow: Nauka 1968.

Gatrell, Peter *The Tsarist Economy 1850–1917*. London: Batsford, 1986.

Gatrell, Peter *Government, Industry and Rearmament in Russia 1907–1914: the Last Argument of Tsarism*. Cambridge University Press, 1994.

Gatrell, Peter *A Whole Empire Walking: Refugees in Russia during World War 1*. Bloomington: Indiana University Press, 1999.

Gatrell, Peter 'Review of Lohr *Nationalizing the Russian Empire*', in *Cahiers du Monde Russe* 44/4 2003 p. 704 (mis en ligne le 19 juin 2009) URL: http://monderusse.revues.org/index4103.html

Gatrell, Peter *Russia's First World War: A Social and Economic History*. Harlow 2004.

Gaza, I.I. *Putilovets v trekh revoliutsiakh*. Leningrad: Kommunisticheskaia Akademiia, 1933.

Geary, Dick (ed.) *Labour and Socialist Movements in Europe before 1914*. Oxford, New York, Munich 1983.

Geldern, James von *Bolshevik Festivals 1917–1920*. Berkeley: University of California Press, 1993.

George, Susan *How the Other Half Dies*. Harmondsworth: Penguin, 1976.

Gerson, L.D. *The Secret Police in Lenin's Russia*. Philadelphia: Temple University Press, 1976.

Getzler, I. *Martov: a Political Biography of a Russian Social Democrat*. Cambridge University Press, 1967.

Getzler, I. *Kronstadt 1917–21: the Fate of a Soviet Democracy*. Cambridge University Press, 1983.

Gill, G. *Peasants and Government in the Russian Revolution*. Rowman & Littlefield, 1979.

Gimpel'son, E. *The Great Soviet Encyclopedia*, 3rd Edition. Farmington Hills, MI: St James Press, 1970–1979.

Gleason A. *et al.* (eds) *Bolshevik Culture: Experiment and Order in the Russian Revolution*. Bloomington: Indiana University Press, 1985.

Gleason, A. *Totalitarianism: the Inner History of the Cold War*. Oxford University Press, 1998.

Gleason, William E. 'The All-Russian Union of Towns and the Politics of Urban Reform in Tsarist Russia', *Russian Review* vol. 35, no. 3, pp. 290–302 July 1976.

Golder, Frank *Documents of Russian History 1914–1917*. Gloucester, MA 1964; Read Books, 2008 (reprint of original edition New York 1927).

Goldman, Emma *My Disillusionment in Russia*. New York 1923; Dover Books, 2003.

Golub, P.A. *et al.* (eds) *Istoricheskii opyt trekh rossiisskikh revoliutsii 3 vols.* Moscow: Politizdat, 1986–1987.

Gorky, M. *Untimely Thoughts: Essays on Revolution, Culture and the Bolsheviks 1917–1918*. London, New York: P. S. Eriksson, 1968.

Gosudarstvennoe soveshchanie (s predisloviem Ia.A. Iakovleva). Moscow–Leningrad: Gosizdat 1930.

Got'e, I.V. *Time of Troubles: the Diary of Iury Vladimirovich Got'e*, (trans and ed by T. Emmons). Princeton University Press, 1988.

Gregory, Paul *Russian National Income: 1885–1913*. Cambridge University Press, 1982.

Grif sekretnosti sniat. Poteri Vooruzhenykh sil SSSR v voinakh, boevykh deistviiakh i voennykh konfliktakh; statisticheskoe issledovanie. Moscow: Voenizdat, 1993.

Grunt, A.Ia. *Moskva 1917: revoliutsiia i kontrrevoliutsiia*. Moscow, Nauka 1976.

Haimson, Leopold 'The Problem of Social Stability in Urban Russia (1905–1917)', *Slavic Review* (Part One) vol. 23, no. 4, pp. 619–642, Dec 1964; (Part Two) vol. 24, no. 1, pp. 1–22 March 1965.

Haimson, Leopold *Russia's Revolutionary Experience, 1905–1917: Two Essays: Two Contemporary Perspectives on the Issue of Power*. New York 2005.

Hamm, M.F. (ed.) *The City in Late imperial Russia*. Bloomington: Indiana University Press, 1986.

Harcave, Sydney *First Blood: the Russian Revolution of 1905*. London 1965.

Hardeman, Hilde *Coming to Terms with the Soviet Regime: The 'Changing Signposts' Movement among Russian Émigrés in the Early 1920s*. DeKalb 1994.

Hasegawa, T. *The February Revolution*. Seattle and London 1981.

Heath, Nick *The Third Revolution? Peasant and Worker Resistance to the Bolshevik Government 1920–22* (pamphlet). London 2010.

Heifetz, E. *The Slaughter of Jews in the Ukraine*. New York 1921.

Hickey, Michael 'Urban Zemliachestva and Rural Revolution: Petrograd and the Smolensk Countryside in 1917', *Soviet and Post-Soviet Review* vol 23 143–169, 1996.

Hirsch, Francine *Empire of Nations: Ethnographic Knowledge and the Making of the Soviet Union*. Ithaca and London: Cornell University Press, 2005.

Hoch, Steven L. 'On good numbers and bad: Malthus, population trends and peasant standard of living in late imperial Russia', *Slavic Review*, 53, 1, (Spring, 1994).

Hoffmann David L. and Kotsonis Yanni (eds) *Russian Modernity: Politics, Knowledge, Practices*. Basingstoke: Macmillan 2000.

Holmes, Larry *The Kremlin and the Schoolhouse: Reforming Education in Soviet Russia 1917–1931*. Bloomington: Indiana University Press, 1991.

Holquist, Peter *Making War, Forging Revolution: Russia's Continuum of Crisis 1914–21*. Harvard University Press, 2002.

Horne, John (ed.) *State, Society and Mobilization in Europe during the First World War*. Cambridge University Press, 1997.

Hosking, Geoffrey *The Russian Constitutional Experiment: Government and Duma, 1907–1914*. Cambridge University Press, 1985.

Ignat'ev, G.S. *Moskva v pervyi god proletarskoi diktatury*. Moscow: Nauka, 1975.

Inozemtsev, M. 'Iz istorii rabochego dvizheniia vo vremia mirovoi voiny', *Krasnyi-arkhiv* 6, pp. 5–27, 1934.

Ioffe, G.Z. *Krakh rossiiskoi monarkhicheskoi kontrrevoliutsii*. Moscow, Nauka, 1977.

Jansen, M. *Show Trial Under Lenin: The Trial of the Socialist Revolutionaries*. Moscow 1922; Amsterdam: Springer, 1982.

Johnson, R. *Peasant and Proletarian: The Working Class of Moscow in the Late Nineteenth Century*. Leicester University Press, 1979.

Jones, Stephen 'The Non-Russian Nationalities', in R.Service (ed), *Society and Politics in the Russian Revolution*. Basingstoke: Macmillan, 1992.

Kabanov, V.V. *Oktiabr'skaia revoliutsiia i kooperatsiia (1917 g.–mart 1919 g.)*. Moscow: Nauka, 1973.

Kabanov, V.V. *Krest'ianskoe khoziastvo v usloviakh 'voennogo kommunizma'*. Moscow: Nauka, 1988.

Kaiser D. (ed.) *The Workers' Revolution in Russia: The View from Below*. Cambridge University Press, 1987.

Kakurin, N.E. *Kak srazhalas' revoliutsiia*, 2 vols, 2nd ed. *Moscow–Leningrad 1926*. Reprinted Moscow: Politizdat, 1990.

Karsch, Stefan *Die Bolschewistische Machtergreifung im Gouvernement Voronez 1917–19*. Stuttgart: Steiner, 2006.

Katkov, G. *Russia 1917: the February Revolution*. London: Collins, 1967.

Katkov, G. *The Kornilov Affair*. London: Longman, 1980.

Keegan, J. in *State, Society, and Mobilization in Europe during the First World War*, ed. John Horne. Cambridge University Press, 1997.

Keegan, J. *The First World War*. London: Pimlico, 1998.

Keep, J.L.H. *The Russian Revolution: A Study in Mass Mobilization*. New York: W.W. Norton, 1976.

Keep, J.L.H. (trans and ed), *The Debate on Soviet Power: Minutes of the All-Russian Central Executive Committee Second Convocation, October 1917–January 1918*. Oxford: Clarendon Press, 1979.

Kenez, P. 'Changes in the Social Composition of the Officer Corps During World War I', *Russian Review*, vol. 31, pp. 369–75.

Kerensky, A. *The Prelude to Bolshevism: The Kornilov Rebellion*. London 1919.

Kerensky, A. *The Catastrophe*. London: T.F. Unwin 1927.

Kerensky, A. *Russia and History's Turning Point*. London: Cassell, 1965.

Khromov, S.S. ed. *Grazhdanskaia voina i voennaia interventsiia v SSSR: entsiklopediia*. Moscow: Sovetskaia entsiklopediia, 1987.

Klier, John Doyle and Lambroza, Shlomo *Pogroms: Anti-Jewish Violence in Modern Russian History.* Cambridge University Press, 2004.

Kneen, Peter 'Higher Education and Cultural Revolution in the USSR', *CREES Discussion Papers, Soviet Industrialisation Project Series, No 5.* Birmingham 1976.

Koenker, D. *Moscow Workers and the 1917 Revolution.* Princeton University Press, 1981.

Koenker, D. *et al.* eds *Party, State And Society in the Russian Civil War.* Bloomington: Indiana University Press, 1989.

Koenker D. and Rosenberg, W. *Strikes and Revolution in Russia 1917.* Princeton University Press, 1989.

Kollontai, A. *Selected Writings.* Westport, CT: Lawrence Hill, 1977.

Kolonitskii, Boris 'Nicholas the Third: Images of Commander in Chief Grand Duke Nikolai Nikolaievich 1914–1915' Paper presented at War Revolution, Civil War: Eastern Europe 1914–1923 conference, Centre for War Studies, University College Dublin 25 March 2011.

Kolonitskii, Boris and Figes, O. *Interpreting the Russian Revolution: The Language and Symbols of 1917.* New Haven and London: Yale University Press, 1999.

Kotel'nikov, K.G. and Meller, V.L. *Krest'ianskoe dvizhenie v gody voiny i pered Oktiabrem 1917 g.* Leningrad: Gosizdat, 1927.

Krasil'nikov, S.A. Morozov A.N. and Chubykin I.B. (eds) *Sudebnyi protsess nad sotsialistami- revoliutsionerami (iun'-avgust 1922g)* Moscow, ROSSPEN, 2002.

Kruchkovskaia, V.M. *Tsentral'naia gorodskaia duma v Petrograda v 1917 g.* Leningrad: Nauka, 1986.

Landis, Eric *Bandits and Partisans: the Antonov Movement in the Russian Civil War.* University of Pittsburgh Press, 2008.

Leggett, G. *The Cheka: Lenin's political police, the All-Russian Extraordinary Commission for Combating Counter-revolution and Sabotage (December 1917 to February 1922).* Oxford University Press, 1981.

Lenin, V.I. *State and Revolution.* Petrograd 1918; London: Penguin, 2009.

Lenin, V.I. *Collected Works* (45 vols). Moscow: Progress, 1960–1970.

Lenin, V.I. 'The Socialist Revolution and the Right of Nations to Self-Determination', London, 1964. http://www.marxists.org/archive/lenin/works/1916/jan/x01.htm

Lenin, V.I. *Selected Works*, 3 vols. Moscow: Progress, 1967.

Lenin, V.I. *Between The Two Revolutions: Articles and Speeches Of 1917.* Moscow: Progress, 1971.

Lenin V.I. i VChK: sbornik dokumentov (1917–1922 gg.). Moscow: Politizdat, 1987.

Levin, Nora *The Jews of the Soviet Union since 1917.* New York University Press, 1990.

Lewin, Moshe *Lenin's Last Struggle.* New York: Pantheon, 1968.

Lieven, Dominic *Nicholas II: Emperor of All the Russias.* London: Pimlico, 1993.

Lih, L. *Bread and Authority in Russia.* Berkeley: University of California Press, 1990.

Lincoln W.B. *Red Victory: A History of the Russian Civil War.* New York: Simon and Schuster, 1991.

'Living History: Wiring the Revolution', *Soviet Weekly* 23 December 1989.

Lohr, Eric *Nationalizing the Russian Empire: the Campaign against Enemy Aliens in World War.* Harvard University Press, 2003.

Longley, D. 'Officers and men: a study of the development of political attitudes among the sailors of the Baltic Fleet in 1917', *Soviet Studies* 25, pp. 28–50.

Luukanen, Arto *The Party of Unbelief: Religious Policy of the Bolshevik Party 1917–29.* Helsinki: Societas Historica Finlandiae, Studia Historica 48, 1994.

Luxemburg, R. 'The Russian Revolution', in *The Russian Revolution and Leninism or Marxism.* University of Michigan Press, 1961 (also at www.marxists.org).

Lyandres, Semion 'The Bolsheviks' "German gold" revisited: an Enquiry into the 1917 Accusations', *The Carl Beck Papers in Russian and East European Studies* no 1106. Pittsburgh 1995.

Lyandres, Semion 'Documents and Politics in 1917', a review essay, *Kritika: Explorations in Russian and Eurasian History* Volume 5 Number 1 Winter (New Series), pp. 169–177 2004.

Lyandres, Semion *The Fall of Tsarism: Untold Stories of the February Revolution.* Oxford University Press, 2012.

Lyandres, Semion and Wulff, Dietmar (eds) *A Chronicle of the Civil War in Siberia and Exile in China: The Diaries of Petr Vasil'evich Vologodskii, 1918–1925*, 2 vols. Stanford University Press, 2002.

Makhno, Nestor *Krest'ianskoe dvizhenie na Ukraine 1918–21: Dokumenty i Materialy* (ed V. Danilov *et al.*). Moscow: ROSSPEN 2006.

Malet, M. *Nestor Makhno in the Russian Civil War.* London: Macmillan with London School of Economics, 1982.

Maliavskii, A.D. *Krest'ianskoe dvizhenie v Rossii v 1917g mart–oktiabr'.* Moscow: Nauka, 1981.

Malle, S. *The Economic Organization of War Communism, 1918–21.* Cambridge University Press, 1985.

Mally, Lynn *Culture of the Future: the Proletkul't Movement in Revolutionary Russia.* Berkeley: University of California Press, 1990.

Manchester, Laurie *Holy Fathers, Secular Sons: Clergy, Intelligentsia and the Modern Self in Revolutionary Russia.* DeKalb: Northern Illinois University Press, 2008.

Mandel, D. *The Petrograd Workers and the Fall of the Old Regime.* London 1983.

Mandel, D. *The Petrograd Workers and the Soviet Seizure of Power.* London: Macmillan, 1984.

Manning, Roberta *The Crisis of the Old Order in Russia: Gentry and Government.* Princeton University Press, 1982.

Markevich Andrei and Harrison, Mark (2011). 'Great War, Civil War, and Recovery: Russia's National Income, 1913 to 1928', *The Journal of Economic History* 71 pp. 672–703.

Marshall, Peter *Demanding the Impossible: A History of Anarchism.* London 1992; PM Press, 2010, pp. 470–75.

Martin, Terry 'Modernization or Neo-Traditionalism? Ascribed Nationality and Soviet Primordialism', in *Stalinism: New Directions*, ed. Sheila Fitzpatrick. London: Taylor and Francis, 2000.

Martin, Terry *Affirmative Action Empire: Nations and Nationalism in the Soviet Union 1923–1939.* Ithaca and London: Cornell University Press, 2001.

Mawdsley, E. 'The Baltic fleet and the Kronstadt mutiny', *Soviet Studies* 24, 4, April 1973.

Mawdsley, E. *The Russian Revolution and the Baltic Fleet, War and Politics February 1917–April 1918.* London: Macmillan, 1978.

Mawdsley E. *The Russian Civil War*. London: Allen&Unwin, 1987.

Mayer, Arno J. *The Politics and Diplomacy of Peacemaking: Containment and Counterrevolution at Versailles 1918–19*. New York: Knopf, 1967.

Mayer, Arno J. *The Furies: Violence and Terror in the French and Russian Revolutions*. Princeton University Press, 2001.

McCauley, M. *Bread and Justice: State and Society in Petrograd 1917–22*. Oxford University Press, 1991.

McKean, R. *St. Petersburg Between the Revolutions*. Yale University Press, 1990.

McNeal, R.H. (ed.) *Resolutions and decisions of the Communist Party of the Soviet Union*, 4 vols. University of Toronto Press, 1974.

Mehlinger, H.D. and Thompson, John M. *Count Witte and the Tsarist Government in 1905*. Bloomington: Indiana University Press, 1972.

Mel'gunov, Sergei *The Bolshevik Seizure of Power*. Santa Barbara, Oxford 1972 (trans of *Kak Bol'sheviki zakhvatili vlast'*. Paris: La Renaissance 1953).

Meller, V.L. and Pankratova, A.M. *Rabochee dvizhenie v 1917 goda*. Moscow–Leningrad: Gosizdat, 1926.

Miliukov, P.N. *Istoriia vtoroi russkoi revoliutsii.*, vol. 1 24.4, Sofia: Rossiisko-Bolgarskoe Izdatel'stvo, 1921.

Miliukov, P.N. (Mendel, Arthur P., ed.) *Political Memoirs: 1905–1917*. University of Michigan Press, 1967.

Miliukov, P.N. *The Russian Revolution*, 3 vols. Gulf Breeze, FL: Ballinger, 1978–1987.

Moon, David *Russian Peasants and Tsarist Legislation on the Eve of Reform, 1825–1855*. London: Macmillan, 1992.

Moon, David *The Russian Peasantry, 1600–1930: The World the Peasants Made*. Harlow: Longman, 1999.

Moon, David *The Abolition of Serfdom in Russia 1762–1907*. Harlow: Longman, 2001.

Mossolov, A.A. *At the Court of the Last Tsar: Being the Memoirs of A.A. Mossolov*. London: Methuen, 1935.

Mullin, Richard 'Lenin and the Iskra faction of the RSDLP: 1899–1903'. Unpublished PhD thesis, University of Sussex. 2010 (pdf download).

Munck, J.L. *The Kornilov Revolt: a Critical Examination of the Sources and Research*. Aarhus University Press, 1987.

Neuberger, Joan *Hooliganism: Crime, Culture and Power in St.Petersburg, 1900–1914*. Berkeley: University of California Press, 1993.

Neumann, J. 'A note on the winter of the Kronstadt sailors' uprising in 1921', *Soviet Studies*, 44, 1, 1992.

Nomad, Max *Apostles of Revolution*. Boston: Little, Brown, 1939.

Nove, A. *An Economic History of the USSR 1917–1993*. Harmondsworth: Penguin, 1992.

Ó Gráda, Cormac 'Making Famine History', *Journal of Economic Literature* 45, 1, 2007, 5–38.

Orlovsky, D. 'State Building in the Civil War Era: The Role of the Lower-Middle Strata', in D.P. Koenker (*et al.*, eds.) *Party, State and Society in the Russian Civil War: Explorations in Social History*. Bloomington: Indiana University Press, 1989, pp. 180–209.

Palij, Michael *The Anarchism of Nestor Makhno, 1918–21: an Aspect of the Ukrainian Revolution*. University of Washington Press, 1976.

Pallot, Judith *Land Reform in Russia 1906–1917: Peasant Responses to Stolypin's Project of Rural Transformation*. Oxford University Press, 1999.

Pallot, Judith and Shaw, Dennis J.B. *Landscape and Settlement in Romanov Russia 1613–1917.* Oxford University Press, 1990.

Paustovsky, Konstantin *Slow Approach of Thunder.* London: Harvill, 1965.

Pershin P.N. *Agrarnaia revoliutsiia v Rossii: kniga 2. Agrarnoe preobrazovaniia velikoi oktiabr'skoi revoliutsii (1917–1918 gg.)* Moscow: Nauka, 1966.

Pipes, Richard *The Russian Revolution.* New York: Random House, 1990.

Pipes, Richard *The Russian Revolution 1899–1918.* London: Harvill, 1992.

Pipes, Richard *Russia Under the Bolshevik Regime 1919–24.* London: Harvill, 1994.

Pipes, Richard *The Formation of the Soviet Union: Communism and Nationalism.* Harvard University Press, 1997.

Pipes, Richard *The Unknown Lenin: From the Secret Archive.* Yale University Press, 1998.

Pirani, S. *The Russian Revolution in Retreat, 1920–24: Soviet Workers and the New Communist Elite.* London: Routledge, 2008.

Pobedonostsev, Konstantin Petrovich *Reflections of a Russian Statesman.* University of Michigan Press, 1965.

Rabinowitch, Alexander *The Bolsheviks Come to Power: The Revolution of 1917 in Petrograd.* New York: W. W. Norton, 1976.

Radkey, O.H. *The Election to the Russian Constituent Assembly of 1917.* Harvard University Press, 1950.

Radkey, O.H. *The Agrarian Foes of Bolshevism.* New York: Columbia University Press, 1958.

Radkey, O.H. *The Unknown Civil War in Soviet Russia, a Study of the Green Movement in the Tambov Region, 1920–1.* Stanford University Press, 1976.

Radkey, O.H. *Russia Goes to the Polls: the Election to the All-Russian Constituent Assembly 1917.* Ithaca and London: Cornell University Press, 1989.

Raleigh, D.J. *Revolution on the Volga: 1917 in Saratov.* Ithaca and London: Cornell University Press, 1985.

Raleigh, D.J. *Experiencing Russia's Civil War: Politics, Society and Revolutionary Culture in Saratov 1917–22.* Princeton University Press, 2002.

Rashin, A.G. *Naselenie Rossii za 100 let (1811–1913 gg.).* Moscow: Gosstatizdat, 1956.

Raskolnikov, F.F. *Kronstadt and Petrograd in 1917.* London: New Park, 1982.

Read, Christopher 'Labour and Socialism in Tsarist Russia', in Geary, D. (ed.) *Labour and Socialist Movements in Europe before 1914.* London: Berg, 1984.

Read, Christopher *Culture and Power in Revolutionary Russia: the Intelligentsia and the Transition from Tsarism to Communism.* London: Macmillan, 1990.

Read, Christopher *From Tsar to Soviets: the Russian People and Their Revolution 1914–21.* Oxford University Press, 1996.

Read, Christopher 'Values, Substitutes and Institutions: Cultural Roots of the Bolshevik Dictatorship', in Brovkin, V. *The Bolsheviks in Russian Society: the Revolution and the Civil Wars.* Princeton University Press, 1997.

Read, Christopher 'In Search of Liberal Tsarism', *Historical Journal* vol. 45 no. 1, pp. 195–210 2000.

Read, Christopher 'Lenin the Stalinist: the Origins of Socialism in One Country' forthcoming.

Read, Christopher *The Making and Breaking of the Soviet System.* Basingstoke: Macmillan, 2001.

Read, Christopher *Lenin: A Revolutionary Life.* London: Routledge, 2005.

236   SELECT BIBLIOGRAPHY

Reed, John *Ten Days that Shook the World.* New York: Boni & Liveright, Inc. for International Publishers, 1919.

Remington, T.F. *Building Socialism in Lenin's Russia: Ideology and Industrial Organization 1917–21.* University of Pittsburgh Press, 1984.

Rendle, Matthew, 'Conservatism and Revolution: The All-Russian Union of Landowners, 1916–1918', *Slavonic and East European Review* 84(3), pp. 481–507 2006.

Rendle, Matthew *Defenders of the Motherland: The Tsarist Elite in Revolutionary Russia.* Oxford University Press, 2010.

Rendle, Matthew 'Revolutionary Tribunals and the Origins of Terror in early Soviet Russia', *Historical Research* vol. 84, no. 226, pp. 693–721, November 2011.

Retish, Aaron B. *Russia's Peasants in Revolution and Civil War: Citizenship, Identity, and the Creation of the Soviet State, 1914–1922.* Cambridge University Press, 2008.

Revoliutsionnoe dvizhenie v Rossii. Dokumenty I materialy, 5 vols. Moscow: Nauka, 1958–63.

Rigby, T.H. *Communist Party Membership in the USSR 1917–1967.* Princeton University Press, 1968.

Rigby, T.H. *Lenin's Government: Sovnarkom (1917–1922).* Cambridge University Press, 1979.

Rodzianko, Mikhail V 'Ekonomicheskoe polozhenie Rossii pered revoliutsiei. Zapiska M.V. Rodzianki', *Krasnyi arkhiv* 10 (1925) pp. 69–86, quoted in English in Vernadsky and Pushkarev 1972, pp. 877–8.

Rogger, Hans *Russia in the Age of Modernization and Revolution 1881–1917.* Harlow: Longman, 1983.

Roobol, W.H. *Tsereteli: a Democrat in the Russian Revolution.* The Hague: Springer, 1976.

Rosenberg, W.H. *The Liberals in the Russian Revolution: the Constitutional Democratic Party, 1917–1921.* Princeton University Press, 1974.

Rosenberg, W.H. 'Russian Labor and Bolshevik Power: Social Dimensions of Protest in Petrograd after October', in D. Kaiser, ed., *The Workers' Revolution in Russia in 1917: the View from Below,* Cambridge University Press, 1987.

Rumiantsev, E.D. *Rabochii klass povolzh'ia v gody pervoi mirovoi voiny i fevral'skoi revoliutsii 1914–1917gg.,* Kazan': Izdatel'stvo Kazanskogo universiteta 1989.

Russell, Bertrand *The Practice and Theory of Bolshevism.* London: Allen and Unwin, 1920.

Sakwa, R. *Soviet Communists in Power: A Study of Moscow During the Civil War 1918–1921.* London: Macmillan, 1988.

Schapiro, L.B. *The Origins of the Communist Autocracy: Political Opposition in the Soviet state: First Phase, 1917–22.* London: Macmillan, 1955.

Schapiro, L.B. *The Communist Party of the Soviet Union.* London: Macmillan, 1963.

Schapiro, L.B. *1917: The Russian Revolutions and the Origin of Present-day Communism.* London: Maurice Temple Smith, 1984.

Semanov, S.N. *Likvidatsiia antisovetskogo kronshtadtskogo miatezha 1921 goda.* Moscow: Nauka, 1973.

Sennikov, B.V. *The Tambov Rebellion and the Liquidation of Peasants in Russia.* Frankfurt: Posev, 2004.

Seregny, Scott J. *Russian Teachers and Peasant Revolution: the Politics of Education in 1905*. Bloomington: Indiana University Press, 1989.

Serge, Victor *Memoirs of a Revolutionary* (trans and ed. P. Sedgwick). Oxford University Press, 1963.

Service, R. *The Bolshevik Party in Revolution 1917–1923*. London: Macmillan, 1979.

Service, R. *The Russian Revolution 1900–1927*. London: Macmillan, 1986.

Service, R. (ed.) *Society and Politics in the Russian Revolution*. London: Macmillan, 1992.

Service, R. *Lenin: a Political Life*, 3 vols. London: Macmillan, 1985, 1991, 1994.

Seton-Watson, H. *The Russian Empire 1801–1917*. Oxford University Press, 1967.

Shanin, T. *The Awkward Class: Political Sociology of Peasantry in a Developing Society Russia 1900–1925*. Oxford University Press, 1972.

Shanin, T. *The Roots of Otherness: Russia's Turn of Century*, 2 vols. Yale University Press, 1985, 1986.

Shepelev, L.E. *Tsarizm i burzhuaziia v 1904–1914gg. Problemy torgovo–promyshlennoi politiki*. Leningrad, Nauka, 1987.

Shliapnikov, A. *On the Eve of 1917*. London: Allison & Busby, 1982.

Showalter, Dennis E. *Tannenberg: Clash of Empires, 1914*. Washington, DC: Potomac, 2004.

Shukman, H. (ed.) *The Blackwell Encyclopaedia of the Russian Revolution*. Oxford University Press, 1988.

Simon, Gerhard *Nationalism and Policy Toward the Nationalities in the Soviet Union*. Boulder, CO: Westview, 1991.

Sirianni, C. *Workers' Control and Socialist Democracy*. London: Verso, 1982.

Skirda, Alexandre *Anarchy's Cossack: the Struggle for Free Soviets in Ukraine 1917–21*. Edinburgh University Press, 2004.

Skocpol, Theda *States and Social Revolutions: a Comparative analysis of France, Russia and China*. Cambridge University Press, 1979.

Slezkine, Yuri. 1994. 'The USSR as a Communal Apartment, Or How a Socialist State Promoted Ethnic Particularism,' *Slavic Review* 53, No. 2 (Summer): 414–452.

Slusser, R. *Stalin in October: the Man who Missed the Revolution*. Baltimore: Johns Hopkins University Press 1987.

Smirnov, N.N. *Tretii vserossiiskii s'ezd sovetov: istoriia sozyva, sostav, rabota*. Leningrad: Nauka, 1988.

Smith, Jeremy *The Bolsheviks and the National Question, 1917–1923*. London: Macmillan, 1997.

Smith, S.A. *Red Petrograd: Revolution in the Factories 1917–18*. Cambridge University Press, 1983.

Smith, S.A. *Revolution and the People in Russia and China: a Comparative History*. Cambridge University Press, 2008.

Snyder, Timothy *Bloodlands: Europe between Hitler and Stalin*. London: Bodley Head, 2010.

Soboleva, G.L. and Smirnov Iu.P. *Aleksandr Kerenskiĭ: liubov' i nenavist' revoliutsii: dnevniki, stat'i, ocherki i vospominaniia sovremennikov*. Cheboksary: Izdatel'stvo Chvashskogo universiteta, 1993.

Solov'ev, Iu.V. *Samoderzhavie i dvorianstvo v kontse XIX veka*. Leningrad, Nauka, 1973.

Spring, D. (ed.) *European Landed Elites in the Nineteenth Century*. Baltimore: Johns Hopkins University Press, 1977.

Stalin, J. 'Marxism and the National Question' 1913 available at Marxists Internet Archive http://www.marxists.org/reference/archive/stalin/works/1913/03a.htm

Startsev, V.I. Russkaia burzhuaziia i samoderzhavie v 1905–1917gg. Bor'ba vokrug 'otvetsvennogo ministerstva' i 'pravitel'stva doveriia'. Leningrad: Nauka, 1977.

Startsev, V.I. *Krakh Kerenshchiny*. Leningrad: Nauka, 1982.

Steinberg, Mark *Moral Communities: the Culture of Class Relations in the Russian Printing Industry 1867–1907*. Berkeley: University of California Press, 1992.

Stites, R. 'Iconoclastic Currents in the Russian Revolution: Destroying and Preserving the Past', in A. Gleason (*et al.* eds) *Bolshevik Culture: Experiment and Order in the Russian Revolution*. Bloomington: Indiana University Press, 1985.

Stone, Norman *The Eastern Front 1914–17*. London: Hodder & Stoughton, 1975.

Strongin, Varlen *Aleksandr Kerenskiĭ: demokrat vo glave Rossii*. Moscow-Vladimir: AST: Zebra E: VKT, 2010.

Subtelny, Orest *Ukraine: A History*. University of Toronto Press, 1989.

Sukhanov, N.N. *The Russian Revolution: an Eyewitness Account*, (trans and ed J. Carmichael, 2 vols). New York: Harper, 1962.

Suny, R. *The Baku Commune 1917–1918*. Princeton University Press, 1972.

Suny, R. 'Toward a social history of the October Revolution', *American Historical Review*, 88, pp. 31–52, 1983.

Suny, R. *The Making of the Georgian Nation*. Bloominiversity Press, 1992.

Suny, R. *The Revenge of the Past: Nationalism, Revolution, and the Collapse of the Soviet Union*. Stanford University Press, 1993.

Suny, R. *The Revenge of the Past: Nationalism, Revolution and the Collapse of the Soviet Union*. Princeton, University Press, 1994.

Suny, Ronald Grigor, and Martin, Terry (eds) *A State of Nations: Empire and Nation-Making in the Age of Lenin and Stalin*. Oxford University Press, 2001.

Swain, G. *Russian Social Democracy and the Legal Labour Movement 1906–14*. London: Macmillan, 1983.

Swain, G. *Origins of the Russian Civil War*. Harlow: Longman, 1996.

Sweetman, John *Tannenberg 1914*. London: Cassell, 2004.

Trotsky, L. *History of the Russian Revolution*, 3 vols. New York 1932. Available at www.marxists.org/archive/trotsky/1930/hrr/ (accessed 27 June 2012).

Trotsky, L. *Literature and Revolution*. University of Michigan Press, 1960.

Trotsky, L. *1905*. New York 1971, London: Penguin, 1972.

Trotsky, L. *Terrorism and Communism*. London: New Park, 1975.

Trotsky, L. *Our Political Tasks*. London: New Park, 1979.

Trotsky, L. *How the Revolution Armed: Military Writings and Speeches* (trans B. Pearce) 5 vols. London: New Park, 1979–1981.

Tsentrarkhiv, *Burzhuaziia nakanune fevral'sko irevoliutsii*. Moscow: Gosizdat, 1927.

Velidov, A.S. *Krasnaia kniga VChK*, 2 vols. Moscow 1920. Reprinted Moscow: Politizdat, 1990.

Velikaia oktiabr'skaia sotsialisticheskaia revoliutsiia: khronika sobytii v chetyrekh tomakh. Moscow: Nauka, 1959.

Vernadsky, G. and Pushkarev, S.A. *Source Book for Russian History from Earliest Times to 1917*. Princeton University Press, 1972.

Verner, Andrew M. *Nicholas II and the Crisis of Russian Autocracy*. Princeton University Press, 1990.

'Voline' [Vsevoled Mikhailovich Eichenbaum] *The Unknown Revolution 1917–21*. Montreal: Black Rose Books, 1982.

Volkogonov, Dmitri *Stalin: Triumph and Tragedy*. London: Weidenfeld, 1991.

Volkogonov, Dmitri *Lenin: Life and Legacy*, trans and ed. by H. Shukman. London: Harper Collins, 1994.

Volkov, E.Z. *Dinamika narodonaselenia SSSR vosem'desiat let*. Moscow: Gosizdat, 1930.

von Geldern, James *Bolshevik Festivals 1917–1920*. Berkeley: University of California Press, 1993.

von Hagen, Mark *School of the Revolution: Bolsheviks and Peasants in the Red Army 1917–1928*. (Unpublished diss. Stanford, UMI) Dec 1984.

von Hagen, Mark *Soldiers in the Proletarian Dictatorship: the Red Army and the Soviet Socialist state 1917–1930*. Ithaca and London: Cornell University Press, 1990.

Vucinich, Wayne (ed.) *The Peasant in Nineteenth-century Russia*. Stanford University Press, 1966.

Vulliamy C.E. *The Red Archives: Russian State Papers and other Documents Relating to the Years 1915–18*. London, 1929.

Wade, R.A. *The Russian Search for Peace: February–October 1917*. Stanford University Press, 1969.

Wade, R.A. *Red Guards and Workers' Militia in the Russian Revolution*. Stanford University Press, 1984.

Wade, R.A. *The Russian Revolution 1917*. Cambridge University Press, 2005.

Waldron, Peter *The End of Imperial Russia 1855–1917*. Basingstoke: Macmillan, 1997.

Waldron, Peter *Between Two Revolutions: Peter Stolypin and the Politics of Renewal in Russia*. London: Routledge, 1998.

Weber, G. and H. *Lenin: Life and Works*. London: Macmillan, 1980.

White, H. '1917 in the rear garrisons', in L. Edmondson and P. Waldron, (eds), *Economy and Society in Russia and the Soviet Union, 1860–1930*. London: Macmillan, 1992, pp. 152–168.

White, James 'The Kornilov Affair. A Study in Counter Revolution', *Soviet Studies* vol. 20, no. 2, pp. 187–205 October 1968.

White, James *The Russian Revolution 1917–1921: a Short History*. London: Hodder Arnold, 1994.

White, James *Lenin: The Practice and Theory of Revolution*. London: Macmillan, 2001.

Wildman, A. *The End of the Russian Imperial Army: the Old Army and the Soldiers' Revolt*, vol 1. Princeton University Press, 1980.

Wildman, A. *The End of the Russian Imperial Army: The Road to Soviet Power and Peace*, vol 2. Princeton University Press, 1988.

Williams, B. *The Russian Revolution, (1917–1921)*. Oxford University Press, 1987.

Williams, William Appelman *The Tragedy of American Diplomacy* (revised edition). New York: W. W. Norton, 1988.

Wirtschafter, Elise Kimerling *Russia's Age of Serfdom 1649–1861*. Maldon, Oxford: Carlton, 2008.

Woods, Alan 'The War Years', in *Bolshevism: The Road to Revolution* London 1999 accessible at http://www.marxist.com/bolshevism-old/part5-5.html

Worobec, Christina *Peasant Russia: Family and Community in the Post-emancipation Period.* Princeton University Press, 1991.

Wright, Alistair 'The Establishment of Bolshevik Power in Karelia 1918–1919'. unpublished PhD thesis Glasgow, 2012.

Yarmolinsky, A. *Road to Revolution: a Century of Russian Radicalism.* New York: Collier, 1962.

Zamiatin, E. *The Dragon and other Stories.* Harmondsworth: Penguin, 1975.

Zhilin, A.P. *Poslednee nastuplenie; (iyun' 1917 godu).* Moscow: Nauka, 1983.

Zhurnal [No. 1] Soveta Ministrov Vremennogo Pravitel'stva 2 March 1917, GARF (State Archive of the Russian Federation), f. 601, op. 1, d. 2103, l. 1 quoted in Wikipedia article 'Russian Revolution', accessed 12 November 2011.

Websites

http://en.wikipedia.org/wiki/Armenian_Genocide/

http://www.armenian-genocide.org/index.htm

http://www.marxist.com/bolshevism-old/part5-5.html

http://www2.stetson.edu/~psteeves/classes/durnovo.html (text of Durnovo memorandum)

WW1WorldWarOneonline

www.mahno.ru (material on Makhno)

www.marxists.org (a massive compilation of writings and documents on the left)

www.nestormakhno.info (material on Makhno)

Index